# Wal-Mart Wars

## *Moral Populism in the Twenty-First Century*

*Rebekah Peeples Massengill*

NEW YORK UNIVERSITY PRESS

*New York and London*

NEW YORK UNIVERSITY PRESS
New York and London
www.nyupress.org

References to Internet websites (URLs) were accurate at the time of writing.
Neither the author nor New York University Press is responsible for URLs that
may have expired or changed since the manuscript was prepared.

LIBRARY OF CONGRESS CATALOGING-IN-PUBLICATION DATA

Massengill, Rebekah Peeples, 1975-
Wal-Mart wars : moral populism in the twenty-first century / Rebekah Peeples Massengill.
pages cm
Includes bibliographical references and index.
ISBN 978-0-8147-6333-9 (hbk. : alk. paper)
ISBN 978-0-8147-6334-6 (pbk. : alk. paper)
ISBN 978-0-8147-6335-3 (e-book)
ISBN 978-0-8147-6336-0 (e-book)
1. Wal-Mart (Firm) 2. Retail trade. 3. Marketing—Moral and ethical aspects. 4. Marketing
—Political aspects. I. Title.
HF5429.M337 2013
658.8'7—dc23

2012040760

New York University Press books are printed on acid-free paper,
and their binding materials are chosen for strength and durability.
We strive to use environmentally responsible suppliers and materials
to the greatest extent possible in publishing our books.

Manufactured in the United States of America
c 10 9 8 7 6 5 4 3 2 1
p 10 9 8 7 6 5 4 3 2 1

*For my family*

# CONTENTS

*Acknowledgments*                                                     ix
*Preface*                                                            xiii

**PART 1   WHY SHOULD WE CARE ABOUT THE WAL-MART DEBATE?**

1  Constructing Moral Markets                                          3

2  Contextualizing the Wal-Mart Wars                                  19

**PART 2   COMPETING FRAMEWORKS FOR MARKET MORALITY**

3  Individuals and Communities                                        45

4  Thrift and Benevolence                                             77

5  Freedom and Fairness                                              115

**PART 3   MARKET MORALITY IN MEDIA AND POLITICS**

6  How Wal-Mart Wins the War of Words                                153

7  Moral Populism in the Twenty-First Century                        175

*Appendix: Methodology*                                              189
*Notes*                                                              195
*Bibliography*                                                       205
*Index*                                                              215
*About the Author*                                                   225

## ACKNOWLEDGMENTS

The research that culminates in this book has unfolded over several years, and that journey has brought me into a series of intellectual communities where my scholarship has been challenged, enriched, and improved. As I always attempt to convince my students, the isolated ivory tower image of scholarship is nothing more than an illusion; research is a collaborative enterprise in which scholars are perpetually engaged with one another in intellectual conversation. I am quite fortunate to be able to thank a multitude of people for their contributions to this book.

In its early form, this project benefited from the advice and mentorship of several members of the Department of Sociology at Princeton University. Bob Wuthnow's interest in and encouragement of my research have been ongoing, and his presence as both scholar and mentor has enriched this project from the start. Conversations with Miguel Centeno shaped this project in a host of ways, and his challenging questions have made my arguments more cogent and, I hope, more convincing. Viviana Zelizer offered vital feedback throughout this project, and I am honored to be able to address even a small portion of the research agenda she has pioneered in economic sociology. At NYU Press, Ilene Kalish was a faithful editor whose enthusiasm for this project helped to shepherd the book from start to finish. Betsy Wells Stokes provided expert editorial assistance in the final stages of revision.

This book also owes a debt of thanks to a number of institutions and individuals who provided financial resources and other forms of assistance. I could not have completed this research without the financial support I received from Princeton University's Center for the Study of Religion during 2005–2008. Anita Kline and Barbara Bermel at CSR deserve special thanks, as do Sarah Chen, Whitney Downs, Greg Kennedy, Amirah Mercer, and Naomi Sugi for the research assistance they provided in working with various documents through the processes of coding and analysis. Portions of this research were also funded through the John Templeton Foundation's support of the Cognition and Religion Initiative at CSR. Later stages of research and writing were supported by the Princeton University Committee on Research in the Humanities and Social Sciences, as well as a Faculty Research Support grant from Swarthmore College. In addition to financial resources, Princeton's Center for the Study of Religion's Cognitive and Textual Methods seminar proved pivotal in shaping both the research questions I eventually embraced in this project and the theoretical approach I use to investigate them. CSR's Religion and Public Life Seminar similarly provided a valuable forum in which to present portions of this project in various stages of completion.

A wealth of colleagues provided various forms of useful feedback at different stages of my research and writing. Ruth Braunstein, Chris Close, Mitch Duneier, Hilary Levey Friedman, Jim Gibbon, Conrad Hackett, David Kozo, Michael Lindsay, Carol Ann MacGregor, Noelle Molé, Caitlin Mollison, Christine Percheski, Amy Reynolds, Rob Smith, Judy Swan, Chris Wildeman, Amanda Irwin Wilkins, and Marian Wren deserve special recognition for helpful conversations about various dimensions of this project along the way. At Swarthmore during 2011–2012, the Junior Faculty Writing Group offered useful feedback on portions of the manuscript, with special thanks going to Rachel Buurma, Laura Holzman, Nina Johnson, Min Kyung Lee, Ayse Kaya Orloff, Mike Reay, and Eric Song.

My work has also been strengthened by the ongoing conversations about Wal-Mart, language, politics, and consumption that have been part of my academic life for the past four years. During this time I've had the opportunity to teach bright and inquisitive students at both Princeton and Swarthmore in my "Wal-Mart Nation" and "Discourse and Democracy" courses. I won't risk trying to thank you all by name, but trust that if you are reading these acknowledgments, then you know who you are! In what I hope is the greatest testament to my students and the strength of their work, I have cited some of their research in the manuscript that follows. Introducing students to the methods of social science research while wrestling with the deep and abiding dilemmas associated with global capitalism have made me a better scholar, writer, and teacher. Thank you, bright and idealistic young ones, for keeping me on my toes.

Much of what I argue in this book has to do with the centrality of the family in economic discourse, so it is fitting that I save this final moment to thank my own family for how they help me to combine love and labor in all aspects of my life. This book is fittingly dedicated to them. To my husband, Sam, my biggest supporter and unfailing encourager, I can think of no more appropriate thanks than that timeless gesture that speaks of love and team-work, equality, and endurance: the fist bump. My parents, David and Emily Peeples, have worn so many different hats—editors, babysitters, discussants, cable news experts—that I truly cannot imagine how I could have finished this book without their help. My children, Haydon and Margaret, have never known a life in which I was not working on this book, and have provided endless but welcome distractions along the way. Roxie Biro is a member of the family in heart, if not blood, and proves on a daily basis just how deeply love flourishes in the lives knit together through paid care work. In all, my family's central presence in my life and my heart always reminds me that the discourses that surround the market and consumption are never far removed from the perpetual minutiae of everyday living: loading children and grocer-ies in and out of shopping carts, preparing a family budget, and answering the age-old question of just what are we all going to have for dinner? You bring me joy, give me perspective, and always spur me to imagine a better world. Thank you.

Writing a book about economic controversies in the early years of the twenty-first century turned out to be a very tricky project. The past several years have witnessed economic events of historic proportions, including a global financial crisis, government intervention in financial firms, and reforms to the nation's health care market that have perhaps been matched in their unprecedented nature only by the subsequent controversies they engendered. New populist movements have erupted in public life, with the Tea Party clamoring for GOP attention on the right, and left-wing groups hoping to convince Occupy Wall Street protestors that they have really been faithful Democrats all along. How does a book about Wal-Mart debates fit into our current economic landscape?

This book argues that we can use the recent controversy surrounding Wal-Mart to explore how conservative and progressive activists talk about controversial economic issues—with regard to both the nation's largest retailer and other recent market controversies. When I became interested in studying economic discourse several years ago, the developing national debate over Wal-Mart emerged as a particularly visible and compelling case study. The public discourse surrounding the retailer produced vivid examples of competing arguments for and against Wal-Mart's often-notorious business practices, which despite their allegedly harmful impacts on workers, the environment, and small retailers, have undoubtedly proved an economic boon for the typical American consumer. I began this research in 2005, tracking closely the developing activities of the organization Wal-Mart Watch, which declared itself to be a novel coalition of community organizations, leaders from various religious groups, and concerned citizens and activists who were united by their desire to pressure Wal-Mart to live up to its potential as a template corporation for the twenty-first century. Although held together by the glue of substantial funding from the Service Employees

International Union (SEIU), Wal-Mart Watch declared its goal to be bigger than simply organizing Wal-Mart's domestic workers in a union; instead, the group sought to prod Wal-Mart toward greater responsibility as the world's largest corporation.

As I argue in the pages that follow, the resulting dialectic between Wal-Mart Watch and Wal-Mart Inc. (which would eventually found its own short-lived "advocacy group," Working Families for Wal-Mart) produced a telling representation of the kind of economic discourse produced on both the right and the left in the present-day United States. Yet this discourse was also created in a particular time and place. Developing in the years 2005 and 2006, Wal-Mart Watch's mission was conceived during a period in which most Americans believed that the nation's economic pie was growing only bigger. In the first half of the decade, for instance, the Panel Study of Income Dynamics found that Americans' net worth increased by almost half, from a median of $87,220 in 2001 to $120,025 in 2007.[1] Of course, this perception of abundance would turn out to be premised on the shaky foundation of the housing sector, with much of this growth in wealth fueled by rising home prices and increasing home equity. Americans' expanded holdings in financial assets were surprisingly paltry by comparison: The median value of financial assets for households in the PSID, for example, increased by only $2,000 between 2001 and 2007. Moreover, incomes were stagnant for the first part of the decade, with the median rising less than $1,000 between 2005 and 2007.

As is still painfully clear as of this writing, the housing bubble that fed Americans' illusion of prosperity (and in many cases, practices of living beyond a household's means through home equity loans that were easily available) could not continue indefinitely, and the string of catastrophes that accelerated in 2008 plunged the entire world into a global financial crisis. The economic context facing groups like Wal-Mart Watch looked radically different, as did the formerly vilified retail behemoth that is Wal-Mart. As unemployment crept into double-digit percentages, Americans watched their retirement investments evaporate, and foreclosures rose steeply with little sign of abatement. A store like Wal-Mart—which had always championed its empowerment of lower- and middle-class American consumers—was well positioned to resume its path to greatness in the name of frugality. Indeed, many of the concessions that Wal-Mart made in 2006 on things like health care (spurred, at least in part, in response to critics like Wal-Mart Watch) would be scaled back in the lean years that followed. Wal-Mart Watch itself would eventually struggle to maintain its identity in the wake of a two-part crisis: unsure, perhaps, of next steps in the wake of having accomplished a number of reforms in areas like employee benefits and environmental sustainability, and facing the unenviable task of maligning the very company that was helping Americans, struggling with basic expenses, to keep food on the table and roofs over their heads.

It struck me as particularly telling, then, that in the final weeks of revising this manuscript I received the following email on March 16, 2012, from the Wal-Mart Watch communications team that had so faithfully filled my inbox for the past seven years:

> For years, Walmart Watch has been one of the leading sources for news on how Walmart is impacting our society and economy. Thanks to your support and interest, the struggle to challenge Walmart to improve its business practices and treatment of workers has grown.
>
> Due to this success, Walmart Watch is joining forces with Making Change at Walmart. Making Change at Walmart is a campaign challenging Walmart to help rebuild our economy and strengthen working families. Anchored by the United Food and Commercial Workers, we are proud to join in this coalition of Walmart associates, union members, small business owners, religious leaders, women's advocacy groups, community groups, multi-ethnic coalitions, elected officials, and ordinary citizens who believe that changing Walmart is vital for the future of our country.

With a new name—and a different source of union-based funding—Wal-Mart Watch has been absorbed and repurposed in a similar struggle to change Wal-Mart in this new economic context. This time, however, its mission is to enlist Wal-Mart's help to "rebuild our economy and strengthen working families"—a sign of the drastic change in the 2012 U.S. economic context as compared to the previous decade, which witnessed Wal-Mart Watch's founding and most visible public presence.

One might be tempted to think that at a time in which unemployment continues to hover around 8%, having a job *at all* may upstage a host of secondary concerns, like whether that job offers affordable benefits. Indeed, most of the official organizations that produced the discourse I study in this book no longer exist in the exact forms I analyze here. Working Families for Wal-Mart was disbanded in late 2007 (when Wal-Mart declared that it could bring the group "in-house" as they were no longer so urgently needed as public ambassadors), and the SEIU-funded Wal-Mart Watch joined forces with its UFCW (United Food and Commercial Workers) counterpart shortly thereafter (they kept the Wal-Mart Watch name until the latest merger with Making Change at Wal-Mart). Even Wal-Mart Inc. would recast its image as

"Walmart" (with no hyphen and a new, no-smiley-face logo) in the years that followed the period I focus on in this study of economic language.

Yet while the actors may have changed and key organizations evolved, a central argument of this book is that the issues and language raised in the debate over Wal-Mart tap into much deeper, symbolic dimensions of Americans' political talk and culture. As I argue in what follows, the debate over Wal-Mart is only one case study of a larger linguistic struggle over the deployment of symbolic language in the discourse surrounding economic issues. If anything, the cleavages I analyze in the Wal-Mart debate have become even *more* visible alongside new controversies concerning corporate bailouts, "Obamacare," the national deficit, and "class warfare." The presence of populist movements on both the right and the left, in the form of the Tea Party movement and Occupy Wall Street protests, serve to further dramatize the distinctions I identify in my analysis of Wal-Mart discourse. (For example, Wal-Mart Watch wasted little time in reminding the readers of its blog that it joined in their ire against the 1%, saying, "No list of major corporations and wealthy individuals distorting our democracy would be complete without Walmart and the Waltons.")[2] Moreover, the example of the Tea Party and OWS illustrate well the enduring cleavages of populism on both sides of the political aisle, as both movements claim to celebrate the "common man" or the "little people" against the oppressive regimes of government (in the first case) and corporations (in the second). In crucial ways, then, such populist movements tap into the same concerns about Americans' economic well-being that occupied the social movement organizations (SMOs) embattled over Wal-Mart just a few years earlier. Accordingly, most analysts who observe the activities of both sides note that while the Tea Party and OWS have many things in common— for instance, both groups are suspicious of established politicians' ability to successfully represent and advocate for "the people"—these two movements show little promise of joining in common cause.

These present permutations of economic discourse illustrate in a pointed way the very contours and conflicts that I find to be central in understanding the Wal-Mart debate of the mid-2000s. As such, my hope is that *Wal-Mart Wars* can serve as a tool for greater understanding of Americans' economic debates, especially those that resonate with core dimensions of populism— celebrating the hard work and patriotism of everyday Americans, and challenging the presumed elitism and dominance of an allegedly privileged form of "the other." Through studying the moving target of political language in our present society, I believe that the arguments I develop in the chapters that follow can be essential for bringing about a greater appreciation for the ideas, values, and moral concepts that animate our economic discourse. As one who must always believe that the future is filled with hope, my deepest desire for this book is that it might help to clarify the political discourse that Americans increasingly find so discordant in public life, which too often leads many Americans to eschew the political process altogether. Understanding our moral language, particularly the language we use to construct and critique the market, may be a first step forward.

PART 1

Why Should We Care about the Wal-Mart Debate?

# 1

## Constructing Moral Markets

Today, we're the focus of one of the most organized, most sophisti-
cated, most expensive corporate campaigns ever launched against a
single company. For whatever reasons, our success has generated a
lot of fear in some circles.
—Former Wal-Mart CEO Lee Scott, Wal-Mart shareholders
meeting, June 2005

Despite what its title might suggest, this is not really a book about Wal-Mart.
Curiosity about the world's largest retailer has prompted a spate of recent
books about the company's business model, history, and influence on the
world's economy—all worthy topics, to be sure. But as a sociologist, I am
less concerned with what Wal-Mart *does* and more with what Wal-Mart *represents*. As a beacon of capitalism in a global marketplace, Wal-Mart invites
both praise and condemnation from entrepreneurs, shoppers, and cultural
critics alike—judgments that tell us more about what we value as a society
than what we might value about any particular corporation. When considered as an icon of economic power, Wal-Mart is but one of a host of economic
symbols that attract enough attention—indeed, much of it negative—to be a
worthy object of investigation in its own right. This book might have been
written about other public examples of controversial economic policy—such
as whether immigrants should be allowed to receive public health services,
or the Tea Party movement's objections to the current tax code. Although
all these controversies raise difficult questions about budgets, taxpayers, and
the sanctity of market freedom, the central premise of this book is that such
economic dilemmas are not really about the policy-specific details of dollars
and cents, taxes or deficits. Instead, this book argues that beneath the surface

of public talk about markets lies a rich moral vocabulary that Americans reference to evaluate these moral dilemmas of modern capitalism. Yet, although
many of the moral concepts that constitute market processes draw on shared
cultural symbols—for instance, the values of freedom, thrift, and individualism—the ways we discuss these values with regard to market society is also
subject to political and moral struggle. The central goal of this book is to
understand that contested process.

The public struggle to moralize the market is an ongoing project with a
rich history in American political life. The availability of socially responsible
investments and the recent proliferation of "fair trade" products are only a
few of the ways that present-day markets represent avenues for moral behavior and social protest. Although such activities have a long and well-estab-
lished history in American public life, debates about the merits of market
logic seem perpetual because the solutions that best serve society's interests
and moral purposes are almost never clear-cut. Further, periodic episodes
of social dislocation and rapid change often prompt a reevaluation of the
market, its rules, and its institutions. For instance, a century ago the development of chain stores incited the ire of progressive activists who worried
that this new form of market organization would threaten small town merchants and, by extension, central values of American life.[1] In a progressive
era where the sacrosanct rights of "the consumer" had yet to become established, this opposition attracted its share of supporters, including Huey Long
and legislators in nineteen states that had levied hefty taxes on chain stores
by 1939.[2] The controversy that surrounded chain store merchandizing in the
early twentieth century reminds us that the issues raised by the growth of
stores like Wal-Mart are echoes of older, long-standing conversations regarding the well-being of consumers, the appropriateness of state power in limiting free markets, and the role of businesses in improving quality of life for
larger communities.[3] Such historical anecdotes also convey just how fluid the
categories of "moral" and "ethical" are, both in actual practice and when considered over time.

Even though this book is not about Wal-Mart, this book *is* about the recent
national debate over Wal-Mart—the pivotal two-year period of 2005–2006,
and the hard-won concessions that Wal-Mart offered to its critics, especially
the union-funded group Wal-Mart Watch. As such, it investigates only a slice
in time, and the public discourse surrounding only one company. But by
focusing on the deeper, perennial themes raised by activists on both sides
of these issues, this book explores the process by which social movements
attempt to offer a moral critique of the darker sides of capitalism, while also
analyzing how these critiques fare in the public sphere. The global financial

crisis notwithstanding, concerns about capitalism endure even in times of plenty, when credit is easy to come by and "market bubbles" seem unthinkable. The debate about Wal-Mart (which continues even as of this writing) challenges us to think about larger questions addressing the relationship between morality and market processes, particularly as they affect a range of people and issues, including low-wage workers, the environment, small businesses, taxpayers, and the array of consumers that make up the American public. Even though critics of capitalism are sometimes quick to accuse the market of immorality, I begin with the premise that markets are actually highly normative institutions that create moral meanings through the words and actions of those who interact with them. In particular, my interest here is in the recurring, patterned ways that Americans articulate different visions of a moral market through the strategic use of language—what sociologists call "public discourse."

In recent years, sociologists have become increasingly interested in showing us just how much of what we call "the market" is subject to this kind of social construction. Fourcade and Healy, for instance, describe economic systems of monetary exchange as "more or less conscious efforts to categorize, normalize, and naturalize behaviors and rules that are not natural in any way, whether in the name of economic principles (e.g., efficiency, productivity) or more social ones (e.g., justice, social responsibility)."[4] In other words, key components of market systems, such as legal forms of exchange, market regulations, and even currency itself, aren't fixed entities at all. Instead, people and societies *use* markets to negotiate moral meanings and obligations, and draw on these webs of significance to justify different kinds of market activities. In fact, we could think of the market as a dependent variable that takes on particular forms of meaning and significance based on the cultural context in which it is situated.[5] A good example of what this might look like in actual practice appears in Weber's classic argument about the Protestant ethic. Fueled by angst over their uncertain salvation, Weber argued, the Calvinists turned to material success as an indicator of their divine status, prompting the savings and reinvestment that created bourgeoning markets in western Europe. The marketplace was considered a moral symbol of divine salvation, and Calvinists saw capitalism and the workings of market society as a place to affirm their individual moral worth.

Other, more recent work demonstrates that human beings do indeed use economic life to create shared expressions of moral significance. As the leading champion of this view, Viviana Zelizer has illustrated this point through her analysis of the social norms and legal codes surrounding intimate relationships.[6] Challenging the "hostile worlds" notion that the caring relationships of love and family need to be kept separate from the presumably rational, unbiased world of market processes, Zelizer demonstrates that both of these things intermingle in actual practice. As she observes of efforts to separate relational ties from economic transactions:

> The surprising thing about such debates is their usual failure to recognize how regularly intimate social transactions coexist with monetary transactions: parents pay nannies or child-care workers to tend their children, adoptive parents pay money to obtain babies, divorced spouses pay or receive alimony and child support payments, and parents give their children allowances, subsidize their college educations, help them with their first mortgage, and offer them substantial bequests in their wills. Friends and relatives send gifts of money as wedding presents, and friends loan each other money.[7]

Moreover, Zelizer goes on to argue that not only do these worlds of money and intimacy intermingle in actual practice, economic activity actually signals the creation of certain kinds of intimate relationships, as when parents choose a paid caregiver for their child, or when one partner gives another an engagement ring. The power of these economic symbols comes from their moral significance in our culture: for instance, nannies are expected to be caring and loving toward the children in their care, and an engagement ring signals a promise to marry. Far from being hostile worlds, Zelizer argues that the framework of "connected lives" better captures how people negotiate moral meanings and economic transactions in everyday social life. In both words and deeds, language and practice, our view of the market is intimately tied up with moral significance.

## Contested Moral Markets

On the one hand, many such moral dimensions of market transactions are shared across whole societies. Most Americans, for instance, would interpret the exchange of an engagement ring as indicating a couple's mutual commitment to marry. We all draw on institutionally embedded meanings like these when we work to understand economic activity. When sociologists speak of culture as a "tool kit,"[8] for instance, they acknowledge that different societies (and the individual members of them) have a set of cultural resources that they draw on to understand, negotiate, and respond to different social situations. For instance, when Americans hear that the U.S. government will be acquiring a majority share of General Motors in order to prevent the company from declaring bankruptcy, they could interpret the situation from a number of vantage points. From one perspective, such interventionist policies could be understood as patriotic acts serving American industry and workers—an interpretation that draws on American legacies of collective accomplishment, national pride, and the historical value of unions in American manufacturing. On the other hand, the federal government's intervention in the looming failure of a privately owned company was interpreted by others as a misguided form of meddling in the workings of the free market. Here, themes of independence, self-reliance, and corporate responsibility could be used to frame this decision as one that indulged a company that had made poor decisions and manufactured inferior products. The point is not that one interpretation is right or that another is wrong, but that both kinds of interpretations are feasible in American politics. Moreover, both interpretations would draw on moral ideals that have long been circulating in American culture—for example, collectivity, independence, patriotism, freedom[9]—in order to justify the interpretation as morally grounded.

Yet, even when activists share a common political history and a common society, their normative views of the world are not always the same. In fact, in a situation such as the government bailout of General Motors, it's precisely because both sets of moral justifications circulate in the public ideology that the decision to assist the struggling company was met with so much controversy. If reasons to support the bailout didn't exist—such as the themes of patriotism or mutual aid—then the decision would have had little chance of even being considered an option by key progressive policy makers in the federal government. On the other hand, the fact that it was met with such opposition from conservatives only underscores how economic dilemmas such as this one resonate with deeper, contested moral values that shape political debates about economic policy. Recognizing the fluid nature of moral debates helps to demonstrate how even aspects of the economic system that seem immutable—such as our abiding endorsement of "free" markets—are actually the result of social construction. Through the repeated interactions of people, institutions, and normative codes, key aspects of our social worlds are taken for granted, masking the degree to which these central features of social life are actually created by human beings themselves.

Morality is a uniquely powerful form of social construction, in that morality is concerned with what should be, and proposes a vision of the world that is ordered according to certain principles that are themselves the product of a particular social order.[10] Put another way, morality "is concerned with broader questions about the modes of reasoning and talking that define things as legitimate,"[11] and the sociology of morality seeks to analyze how different societies establish common values that grow out of their own history and culture.[12] When activists put forward moral arguments about a political issue, for instance, they present an ordered vision of how the world ought to be (e.g., terrorists should not have the same rights to due process as citizens), and invite onlookers to consider the merits of their respective arguments (e.g., detaining suspected terrorists indefinitely does not violate their constitutional rights). An infinite number of moral arguments such as these—both those that are overt as well as more subtle varieties—are a perpetual part of the social order that constitutes our common political life.

The tricky thing about moral arguments, however, is that a growing body of research suggests that the intuitions that shape our moral frameworks are just that—intuitions, rather than the result of conscious, deliberate thought processes structured by logic and reason.[13] The cognitive linguist George Lakoff argues this very point when he posits that Americans don't think rationally when they evaluate political issues, but instead understand the nation primarily through two competing metaphors for the nuclear family: the conservative framework of a "Strict Father," and the progressive vision of a "Nurturant Parent." In the former, people see the world as a dangerous place in which individuals must learn self-reliance and discipline in order to be safe—thus Republicans tend to dislike expansive collective entitlement programs and support individuals' rights to carry firearms. Progressives, on the other hand, prioritize nurture through collective care and empathy, supporting welfare programs and opposing capital punishment. At the same time, we are often unaware of how these moral metaphors affect how we actually think and talk about political issues in American life. Thus Lakoff argues that most Americans aren't aware that they are guided by these moral metaphors for the family when they form political opinions—instead, most people prioritize one model over the other because it feels right at a deeper, intuitive level.[14]

If political discourse is indeed founded on moral metaphors that often escape our conscious recognition, it's no surprise that most observers of American culture find our political discourse increasingly noisy and conflicted, with little promise for meaningful, lasting resolution. Even though most survey research shows that Americans aren't nearly as divided on "culture war" issues as the media might suggest,[15] most scholars agree that the elites and social movement organizations that increasingly dominate national media outlets have become more polarized.[16] In fact, the perception that elites' and political actors' discourse has itself become more strident has been suggested by scholars as one reason why many Americans—academics and the lay public alike—have been so quick to accept this appearance of division as representative of the American public at large. When elites control the issues discussed, set proposed agendas, package candidates, and craft "talking points" that are reiterated across multiple forms of media, voters' choices become increasingly circumscribed.[17]

What is the consequence of this polarized public sphere for the American people, and what difference does polarized market discourse make for our political culture? In the pages that follow, I take the position that this kind of discursive polarization matters a great deal for the way that Americans think and reason through complex social problems, particularly those that have to do with the economic dilemmas created by globalization and free market capitalism. Examining how activists invoke moral arguments in their discussions of the capitalist marketplace helps us to identify some of the ways that Americans, in turn, may think about economic dilemmas. As Christian Smith writes of the moral social order, "The moral orders animating social institutions also find imperfectly corresponding expression within human actors—in the assumptions, ideas, values, beliefs, volitions, emotions, and so on of human subjectivity."[18] Polletta comes to a similar conclusion in her study of narratives in the social movements setting, observing that "stories make explicit the cultural schemas that underpin institutional practices."[19] These cultural schemas are particularly important in understanding how we, as Americans, create shared understandings about the moral dimensions of key institutions, such as the capitalist marketplace. Wagner-Pacifici's theoretical discussion of discourse thus emphasizes the importance of the relationship between larger institutions and this symbolic aspect of language. In her view, discourse analysis is that which analyzes the relationships between "systems of symbolic representation (most notably speech) and the organizations and institutions of the social world through which such symbol systems flow."[20] Analyzing explicitly moral discourse allows us to better identify the moral ideas that lurk beneath the surface of our public discussions of contentious social issues, as well as the larger, often competing moral frameworks that Americans use to understand our relationships to the institution of the market. Particularly in economic situations—where many worry that the sphere of the market has become too powerful in both theory and practice—discourse is a key place to look for a deeper understanding of the ways that the American people evaluate contentious dilemmas that raise moral concerns about justice, fairness, and equality.

Considering the complex moral aspects of market society, it's not surprising that economic issues prompt some of the most polarizing debates that have faced the American public. In fact, close examination of many of the most contentious political issues in recent memory concern economic issues and market systems. Should businesses be allowed to employ undocumented immigrants? Has globalization been good for the United States? Can we depend on the market to distribute health care, or should the government intervene? A common theme in these and other similar debates concerns the extent to which our society should rely on the market (or market logic) to create social progress and effect moral ends. Accordingly, this book seeks to understand the conflicting moral foundations that underlie Americans' discourse about contentious economic issues. In doing so, I analyze how activists talk about morality in market settings, and offer an explanation for why Americans seem to arrive at such different conclusions about what we should prioritize in economic policy.

Wal-Mart Wars

Although many current issues would make suitable case studies for studying how economic morality is constructed and contested in public discourse—for instance, the health care reform debate, or the government bailouts of the large banks during the 2008 financial crisis—I choose to explore these issues by studying the public debate over Wal-Mart, one of the country's most popular and most controversial companies. Whatever people think about Wal-Mart, the chain is ubiquitous in the United States. For instance, table 1.1 examines data collected by the Pew Research Center, which demonstrates that 93% of Americans live close enough to shop at a Wal-Mart if they wanted to, and 84% of those had done so in the past year (with about half that group shopping there on a regular basis). Yet, even though most Americans had some contact with Wal-Mart in the year prior to the survey, they don't always rate all aspects of the retailer positively. While almost all Americans approve of the retailer as a shopping venue (about 80% rate Wal-Mart a good place to shop), the store's popularity begins to decline when respondents are asked to rate the store in other ways: 62% judge Wal-Mart to be good for the United States, and only about half of the population, 54%, considers Wal-Mart a good place to work. These data suggest that most Americans recognize that Wal-Mart's role in the national economy has brought with it good things—in part, a positive consumption experience for individuals—even though its merits for other groups, such as workers, are more debatable.

We get a better picture of how Americans think about Wal-Mart when we compare ratings of Wal-Mart to other comparable, national corporations. Again in table 1.1, we see that Wal-Mart generally earns somewhat mixed reviews: on a scale of 1 to 4, with 1 meaning "not at all favorable" and 4 meaning "very favorable," Americans give Wal-Mart an average of

*Table 1.1. Americans' attitudes about Wal-Mart and other corporations*

| Think Wal-Mart is a . . . | |
|---|---|
| Good place to shop* | 79% |
| Bad place to shop | 15% |
| No opinion | 6% |
| Good place to work | 54% |
| Bad place to work | 36% |
| No opinion | 11% |
| Good for the United States | 62% |
| Bad for the United States | 26% |
| No opinion | 12% |
| Other | |
| Live near a Wal-Mart | 93% |
| Shop at Wal-Mart | 84% |
| Regular Wal-Mart shopper | 43% |
| Ratings of corporations, 1 to 4 (S.D.) | |
| Wal-Mart | 2.74 (.99) |
| Target | 3.00 (.75) |
| Home Depot | 3.15 (.65) |
| Exxon | 2.29 (.97) |
| McDonald's | 2.84 (.81) |

* Asked only of those with a Wal-Mart nearby.

Source: Pew Research Center, December 2005.

2.74, higher than Exxon (2.29), but a bit lower than McDonald's (2.84)—two other corporations with a history of controversy. When compared to other big-box retailers, however, Wal-Mart receives lower ratings than either Target or Home Depot, making it the lowest-rated big-box store considered in this survey. While it's difficult to know if respondents rate Wal-Mart poorly because of its treatment of employees or store-specific issues (e.g., poor customer service or long checkout lines), other evidence suggests that Wal-Mart is indeed a controversial entity. One such indicator appears in the standard deviations for these ratings, which is one way that we can determine how much variation exists in respondents' ratings of these various corporations. For ratings of Wal-Mart, for instance, the standard deviation is almost an entire point (.99), which suggests that ratings of the retailer are more dispersed across the four-point spectrum than they are for Home

Depot, which has a standard deviation of only .65. In this way, Wal-Mart is somewhat similar to Exxon, which still invites polarized ratings from the public (a standard deviation of .97) even though more than two decades have passed since the *Exxon Valdez* oil spill.

We can better understand some of the reasons *why* Wal-Mart is so polarizing by examining how ratings of Wal-Mart as a place to shop and work, or as an influence on the country, vary according to key demographic characteristics. Table 1.2, for instance, shows that support for Wal-Mart is not distributed evenly among the American population. Instead, we see that certain groups tend to rate Wal-Mart favorably: in particular, Republicans, African Americans, and those without a college degree tend to be much more supportive of Wal-Mart than Democrats, whites, and respondents who have finished college. Among Democrats, for instance, only 47% think Wal-Mart is a good place to work, while almost 62% of Republicans think the same. Likewise, clear divisions emerge among those with and without a four-year college degree: with regard to Wal-Mart as an influence on the country, 54% of those with a bachelor's degree rate Wal-Mart positively, compared to 66% of those without a bachelor's. Finally, the clearest divisions in the American population emerge with regard to race: African Americans are consistently the most likely to rate Wal-Mart favorably, giving the company an average 3.15 on the four-point scale. Clearly, Wal-Mart invites diverse responses from the American public that have clear roots in social status divisions and political party identification.

In addition to inviting divided responses from the American public, Wal-Mart warrants sociological research due to the public controversy it has recently engendered, most notably, the largest class action suit in history, *Dukes vs. Wal-Mart Inc.*, filed on behalf of female workers alleging that they

*Table 1.2. Demographic characteristics and Wal-Mart attitudes*

|  | Democrats | Republicans | BA degree | No BA degree | White | Black |
|---|---|---|---|---|---|---|
| % that thinks Wal-Mart is a good place to shop | 67.72 | 78.24 | 62.78 | 78.75 | 72.84 | 83.87 |
| % that thinks Wal-Mart is a good place to work | 47.26 | 61.76 | 44.17 | 58.84 | 51.99 | 71.77 |
| % that thinks Wal-Mart is good for the country | 55.97 | 68.13 | 54.81 | 66.07 | 60.38 | 79.03 |
| Rating of Wal-Mart (1 to 4) | 2.63 | 2.91 | 2.51 | 2.87 | 2.69 | 3.15 |

Source: Pew Research Center, December 2005.

were systematically overlooked for promotions at Wal-Mart. (Although the U.S. Supreme Court would eventually rule in Wal-Mart's favor by denying the plaintiffs' request for class action certification, the case was tied up in court proceedings for the better part of a decade.) In addition to fending off the *Dukes* lawsuit after it received class action status in June 2004, the middle part of the decade saw numerous additional public embarrassments for the giant company. In late 2005, a leaked memo from a Wal-Mart VP found its way into the *New York Times*, revealing that nearly half the children of Wal-Mart's hourly workers were either uninsured or on Medicaid.[21] By July 2006, the company's desire to enter the banking industry by way of store credit cards had prompted more negative public response than any other ILC application in the FDIC's history.[22] The next month, former ambassador Andrew Young, who had only recently been drafted to head the Wal-Mart-backed advocacy group Working Families for Wal-Mart, resigned under a cloud of controversy after making racially charged remarks about Jewish, Korean, and Arab entrepreneurs in African American neighborhoods.[23] And in October, the company was ordered to pay $78.5 million to workers in a class action suit in Pennsylvania, who sued Wal-Mart for compensation owed to them for being forced to work off the clock.

Yet at the same time, Wal-Mart's own blunders were amplified by the activities of Wal-Mart Watch, a progressive organization founded in 2005 with partner organizations like the Service Employees International Union, the Sierra Club, and Sojourners. With a self-proclaimed mission of challenging Wal-Mart "to embrace its moral responsibility as the nation's biggest and most important corporation," Wal-Mart Watch remained poised to call public attention in national media venues to any and all of the company's missteps. The organization's media-heavy strategy was announced in two full-page ads published in national newspapers shortly after its 2005 founding—one declaring "It's Time to Roll Back Wal-Mart" (focusing particularly on Wal-Mart's cost to taxpayers), and another asking "What Happened to the Wal-Mart 'Buy American' Program?" By strategically using the media along with Internet venues, Wal-Mart Watch brought a new level of facts and insider information about Wal-Mart directly to its shopping public. The health care memo published in the *New York Times*, for example, was first leaked to the press by Wal-Mart Watch.

Although Wal-Mart attempted to maintain a calm public face amid these storms, the company's actual behavior revealed its growing concern for its public image. The company hired former Clinton adviser Leslie Dach to direct a political-style campaign to respond to these new attacks, and recruited Al Gore to screen *An Inconvenient Truth* at a Wal-Mart shareholders' meeting.[24]

In late 2006, Wal-Mart issued wage increases for new hires at a third of its stores,[25] and in early 2007 then-CEO Lee Scott met with the SEIU's Andy Stern to kick off the "Better Health Care Together" campaign, which brought together these unlikely allies with the goal of working more collaboratively to solve the nation's health care crisis.[26] Wal-Mart also withdrew its FDIC application to acquire a bank charter,[27] and a few months later announced that it would begin asking suppliers to improve their energy efficiency, using its market power to encourage its competitors to make additional environment-friendly reductions in packaging and production waste.[28] Even more important, the giant retailer announced improved health care additions for its associates in September of the same year, lowering premiums in some plans, reducing or eliminating hospital deductions in others, offering four-dollar generic drug prescriptions, and making health care more accessible to part-time workers and their children.[29] These changes are notable not only for their substance, but also because they were not foregone conclusions: the company's decision to alter some of its business operations was surely influenced, at least in part, by the ability of its opponents to create an anti-Wal-Mart campaign that found resonance with both the public and the national media.

The considerable successes of Wal-Mart Watch aside, my goal is not to explain how one activist group was able to secure concessions from a global corporation, but rather to understand the moral foundations of this larger struggle. In the coming chapters, I argue that market conservatives and progressives talk about many of the same concepts, but deploy them with reference to radically different core categories in ways that appeal to largely separate audiences. In particular, economic progressives adopt language that emphasizes the *benevolent citizen* in their criticism of Wal-Mart's alleged selfishness and monopolistic perversion of market freedom. For these activists, Wal-Mart's size and scale renders the marketplace inherently unfair to entire classes of people—particularly women, African Americans, and small business owners who are forced out of business by Wal-Mart's relentless bottom line. Instead, the company's critics call on Wal-Mart to use its market power to promote progressive reforms (such as setting higher labor standards for suppliers in the developing world) and to "use some of its profits to help some of its people." Wal-Mart's most public detractors talk less about families in lieu of a focus on larger societal categories such as the worker, the taxpayer, and the citizen—all of whom are deprived of revenue and freedom due to Wal-Mart's allegedly poor care and provision for its employees.

Conversely, Wal-Mart and its supporters build a moral framework around individual freedoms and the central category of the *average working family*, which helps explain why many of Wal-Mart's most ardent supporters are those same workers whose jobs have been displaced in the wake of larger forces of globalization, outsourcing, and corporate downsizing—trends that Wal-Mart itself has arguably helped to perpetuate. When framing economic hardship as something experienced primarily within one's family (rather than the result of larger economic forces or corporate policies), a store like Wal-Mart helps families make ends meet, and thus becomes a savior instead of a villain. But lest one assume that conservatives' "close to home" rhetoric is more simplistic, I also argue that conservative rhetoric tends to draw on a broader range of moral values than the progressive language illustrated by Wal-Mart's critics. Situating their language and arguments within the deep bonds of family and community, conservative activists are better able to appeal to the lived experiences of Americans than are progressives, whose rhetoric centers on broader, rationalized categories of modern society. Given this shortcoming, one strategy that might create a richer, more productive public discourse is one that creates more links between cognitive categories (e.g., workers, consumers, and families), although my research suggests that progressive groups like Wal-Mart Watch have not yet made extensive use of this approach.

## Outline of the Book

The book is divided into three main parts. Together with this introductory chapter, chapter 2 completes part 1 by placing the present-day debate over Wal-Mart within the larger context of the company's own history, as well as key developments in global retailing and manufacturing that make Wal-Mart a particularly useful case study of key dilemmas of modern capitalism. I also introduce the reader to the main actors in the Wal-Mart debate, as captured in a period of explosive media attention in 2005–2006: Wal-Mart Watch, Wal-Mart Inc., and the company's homegrown advocacy group Working Families for Wal-Mart. This chapter also describes the larger themes around which both sides of the debate structure their moral claims; these pairs of moral ideas—what I call "moral dialectics"—help to anchor the subsequent analysis of the moral discourse created by these groups: individualism and community, thrift and benevolence, and freedom and fairness.

Part 2 considers the kinds of moral arguments that these social movement organizations use to construct very different frameworks for understanding the morality of market processes. Although the chapters focus on data drawn from the Wal-Mart debate, each chapter also relates my interpretive arguments to other public, economic events in recent political history, including the Tea Party movement, health care reform, and the government's pledge of assistance to General Motors during the financial crisis of 2009. Chapter 3 considers the different audiences that each side of the Wal-Mart debate refers to and speaks to—what scholars of social movements call "imagined communities of reference." Examining these categories carefully reveals that both sides of the debate prioritize radically different audiences, which helps to explain why the moral visions of the market articulated by each side seem so diametrically opposed to each other. For Wal-Mart's supporters, this core category is the "average working family," while Wal-Mart's critics invite potential supporters to think of themselves primarily as citizens and activists. Chapter 4 explores how the same moral values can be invoked in very different contexts by analyzing how both groups approach the moral ideas of thrift and benevolence. When considered in the context of the family, for instance, Wal-Mart's supporters claim thrift as a moral virtue. This rhetoric looks profoundly different from that of Wal-Mart's opponents, who tend to argue that Wal-Mart is too thrifty and should instead act more benevolently, creating a discourse that focuses on larger societal categories such as the worker, citizen, and taxpayer. For Wal-Mart's supporters, focusing on families and their need to practice thrift explains why many of the same workers who have allegedly been harmed by Wal-Mart and its "race to the bottom" are also the company's most loyal shoppers. When one evaluates the market through the lens of the family, Wal-Mart becomes a lifeline instead of a threat, leading many supporters to describe Wal-Mart's low prices as central to their family's survival strategies. Finally, chapter 5 explores how the moral rhetoric of each side addresses broader market processes—in particular how both sides of the debate use ideas about freedom and fairness in their language about markets and their distributive outcomes. The rhetoric of Wal-Mart's supporters describes a wide range of individual freedoms that are tightly linked to the central value of market freedom, in which individuals need only to try hard in order to get ahead. In contrast, because Wal-Mart's critics tend to focus less on individuals and more on institutions (e.g., state governments and groups of small businesses), they reach a very different conclusion that warns of the dangers of Wal-Mart's activity in a laissez-faire market—for instance, alleging that Wal-Mart's practice of shifting health care costs onto taxpayers was simply unacceptable.

Part 3 looks beyond the focused language of SMOs to consider the significance of these contested moral frameworks in media and politics more broadly. In chapter 6, I examine roughly 1,200 articles sampled from the *New York Times*, the *Wall Street Journal*, and *USA Today* that mention Wal-Mart during the period 2000–2006. This analysis shows that during the period in which the union-funded Wal-Mart Watch was most active, these national newspapers made increasing mention of workers' issues in their coverage of Wal-Mart. At the same time, a closer examination of how national newspapers write about Wal-Mart Watch reveals that the larger forms of narrative and metaphor that shape this journalistic coverage actually serve to Wal-Mart's advantage in the national press. Framed within the larger metaphor of political struggle, Wal-Mart Watch's campaign against Wal-Mart fits into a narrative structure in which Wal-Mart can ironically present itself as something of a misunderstood victim, or at least a wayward company that eventually realizes the error of its ways and emerges as a changed hero on behalf of consumers as a result.

In the book's final chapter, I argue that the discourse produced by both sides of the Wal-Mart debate offers a telling portrait of how "the family" itself can become a discursive context for discussing economic issues. Alongside the sexually charged issues of reproductive freedom and same-sex marriage, conservative voices like those from Wal-Mart and its allies construct a moral worldview that places a particular understanding of the family at the center of their economic language. Drawing on deep institutional roots in the American South, evangelicalism, and the family-centered practice of consumption, Wal-Mart and its supporters speak a very different language than the union-funded Wal-Mart Watch, which tends to focus on larger collective categories of social organization. In discussing these institutional legacies, I also consider more productive possibilities for economic discourse, particularly public language that could effectively create more linkages between the categories of families and workers, consumers and citizens.

# 2

## Contextualizing the Wal-Mart Wars

The retail giant has launched a massive PR campaign to combat a
recent wave of negative stories, ranging from being sued for allegedly making employees work off the clock, to being sued for allegedly paying female workers less than men, to being sued for allegedly hiring illegal aliens. And it's also building a superstore next
to an ancient Mexican pyramid. And another one over a Hawaiian
burial ground. And I guess you could say they've destroyed the fabric of small town America. But on the positive side, three dollars
for a refrigerator? What? That's awesome!
—Jon Stewart on Comedy Central's *The Daily Show*

December 22, 1992, turned out to be an important day for both the history and the future of the Wal-Mart corporation. As Robert Slater tells the
story, shortly before Sam Walton died, he had reluctantly agreed to give a
pre-Christmas interview to *Dateline NBC*'s Jane Pauley, whose producers pitched the story as a positive exploration of Wal-Mart's winning retail
strategies. Keeping the company's commitment after Walton's death, the
company's new CEO David Glass gave the interview, only to be surprised
midway through by footage from a Bangladesh factory in which children
were making garments that would later be found under a "Made in the
USA" shelf label at a local Wal-Mart. Glass ended the interview immediately, and returned days later for a scheduled rebuttal in which he assured
viewers that the company had handled the situation, and that any allegations to the contrary might result from disagreement concerning what age
group constituted "children."[1] Although surprisingly little fallout occurred
from the *Dateline* story in terms of sales, the event marked Wal-Mart's real-
ization that it could no longer fly under the radar when it came to public opinion. While Sam Walton had managed to present the company as
something of a quirky underdog—aided by Walton's public image as a back-
woods billionaire who drove an old pickup truck, got five-dollar haircuts,

and borrowed change to make phone calls—Wal-Mart had entered the big leagues of muckraking journalism.

According to Slater, Wal-Mart's senior leadership viewed these criticisms as mere pitfalls of the notoriety that necessarily comes with success. "Though we were a $43 billion company when Sam passed away," Lee Scott explained to Robert Slater, "we were still able to avoid much notice; we were seen as the underdog, as a small-time company. We were the people from Bentonville, Arkansas, who had a pretty good company."[2] Don Soderquist, another longtime Wal-Mart executive, concurred when he considered the company's growing criticisms: "Like any successful company or organization, the company faces challenges from a host of detractors who want to slow or completely stop the company's growth." Soderquist went on to suggest that Wal-Mart was merely a scapegoat for a larger set of problems facing the country: "Because of the company's size and success, it has become a lightning rod for some of the most challenging issues we face as a society and country."[3]

The events of December 1992 notwithstanding, the first decade of the twenty-first century was surely the most difficult in the country's history.[4] Although NIMBY-type movements opposing Wal-Mart construction began appearing in the late 1980s and early 1990s,[5] Wal-Mart's newer criticisms have less to say about putting mom-and-pop retailers out of business at a local level and more to say about the company's broader labor practices, environmental impact, and subsidization by public tax dollars. While Wal-Mart could more easily respond to criticisms about undermining smaller retailers with its standard reply that these merchants had only themselves to blame for not adequately serving the customer's needs,[6] the criticisms facing the company in more recent years strike right at the heart of Wal-Mart's very identity as a cost-cutting, efficiency-obsessed mega-retailer.[7] Particularly during the time period under scrutiny in this study—a time of sustained economic gains following the post-9/11 recession, before the housing bubble burst and the financial crisis of 2008 developed—criticisms of Wal-Mart evolved into a sustained public debate that attracted the attention of national newspapers and presidential hopefuls. This public debate in the mid-2000s found a multitude of voices chiming in on all sides, with labor advocates alleging that Wal-Mart had decimated decades of hard-won union gains, environmentalists worrying about Wal-Mart's role in creating waste and suburban sprawl, economists crediting Wal-Mart with lowering inflation, and shoppers raving about how much they saved on groceries. As *The Economist* noted wryly in late 2006, even evangelical Christians found fault with some of the retailer's recent attempts to attract higher-income, progressive urban shoppers:

America's biggest retailer has become everybody's favourite whipping boy. The left decries the firm's stingy pay and health benefits. Mr. Obama last week declared that the "battle" to force the firm to examine its policies towards its workers was "absolutely vital." The Christian right is appalled at Wal-Mart's godless depravity, in particular its decision to sign up with the National Gay and Lesbian Chamber of Commerce in August and (horrors) to stock the totally legal morning-after pill.[8]

Even former presidential candidate John Kerry issued a statement after a member of a pro-Wal-Mart group used the term "Hezbocrats" to refer to Democrats who had been critical of the company. Kerry took care to emphasize Wal-Mart's responsibility to American workers, saying, "Make no mistake, those who push and prod Wal-Mart to be a decent corporate citizen are standing up for the American worker. Decent wages and afford-able health care aren't too much to ask for from the largest employer in the United States."[9] Like Kerry, other progressive advocates at the time framed the issue as one largely about the rights and well-being of workers in retail service jobs, most of whom are unorganized and earn wages too low to sup-port families with children. For these advocates, such shortcomings seem simply unacceptable in the comparatively prosperous era in which Ameri-cans now live. An editorial in *The Nation* compared Wal-Mart's cost-cutting strategies to antebellum slavery, concluding, "Wal-Mart's strategy of keeping costs down by exploiting sweatshop suppliers abroad while undermining unions and paying less than living wages in this country should be deemed unacceptable in the twenty-first century."[10]

For Wal-Mart's supporters, however, the issue is one of perspective and market realism. The *New York Times* columnist John Tierney, for example, argued that the protectionist rhetoric of the Wal-Mart critics privileged the rights of American workers over those of laborers in developing countries, where industry and manufacturing plants for Wal-Mart's suppliers (and other similar retailers) have encouraged unprecedented economic develop-ment. "If you want to help them," Tierney concluded, "remember the new social justice slogan proposed by [entrepreneurial activist Michael] Strong: 'Act locally, think globally: Shop Wal-Mart.'"[11] Others who have been critical of Wal-Mart's detractors emphasize that Wal-Mart, as merely one actor in the free market, offers jobs to those who would not otherwise be employed, lowers prices for families who are trying to make ends meet, and serves the well-being of large groups of consumers through actions such as low-ering prices on many prescription drugs to just four dollars. An editorial in the *Wall Street Journal* rationalized Wal-Mart's decision to undercut its competitors on prescription drug prices thus: "Wal-Mart isn't a charity, and its $4 decision is designed to lift its own sales by undercutting prices at competing retailers. But that's the way the market works, driving prices lower with competition. It turns out that Wal-Mart's critics really didn't care about prices; what they want is more union clout, and more government control over health care."[12] From this perspective, Wal-Mart's critics are foolishly asking Wal-Mart to ignore the rules of market competition, and are motivated by their own ideological desire to see more government intervention in labor laws and health care.

Thoughtful observers of this debate will find aspects of both perspectives compelling. But however convincing the arguments on all sides of an economic dilemma such as this might be, the Wal-Mart debate is of theoretical interest for another reason entirely: the debate over Wal-Mart offers an auspicious opportunity to study the language that both conservative and progressive Americans use to construct different frameworks of economic morality in the public sphere. Much in the same way that immigration reform elicits impassioned arguments about undocumented workers' connections to the American economy, or that President Bush urged American consumers to go shopping in order to ward of recession in the wake of 9/11, the Wal-Mart controversy represents just one of many current public issues in which the American public is invited to consider the ameliorative potential of "market logic"—in other words, a conceptual framework in which the laws of economics and capitalist markets are considered as potential agents in the solution of larger social problems.

The Wal-Mart debate is also a valuable case study of two competing versions of populist politics, each contending that their constituency is a moral and virtuous representation of "the people" against "the powerful." In defining populism, the historian Michael Kazin has emphasized the significance of rhetoric itself in communicating populist goals: populism is therefore "a language whose speakers conceive of ordinary people as a noble assemblage not bounded narrowly by class, view their elite opponents as self-serving and undemocratic, and seek to mobilize the former against the latter."[13] Although whom each side of the Wal-Mart debate frames as their allegedly selfish and undemocratic opponents differs considerably, both activist groups seek to define their opponents in broadly populist, people-against-the-powerful terms. Thus, while the issues at the center of the Wal-Mart debate revolve largely around matters of economics (e.g., how much employers should be required to contribute to health care, or the fine line between acceptable success in the free market and unacceptable monopoly dominance), the debate captures our attention because these market issues are directly connected to larger questions about the nature of the common good and the well-being of ordinary people in the wake of capitalism's intractable inequalities. And, as I shall argue further in this chapter, the debate over Wal-Mart is also an excellent case study of economic political discourse for three main reasons: Most important, for its public presence and relevance. In addition, Wal-Mart itself represents an embodiment of several key issues in larger debates about globalization and capitalism that confront us, as Americans, in the twenty-first century. Finally, Wal-Mart itself can be understood as representing both the best and the worst of capitalism and market logic. In this chapter, I discuss each of these three reasons in turn, and in the process introduce the major issues and actors in this particular political struggle.

## Wal-Mart in the Public Eye

A quick survey of recent newspaper stories alone would convince most anyone that Wal-Mart is indeed teeming with public relevance. In the spring of 2007, for example, Democratic presidential hopefuls like Joe Biden, John Edwards, and Barack Obama joined a cross-country campaign denouncing the retailer for being, in the words of Indiana senator Evan Bayh, "emblematic of the anxiety around the country, and the middle-class squeeze."[14] Following suit, Hillary Rodham Clinton returned a $5,000 campaign contribution from Wal-Mart that same summer, and attempted to downplay her tenure as the company's first female board member during the 1980s.[15] Wal-Mart has also been an issue for state and local governments during the past several years, such as when the Chicago city council and the state legislature of Maryland both passed legislation forcing Wal-Mart to pay higher wages and fund state health care initiatives, respectively (both pieces of legislation were later overturned, the former by mayoral veto, the latter in federal court).

A central issue in these political debates is Wal-Mart's compensation of its employees. Working full-time in 2006, the average Wal-Mart worker made around $21,000 a year—which still traps families with children near the federal poverty line ($20,650 for a family of four in 2007).[16] To be fair, Wal-Mart's hourly wage was slightly higher than the 2005 BLS median hourly estimate of $9.20 for retail salespersons, and Wal-Mart consistently reports that most of its associates have health insurance (though not necessarily through Wal-Mart). At the same time, critics argue that a company of Wal-Mart's size and stature could afford to do better by its employees. Further, Wal-Mart's detractors claim that the company's health care plans were not affordable for the typical Wal-Mart worker: in 2007, for instance, the 80/20 coverage on the cheapest plans required that the associate first meet a sizeable deductible, typically $1,000 for an employee and $3,000 for a family.[17]

This has led many of Wal-Mart's critics to publicly accuse the company of shifting health care and other costs to state and local governments. Because so many of Wal-Mart's associates live on meager incomes, critics allege, they must rely on public assistance programs such as food stamps or Medicaid, a move that ultimately shifts costs from businesses to taxpayers. This argument gained further traction in 2003 when California assemblywoman Sally Leiber received leaked Wal-Mart documents explaining to its workers how to apply for public assistance. Adding insult to injury, this came to light amid a severe state budget crisis.[18] The costs were not insignificant: a UC Berkeley study reported that Wal-Mart workers cost California taxpayers around $86 million in both health care costs and other related fees.[19] Similar issues face taxpayers at the national level: Democratic staff of the House Committee on Education and the Workforce found that federal taxpayers had spent as much as two thousand public dollars on every Wal-Mart employee. And in states like Tennessee and Georgia, Wal-Mart workers were by far the largest contingent to have enrolled their families in state-funded health insurance programs for the poor.[20]

In the mid-2000s, Wal-Mart was also plagued with another kind of high-profile censure: the class action lawsuit. Two issues were particularly relevant: gender discrimination and failure either to pay employees for time worked off the clock, or to provide employees with required rest breaks. The lawsuit *Dukes vs. Wal-Mart Stores Inc.* was awarded class action status on June 22, 2004, three years after Betty Dukes filed as the lead plaintiff in what would become the largest civil rights class action suit in history.[21] And in the fall of 2006, Wal-Mart was ordered to pay $78.5 million in a class action verdict on behalf of Pennsylvania employees who were not paid for rest breaks during which they continued to work.[22] The decision followed a $172,000 verdict on lost meal breaks in California in 2005 (Wal-Mart has since appealed), and preceded similar lost pay lawsuits filed in Illinois[23] and Minnesota.[24]

Echoes of all these allegations resurfaced in a very public way when Wal-Mart filed an Industrial Loan Corporation charter application in the summer of 2005. ILCs are banks that serve the limited function of offering small loans to their customers—practices that have become commonplace for corporations like automotive companies and other retailers.[25] Like its competitors Sears and Target, Wal-Mart filed an ILC application with the Federal Deposit Insurance Corporation in order to be able to process credit and debit transactions "in-house," saving the company the processing fees it currently pays to outside services for such transactions.[26] The normally routine application drew so many comments—overwhelmingly against Wal-Mart—that the FDIC held three days' worth of hearings on the application, drawing comment from a diverse coalition of community bankers, retailers, and grocers' organizations, as well as union-based and other citizens' advocacy groups.[27] After hearing this testimony in July of 2006 (and receiving more than one thousand additional statements and letters), the FDIC issued a six-month ban on all ILC applications, which it extended for an additional year the following January.[28] Faced with these obstacles, Wal-Mart quietly withdrew its application, and the FDIC was spared from making a decision in the controversial matter.

Amid the controversy surrounding its labor and business practices, however, Wal-Mart has recently garnered public acclaim for supporting a cause close to the heart of progressives everywhere: protecting the environment. To be sure, for most of its history Wal-Mart's reputation on environmental issues has been anything but admirable. In fact, Wal-Mart was more likely to be associated with the kind of embarrassing environmental violations for which it was fined in 2004—to the tune of $3.1 million for violating the Clean Water Act at twenty-four sites across nine different states.[29] In the fall of 2005, however, Lee Scott issued a series of pledges designed to make the company more environmentally efficient while using its market clout to encourage similar modifications throughout the industry, prompting headlines like "The Green Machine," and "Build Green, Make Green," as various journalists began chronicling Wal-Mart's nascent environmental reforms.[30] Wal-Mart's strategy could be described as threefold: to make modifications at its store locations that promote efficiency, to encourage similar reductions among its employees and shoppers, and to be a trendsetter that encourages environmentally friendly initiatives at every step of its global supply chain. The common denominator in all these efforts is Wal-Mart's massive size: if Wal-Mart could use its power to promote positive social change among individuals, the effects could reverberate throughout larger collectivities.

### Wal-Mart Watch and Working Families for Wal-Mart

In addition to facing political debates, public referendums, class action lawsuits, FDIC hearings, and environmental pressures, in 2005 Wal-Mart began taking heat from social movement organizations whose sole purpose was reforming Wal-Mart, such as Wake Up Wal-Mart and Wal-Mart Watch. Both groups were vigilant about publicizing Wal-Mart's shortcomings by leaking insider memos and emails, issuing media releases, and speaking to the press. The public nature of this debate was critical, because although both groups wanted to change the country's largest employer, they sought to do so primarily through the means of public opinion, hoping to motivate the public by emphasizing the moral contours of this debate. While Wake Up Wal-Mart remained closely affiliated with the United Food and Commercial Workers (the two groups shared office space and Wake Up's funding came almost entirely from the union), Wal-Mart Watch was founded in the spring of 2005 by a coalition of progressive organizations, including the Service Employees International Union, the Association of Community Organizations for Reform Now (ACORN), Sprawl-Busters, and the Sierra Club. Although both groups worked separately (and sometimes even in contention with each other) for the time period primarily under study in this book, Wake Up Wal-Mart and Wal-Mart Watch would eventually join forces under the Wal-Mart Watch name in 2007.

In its public censure of the retailer, Wal-Mart Watch took a strategic approach that emphasized carefully crafted press releases and media statements designed to draw public attention to some of Wal-Mart's most controversial features, particularly its employee benefits policies. This strategy seemed to pay off: in early 2007 Wal-Mart CEO Lee Scott joined with SEIU president and Wal-Mart Watch board member Andrew Stern to announce the "Better Health Care Together" campaign, calling on businesses, individuals, and government to collaborate in providing health insurance for all Americans by 2012. Given that Stern and Wal-Mart had been longtime antagonists, NPR correspondent Len Nichols quipped, "This was equivalent, in my view, to Anwar Sadat going to Jerusalem to shake hands with Menachem Begin."[31]

Wal-Mart Watch also focused its efforts less on dramatic organized actions and attention-grabbing television advertisements and more on language itself, as communicated through newspaper advertisements, press releases, and its website, walmartwatch.com. The centerpiece of the organization's public relations campaign was its press releases and media campaigns—appropriately, the organization inaugurated its attack on Wal-Mart in April 2005 with two full-page ads in the *New York Times* and *USA Today*. One advertisement asked, "How Much Does Wal-Mart Cost American Taxpayers Each Year?" and countered that it was time to "Rollback Wal-Mart" (a clever wordplay on the retailer's well-known strategy at the time of "rolling back" prices). The other asked, "What Happened to the Wal-Mart 'Buy American' Program?" atop a photo of a Wal-Mart store rife with signs indicating goods made in China. Both ads followed with facts and supporting documentation, and invited readers to join Wal-Mart Watch in "taking on the largest corporation in the world."

Of course, Wal-Mart would not be content to accept this assault without responding in kind, and the company did so by founding its own "grassroots" group, Working Families for Wal-Mart, which issued its own statements and maintained a website for nearly two years, ending in December 2007 (when Wal-Mart announced that it would bring the organization in-house shortly before Christmas). Like Wal-Mart Watch, Working Families for Wal-Mart existed primarily as a "paper" advocacy group, with large lists of email supporters and funding from a larger, influential organization. On its website, the group declared, "Working Families for Wal-Mart is a group of leaders from a variety of backgrounds and communities all across America. Working Families for Wal-Mart are customers, business leaders, activists, civic leaders, educators and many others with first-hand knowledge of Wal-Mart's positive contributions to communities." Further, the organization described its mission as "fostering open and honest dialogue with elected officials, opinion makers and community leaders that conveys the positive contributions of Wal-Mart to working families," because "we believe that Wal-Mart provides value to its customers, to its associates and to the communities it serves."

At the same time, the group seems to be the epitome of a phenomenon called "astroturfing," in which corporations create front groups billed as grassroots organizations. To illustrate, Wal-Mart's PR firm, Edelman, was the chief recruiter of Working Families for Wal-Mart's steering committee members, many of whom had business connections with Wal-Mart.[32] At the same time, the organization solicited hundreds of stories from real-life consumers, employers, suppliers, and beneficiaries of Wal-Mart's corporate philanthropy, using their own words to describe the difference that Wal-Mart has made in their lives. The stories were varied in their content, style, and length, and contain a range of errors in spelling and punctuation that point to their authenticity. Although it is impossible to know if some or all of these narratives might be counterfeit, the depth of the stories and the personal histories embedded within them—describing single motherhood, sick spouses, military relocation, and family struggle—either speak to Working Families for Wal-Mart and Edelman's tireless devotion to screening/crafting a particular message, the importance that Wal-Mart holds in the lives of many Americans, or both.

## Wal-Mart and Twenty-First-Century Capitalism

Despite the storm of controversy surrounding the retailer in recent years, one of the ironies of the Wal-Mart debate is that neither Wal-Mart's size nor its business practices are particularly novel in American history.[33] Although a lightning rod for such criticisms, Wal-Mart is not alone in the retail industry in paying low wages and offering scanty benefits, squeezing the global supply chain, or leaving a larger-than-average "carbon footprint." As Petro-vic and Hamilton observe of recent developments in the big-box industry, "Wal-Mart may have the starring role, but it is surrounded by a very talented cast," including retailers like Target, Home Depot, and Best Buy.[34] Yet even as it is surrounded by a gallery of similarly placed competitors, Wal-Mart remains a "template corporation" whose size and innovations have indisput-able implications for its competitors, making it difficult to accurately specify where Wal-Mart's influence ends, where patterns within the larger industry begin, and vice versa.[35]

Thus, in addition to its public relevance, Wal-Mart is an ideal topic for the study of political discourse about capitalism simply because its sheer size and market influence place it at the heart of debates over globalization, deregula-tion, and capitalism itself in the twenty-first century. Wal-Mart has been an unparalleled success in the retail industry in part due to its distinctive strate-gies, in which the retailer pioneered techniques that have diffused through-out the industry to the point that they are now taken for granted—indeed, now required—for market success in a highly rationalized, globalized, retail marketplace. The Wal-Mart model illustrates the importance of at least four main trends in twenty-first-century capitalism: competing in a global mar-ket, the importance of technology in managing an increasingly rationalized supply chain, the shift from "push" to "pull" systems of marketing, and a new team-centered model of service work in which workers are discouraged from collective bargaining.

*The Global Market*

To be a retailer in the twenty-first century means being a part of an increas-ingly integrated global supply chain. Thus arguments about Wal-Mart's busi-ness practices—in which, for example, critics allege that Wal-Mart takes jobs away from Americans by forcing manufacturers to relocate overseas—are effectively arguments about globalization itself. In particular, the past three decades have witnessed increasing integration between the developed world and industrializing nations in the developing world. This global supply chain connects nations through the trading of commodities so diverse as to include textiles, manufactures, food, livestock, and direct services.[36] And while glo-balization itself is not necessarily a new phenomenon (nations have been trading with one another for centuries), the important change for under-standing the Wal-Mart debate concerns the *kinds* of goods that are presently traded among nations. By 2001, for example, the World Bank's estimates of imports and exports suggested that most exports from the developing world were no longer primary products, like food or raw materials, but manufactured goods that make up more than half the exported goods everywhere in the world, except for its poorest regions.[37]

Discourse on globalization reveals a deep ambivalence about this process. Many of globalization's critics hail, ironically, from the developed countries who are presumed to be the beneficiaries of the cheaper labor available overseas.[38] Even so, investigations of the data on global income inequality suggest that developing countries have experienced real income growth in the wake of globalization—for example, the poverty rates in China and India have declined by twenty and fifty points, respectively, between the late 1970s and the late 1990s,[39] indicating that inter-nation inequality is actually on the decline as a result of the rapid industrialization in China and Southeast Asia, the world's most populous poor regions.[40] Even studies that find increasing wage inequality within countries note that its effects remain quite modest overall, because the gains from even a small percentage of wage earners may be spread throughout families and regions that benefit from cheaper raw materials (such as fertilizer for farming) and increased production that brings higher prices for agricultural goods.[41] This has led some to observe that the real critiques of globalization may emerge from the lower-skilled laborers in developed countries who do find themselves on the losing end of an integrated global supply chain.[42] In the discount industry, where retailers make pennies on each sale, reducing manufacturing costs is an unavoidable reality that does place American manufacturers in a much weaker bargaining position.

By participating in these global trends, many argue that Wal-Mart is merely following the new rules of the global marketplace, in which technology and policy changes have removed many of the barriers that previously urged more protectionist approaches to international trade. China's opening of its markets in 1978, falling shipping rates by both sea and air, reduced subsidies and tariffs, and treaties such as the GATT and NAFTA all helped companies like Wal-Mart take advantage of the global supply chain, because manufacturers recognized opportunities for cheaper production in industrializing nations, particularly in China, India, and Southeast Asia.[43] Technological advances also played a role, particularly innovations such as intermodal transportation (packing goods in mobile containers), making it easier and less costly to ship goods from the manufacturer to ports and directly onto transport trucks destined for retail distribution centers.[44] The resultant cost savings, Wal-Mart and its supporters argue, can then be passed on to consumers.

Globalization also creates reciprocal opportunities for Wal-Mart, which benefits from offering stores to emerging wage-earning classes in places like

China, India, and Mexico—ironically, the very countries where new groups of workers have the buying power to shop at larger retailers precisely because they are working at manufacturing plants that produce the kind of goods sold there. Accordingly, Wal-Mart and its global competitors Carrefour and Tesco have lately begun competing for the grocery and general goods market in China and India.[45] For a company that faces potential saturation in the United States, entry into these global markets proves critical. And the ironies of globalization persist: its Chinese stores are unionized (according to the Chinese Communist Party law), and while Wal-Mart's attempt to receive an ILC charter met incessant obstacles in the United States, it has long offered consumer credit cards to shoppers in China and Mexico, where it has also entered the banking industry.[46]

*Technological Innovation*

In this global environment, Wal-Mart's pioneering use of technology has been a key feature of retailers' growing ability to manage their inventory, respond to consumer demand almost instantaneously, and keep labor costs low through the control of information. From its early days as a discount retailer, Wal-Mart led the industry by emphasizing the role of technology in creating ever-more efficient systems of distribution.[47] As early as 1977, Wal-Mart instituted an electronic data interchange (EDI) system that brought automation to key aspects of the distribution system, such as ordering and tracking merchandise and issuing payments. In the pre-Internet decades, this EDI system connected store phone networks with two IBM mainframe computers at Wal-Mart's headquarters that stored payroll data along with inventory and financial information.[48] Thus it followed perfectly that Wal-Mart led the industry in adopting UPC scanners in 1983, shortly after the innovation began to filter through grocery stores, where they were often met with resistance.[49] By 1987 Wal-Mart had further refined its technological nerve center by building the largest private satellite network in the country, which allowed the company to track every sale at every store and analyze them alongside a series of variables such as the store's demographics (did it attract students or retirees?) and climate (was there a hurricane or a heat wave?), which would then suggest locally tailored inventory. More recently, Wal-Mart's move toward RFID (radio frequency identification detection) technology promises to streamline the company's inventory management even further, allowing stock workers to determine how many items of certain types are present in any given warehouse at any given time. Wal-Mart (along with other retailers) will literally be able to monitor and chart the progress of goods as they cross the Atlantic Ocean.

New technology has also proven essential in the retail industry's ability to keep labor and management cost increases to a minimum, belying the conventional wisdom that says the more productive firms are those that lower transaction costs through reducing firm size.[50] By keeping the costs of moving goods and paying workers to a minimum, retailers like Wal-Mart manage to avoid some of the pitfalls associated with large-scale corporations: they can respond more quickly to change, challenging a premise in organizational ecology that large size tends to make it more difficult for organizations to adapt and innovate.[51] For example, Wal-Mart adopted a scheduling policy in 2006 in which computerized technology would chart store traffic and ask employees to be "on call" to come in when foot traffic required more workers.[52] Big-box retailers' use of technology to streamline efficiency accordingly places merchants like Wal-Mart in quite a predicament when facing current criticisms, particularly those addressing wages and benefits. In large part *because* Wal-Mart is so efficient, profit margins are trimmed so close to the bone that the company literally can't raise wages without raising prices. To illustrate, Wal-Mart makes about $3 an hour per associate per year—to raise the average $10.11 hourly wage by a mere $1.50 per hour would cut the company's profits in half.[53]

### From Push to Pull Systems of Merchandising

The consequences of these technological innovations are not limited to employees. In fact, one of the most important consequences of retailers' growing technological readiness is the shift from a "push" to a "pull" system of merchandising. While manufacturers once approached retailers with products and price points, in the post-Wal-Mart economy this relationship has been reversed. Terming this change the "logistics revolution," Edna Bonacich describes the complete overhaul of the production and delivery of retail goods that has taken place over the past thirty years, a period during which Wal-Mart has been the leader by virtue of its commanding use of technology and its massive scale.[54] Because profit margins in the retailing business are merely pennies on the dollar, ensuring unflagging efficiency is a key feature of remaining profitable, and this means controlling as many details of the logistics operation of the supply chain as possible. Aided by technology that tracks consumer purchases and inventory trends, large retailers like Wal-Mart control ever more features of the supply chain, right down to where identification stickers are placed on cartons of inventory.[55]

Where manufacturers once "pushed" inventory onto retailers with suggested price points (and often costly overstocks that mis-estimated consumer preferences), the "pull" system delivers orders to vendors based on consumer preference data and keeps orders to a minimum to cut down on the costly process of dealing with those overstocks. This has increased "just in time" merchandising that restocks items overnight in order to respond to up-to-the-minute consumer demands.[56] Thus retailers are able to keep strict tabs on the quantities of items sold, adjusting their requests of suppliers often on short notice to fill vacant shelves and replace depleted inventories. This means that manufacturers, not retailers, are stuck with the excess goods. Further, by virtue of its sheer size Wal-Mart in particular is able to set the opening price point and ask manufacturers to meet it—or else. Like other big-box retailers, the concentrated volume of sales at Wal-Mart means that the retailer increasingly sets the price for specific goods and expects that the manufacturer will deliver them as requested.[57]

Doing business with a retailer the size of Wal-Mart is thus a mixed blessing for suppliers. Given Wal-Mart's size and market share, most companies can't afford *not* to sell their products at a retail chain that by some estimates controls 16% of the national grocery market,[58] is the largest toy retailer in the United States,[59] and sells 10% of all products made by suppliers like Proctor & Gamble.[60] Charles Fishman recounts the semi-tragic story of Vlasic pickles, which agreed to Wal-Mart's offer to sell a gallon of pickles for $2.97—a price so low that Wal-Mart and Vlasic each made about one cent per jar in profit. While pickles flew off the shelves faster than families could consume a gallon's worth, the low prices at Wal-Mart began to eat into Vlasic's non-Wal-Mart shares.[61] By the time they agreed to a $2.49 half-gallon jar, pickle profits had declined by 50%. Other stories of this same kind of process are much less benign than pickle profit slashing—Fishman also recounts the story of the L. R. Nelson sprinkler company, which shut down most of its U.S.-based manufacturing division in favor of relocation to China, leading company president Dave Eglinton to explain, "Wal-Mart has said that they would love to buy from us because some of the production is done in the United States, but the cost differential is so great that they told us that unless we supply them out of China, we couldn't do business."[62] Viewed in this way, the new pull system of manufacturing is inextricably linked to the decline of American manufacturing jobs—many of which had formerly been unionized.

Of course, this "Wal-Mart effect" arguably creates winners alongside losers like Vlasic and L. R. Nelson. Wal-Mart has also been credited with such accomplishments as single-handedly creating the burgeoning salmon farming industry in Chile, which supplies Wal-Mart Supercenters with salmon filets that retail for less than five dollars per pound. While the factory hours and work requirements at the accompanying processing plants would incite the ire of even lukewarm Marxists, the industry has raised the standard of living for hundreds—perhaps even thousands—of workers who formerly based their precarious survival on subsistence farming, or worse.[63] Soderquist offers an even more positive spin on the buyer–supplier relationship, emphasizing Wal-Mart's role in helping companies identify their own inefficiencies and address them so that cost savings may be shared with the consumer. More important, Soderquist frames these relationships as just that—relationships that bring team members together toward their common goal, which is serving the customer by eliminating waste and improving efficiency. Yet others maintain that the true cost of the resulting products is much higher than that borne by any of the parties involved. In the case of the salmon industry, for example, activists warn that Wal-Mart can afford to retail salmon at such low prices because they do not absorb all of the costs associated with the industry, particularly the pollution resulting from over-farming and the medical and other costs of factory employees.[64]

## The New "Teamsters"

Finally, in addition to its innovative approaches to merchandising, technology, and the global supply chain, Wal-Mart represents a new approach to service work itself that stems at least in part from its own particular corporate culture and the enduring legacy of its charismatic founder.[65] Sam's credo could be summarized as a mix of old-fashioned populism (exemplified by the Wal-Mart tagline, "Who's number one? The customer, always"), down-home friendliness (expressed in slogans on associates' vests such as "Our people make the difference" and "How may I help you?"), and, of course, relentless cost-cutting. In the spirit of this folksy culture, Wal-Mart's front-line hourly workers are called "associates," not employees, and wear name tags with only their first name—and some of them have even earned starring roles in Wal-Mart's television ads.[66] When associates commit an infraction, they are "coached," not disciplined, and the company cites its "open door policy" as a central reason for the uselessness of a union—employees with a grievance may complain directly to management, at any time.[67] Such techniques are now quite common in the retail industry, with stores like Target, Home Depot, and the like following suit as they hire "associates" and "team members" instead of "employees."

Moreover, Wal-Mart's workforce is of particular interest because not one of its 1.4 million domestic workers is a member of a union. Wal-Mart's workers are thus emblematic of the steep challenges facing organized labor today: while one in three Americans carried a union membership card in 1950, only about one in ten are organized today.[68] Former SEIU president Andy Stern (and a founding board member of Wal-Mart Watch) cited Wal-Mart as an example of the kind of industry that the labor-establishment breakaway Change to Win Coalition planned to target in its future organizing endeavors, arguing, "If we're going to change the size and the shape of the American union movement and change workers' lives, we have to get away from this shop-by-shop, small organizing and really take on the largest employers in our country today, like Wal-Mart."[69] Accordingly, Wal-Mart's own advocates have leveled charges at Stern and Wal-Mart Watch, alleging that these and other activist groups don't have the welfare of workers in mind, but only want to tap into Wal-Mart's workforce as a new source of revenue to replace shrinking union dues.

## Wal-Mart and Populist Discourse

As the preceding discussion has argued, Wal-Mart is clearly a lightning rod for public debate about many of the core dimensions of the reorganization of labor and manufacturing that have accompanied globalization in recent decades. But more important (and of special interest to sociologists studying the relationship between culture, morality, and economics), the debate over Wal-Mart illustrates both the best and worst potential inherent in the very idea of American capitalism. Discussions about Wal-Mart's consequences for the American economy—both positive and negative—call on deeper, more widely shared cultural understandings of the appropriate moral boundaries of economic activity, particularly for average American citizens. Three pairs of moral dialectics prove particularly relevant when considering Wal-Mart's history, its core values, and the themes that repeatedly surface in the current discourse regarding the company: *individuals and communities, thrift and benevolence,* and *freedom and fairness.*

Although other moral concerns could surely be raised when evaluating capitalist activity (e.g., concerns about exploitation, equality, justice), the three pairs identified here are sufficiently broad to encompass many other moral values: exploitation might be considered a result of stymied freedom, equality an outcome of one conception of fairness, and so on. These themes also have a long and distinguished history in American political culture, and are of particular interest because while they are not necessarily contradictory, an excess of one may inhibit the other. Situations that work for the advantage of individuals, for example, may not necessarily serve the interests of a community or collective as a whole. Similarly, excessive thrift may inhibit opportunities to express benevolence, and some conceptions of fairness (e.g., certain ways of leveling the playing field, such as affirmative action) may threaten other understandings of freedom. Of course, these dialectical themes are partially overlapping, but they are also distinct enough to be identified separately in empirical analysis, as I will argue in chapters 3–5. As analytical constructs, they help to make the Wal-Mart debate intelligible while also connecting this particular case study to larger ideals that have a longer history in American political culture. Below, I discuss each of these moral dialectics—their relationships to the company and its history, along with some of their connections to the current discourse.

## Individuals and Communities

First and foremost, Wal-Mart raises the perennial question of how to evaluate the well-being of individuals alongside the well-being of collectivities. Perhaps more so than any other source of thematic resonance in American culture, the dichotomy between individualism and communitarianism has received unwavering attention in the social sciences.[70] More often than not, sociologists have warned of the dangers of unchecked individualism, which critics view as putting one's own personal needs ahead of the concerns of larger collectivities. Hence, a spate of recent studies examine social capital, volunteerism, and participation in institutional avenues that help individuals overcome myopic self-absorptions.[71] Yet individualism—understood as self-reliance, self-expression, or self-advancement by achieving the American Dream—also has a long and cherished place in American political culture, which places its critics in a difficult predicament. Individualism need not be self-absorbed and selfish; in fact, individualism is consistently linked with traits that many Americans admire and seek to emulate. Through being strong and self-reliant, for example, the individual develops the self-control and resolve that prove necessary for success and leadership; people are accountable for their own behavior and receive the benefits (or the consequences) of their actions.[72] In American political culture, then, many social problems such as drunk driving[73] and fetal alcohol syndrome[74] are framed in the media and in public discourse as individual-level issues.

Of course, the community has an equally notable role in American history and political thought—ranging from small town America to the current fury of civic revival that hopes to preserve community's place of pride in American political consciousness. Thus it comes as no surprise that a key realm of debate over Wal-Mart concerns the relationship between the individual and the community. In fact, much of the substance of the debate over the country's largest retailer concerns how individuals' pursuit of lower prices on consumer goods affects larger groups of Americans—whether smaller merchants, laborers whose jobs are affected by outsourcing, or the growing ranks of service workers employed at big-box retailers. There's no denying, for example, that Wal-Mart has succeeded in its mission of bringing everyday low prices to consumers across the United States. According to the research firm Global Insight, Wal-Mart saves the average consumer over $2,300 a year.[75] Similarly, other studies suggest that CPI estimates may overstate even the modest inflation rates of the past decade by as much as 15% due to not correctly estimating the effect of Wal-Mart on lowering grocery prices.[76] Clearly, Wal-Mart does make good on its claim to help working families stretch their dollars further each month.

Yet critics of consumption like Benjamin Barber worry that the capitalist engine has been so successful in the American economy that marketers must now convince consumers that they have more need of more goods more frequently than ever before. Thus Barber argues that the market feeds the very worst kind of individualism possible in American life—a self-centered, infantilizing consumerist ethos that seeks immediate satisfaction that is never fully apprehended.[77] Other critics ask about the potentially high cost of the individual savings that Wal-Mart proffers—as noted earlier, many of Wal-Mart's critics allege that Wal-Mart can offer these low prices only by taking advantage of both people and natural resources, keeping labor costs low, offering skimpy benefits, using sweatshop labor, and ignoring environmental concerns such as waste and stormwater management.

One difficulty in the Wal-Mart debate, however, is that it is sometimes challenging to identify just who the individuals and communities are that are being alternately well served or abused by Wal-Mart's success. Charles Fishman, a journalist whose recent writings have been mostly critical of the retailer, concludes that "at the moment, we are incapable as a society of understanding Wal-Mart because we haven't equipped ourselves to manage it. That is the reason for our ambivalence, our appreciation and aversion, our awe and our nervousness, our confusion."[78] As Fishman goes on to explain, part of the difficulty with Wal-Mart is that unlike the giant oil trusts that were successfully foiled in the progressive era, Wal-Mart doesn't claim its profits on its own behalf, but champions the consumer in populist terms—the "little guy" who's just trying to stretch a dollar a bit further.[79] Don Soderquist similarly writes, "Recognizing that many of our customers are average American families working hard to make ends meet, we believe that low prices are essential, and we never stop working to keep our prices low."[80] Just whom Americans should be loyal to—the company that helps an individual family save 15% on groceries every month, or the activists who accuse that same company of siphoning money away from the heads of other families in the community who are un- or under-employed as a result—remains unclear. How different groups of activists appropriate these twin themes will explain much of how they understand their audience, and how that audience relates to their larger mission and moral perspective.

## Thrift and Benevolence

Any discussion of economic debate in modern America would be incomplete without considering thrift and benevolence. In his classic treatise *The Protestant Ethic*, Weber argues that capitalism emerged in western Europe due an elective affinity with Protestantism, particularly Calvinism, in which believers who were unsure of their salvation eased their anxiety by achieving financial success in their worldly activity. Ascetic lifestyles, hard work, thrift, and reinvestment created burgeoning entrepreneurs whose wealth and business acumen spawned the modern capitalist enterprise. Of course, Weber did not view this development with wholehearted admiration, ending his study by warning that while Calvinists *chose* to live in the manner described in his analysis, modern-day individuals are *forced* to do so. Once established, the system no longer needed the Protestant ethic to be the steam in its engine—capitalism took on a life of its own, which created an "iron cage," forcing future generations to accept its principles without question.

It would be difficult to imagine a company that exemplified the Protestant ethic more completely than Wal-Mart. At the very heart of its identity is the value of thrift—Wal-Mart's profits come from selling large volumes of merchandise priced at pennies below its competitors. For this reason, and as discussed above, squeezing waste and inefficiency out of its supply chain is an essential part of the Wal-Mart business model. And so it comes as little surprise that Sam Walton was widely regarded as an evangelical Presbyterian who experienced his first entrepreneurial success by trimming costs throughout his small franchise of Ben Franklin variety stores. The ethic of thrift pervades not only the prices on Wal-Mart merchandise but also the larger Wal-Mart culture. Even today, decades after Walton's death, Wal-Mart headquarters do not have any executive dining rooms or bathrooms, the office furniture is often leftover samples from furniture vendors, and executives follow the "two to a room" rule when on company travel.[81] Underscoring executives' loyalty to this aspect of the company credo is the story of how company vice chairman John Menzer served Henry Kissinger a Subway sandwich with chips during the former diplomat's visit to Wal-Mart company headquarters.[82]

This pseudo-Protestant ethic finds further expression in the company's strict ethics policy. Wal-Mart's executive employees must adhere to strict guidelines prohibiting them from giving or accepting gifts from suppliers—even something as small as a cup of coffee. Further, in "Action Alley" (the section of Wal-Mart headquarters where company buyers negotiate with suppliers) buyers are discouraged from forming relationships with suppliers that might cloud their judgment through the practice of rotating buyers among different departments.[83] And the seriousness with which Wal-Mart takes its corporate ethics policy was underscored by the controversy surrounding the departure of ad execs Julie Roehm and Sean Womack amid allegations that the two had engaged in an extramarital affair and accepted improper gifts from ad agencies hoping to land Wal-Mart's $580 million account.[84] Wal-Mart has even gone so far as to trail upper-level employees on business trips to confirm suspected affairs with subordinates.[85] Wal-Mart's longstanding affinity for thrift and asceticism helps explain its recent embrace of environmental conservation efforts, such as promoting compact fluorescent bulbs that—if purchased by every one of Wal-Mart's weekly customers—could save a total $3 billion in electricity costs and preserve fifty billion tons of coal used to create electricity, not to mention creating less solid waste due to the long lasting nature of these bulbs when compared to their traditional incandescent counterparts.[86]

At the other end of the continuum is Wal-Mart's well-publicized benevolence. In 2006, for example, Wal-Mart increased its charitable giving by 10% to $272.9 million, placing it at the top of American corporations in terms of cash donations.[87] And Wal-Mart is frequently cited as a headline contributor in the wake of disasters such as tornados and hurricanes, providing both cash and in-kind donations of merchandise. In fact, Wal-Mart's success in delivering supplies distributed after Hurricane Katrina was often hailed as superior to the comparatively inept response of government entities such as FEMA. At the same time, however, others point out that the Walton Family Foundation (which makes charitable contributions separate from Wal-Mart Inc.) appears rather paltry in size when compared to other foundations. Although the Walton family owns stock worth more than twice as much as the Gates' personal holdings in Microsoft, the Bill and Melinda Gates Foundation is an estimated thirty-five times as large as the Walton Family Foundation.[88] Not surprisingly, Wal-Mart's critics have sought to make benevolence an issue in the Wal-Mart debate: if the Waltons are so rich, and Wal-Mart reaps billions of dollars in profit each year, couldn't the company just trim its profits a bit in order to be more generous to its employees?

## Freedom and Fairness

Echoes of a final pair of themes, freedom and fairness, appear throughout both the current debate as well as the personal story of Wal-Mart's founder, Sam Walton. The story of Wal-Mart's founding is itself a tribute to two cherished ideas in American political culture: free enterprise and the American Dream. The young Sam Walton got his start as the owner of a Ben Franklin franchise—the small town variety stores founded by Butler Brothers wholesalers that focused on the smaller, rural markets that were often overlooked by larger merchandisers such as Sears and Woolworth's. But in his years as a variety store owner, Walton became disillusioned with the model when he compared it to the emerging phenomenon of discount merchandising, which he had observed on his travels around the South and Midwest. Don Soderquist—longtime friend of Walton's and retired COO of Wal-Mart Stores—tells how Walton forged his own path with an elementary simplicity that reads like a prophet's tale straight from the Good News Bible:

> The man [Walton] needed to change and grow along with his dream to get where he wanted to go, and he asked for help. "Mr. Ben Franklin Company," Sam said, "please help me build larger stores in my small towns. I know it's not been done before, but my people are asking for more assortments and lower prices. I've got an idea for them. Will you work with me and franchise these larger stores? Will you sell the merchandise to me at a lower price since I need to reduce the prices to my customers? You'll do okay, too, because I'll be buying a lot more merchandise."
>
> "It will never work," they said. "We can't do that. There are not enough people out there for discount stores. You will never be able to generate enough business in those small towns. Larger stores work in the larger cities. Smaller stores for smaller towns. Everyone knows that. Be content. You're already the biggest and best at what you do. And by the way, we can't sell the merchandise to you for a lower price than we sell it to everyone else. The risk in this plan is too great for everyone—including you."

Soderquist concludes that "he [Walton] knew that change was necessary to follow his dream—a simple dream that had stayed true to its ideals—and he wasn't going to give up now."[89] And, to be sure, Walton did not give up— he parted ways with Butler Brothers and opened the first Wal-Mart Discount City in Rogers, Arkansas, in 1962—incidentally, the same year that saw the founding of Kmart, Target, and the Woolworth's spin-off Woolco. Walton refused the constraints placed on him by the Butler Brothers conglomerate that supplied Ben Franklin, and chose instead the way of free enterprise.

Of course, Walton's gamble paid off. By 1967 he owned 24 Wal-Mart stores, earning over $12 million in sales per year; by 1979 those numbers had expanded to 276 stores in eleven states, and Wal-Mart had broken records by posting $1 billion in sales in its comparatively short seventeen-year history. The expansion continued at breakneck pace: in another decade Wal-Mart had more than quadrupled in size with more than 1,400 stores—and in an even more noteworthy accomplishment, it posted $25.8 billion in sales. By 1991 Wal-Mart was (and has since remained) the largest retailer in the United States.[90]

Wal-Mart's success story is one championing the power of free enterprise and the triumph of unfettered market competition. Wal-Mart's exploitation of free enterprise, however, was met with even greater concern when Wal-Mart started to adapt its "everyday low prices" model to the grocery business—which spelled trouble for established grocery chains that were largely regional conglomerates (leaving more than enough room for Wal-Mart's price-cutting) and still heavily unionized as an industry. Preceding Wal-Mart's present difficulties in entering untapped California markets was a bitter grocer's strike that ended with few gains for unionized workers, whose position had been rendered precarious by the mere threat of Wal-Mart's arrival.

The irony is that while Wal-Mart has free enterprise to thank for its success, its very size and scale question the very nature of free competition for other merchandisers. This was the argument advanced by Barry Lynn in a 2006 *Harper's* essay titled "Breaking the Chain: The Antitrust Case against Wal-Mart." Lynn contends that Wal-Mart has consolidated so much power that the retailer can now control the actions of its suppliers—in dictating the price of pickles, for example—in ways that pervert the free and fair working of market competition. The basic problem is that Wal-Mart's size distorts the freedom of the market—smaller retailers simply can't match its prices, and thus cannot compete in a Wal-Mart world. Further, Wal-Mart's market power actually micromanages parts of the market that are separate from its own activities—dictating to suppliers how items should be packaged, for example, and even encouraging mergers among large suppliers (such as Kellogg's and Keebler, Gillette and Procter & Gamble) who are desperate to shore up their position in negotiations with the retailer about the pricing and display of their products. The basic argument, then, is that by perverting freedom, Wal-Mart ushers in a market that is no longer fair.[91]

This was much the same argument advanced by the independent bankers and other smaller retailers who testified before the FDIC to protest

Wal-Mart's application for an ILC charter. As Tom Wenning of the National Grocers Association explained, "Community focused businesses like grocers and others depend on local banks for financial services and capital resources, not competing retailers. If the world's largest retailer is permitted to open branch banks, then the separation of the banking and commerce will no longer exist and there will be an even more fundamental shift to enhance the company's economic power."[92] This notion of fairness extends beyond market competition as well. A central question concerns whether Wal-Mart is free to compensate its workers according to prices set by the market, or if the principles of fairness dictate that a living wage—one that includes benefits like health insurance—are the necessary minimums that workers can expect from their employers.

Conclusion

When surveyed from all angles, Wal-Mart is a company to be viewed with both admiration and apprehension, to be both respected and reviled. On the one hand, Wal-Mart alone seems to have been singled out among its similar big-box competitors as the target of a well-organized national campaign alleging that the retailer shortchanges its employees, abuses public subsidies, and has for too long ignored the environmental consequences of its expansion. At the same time, Wal-Mart has earned itself this unwanted starring role in large part because its success has redefined many aspects of merchandizing in the twenty-first century, among them how goods are manufactured and transported across the globe, and the way that both manufacturing and service jobs are distributed and organized. By virtue of its importance to twenty-first-century retailing, its recent public notoriety, and its potential to represent both the best and worst possibilities of American capitalism, Wal-Mart is an excellent case study for the discourse of economic morality.

The debate also emphasizes three pairs of moral dialectics that illustrate the connection of this particular case study to debates about economic policy more generally. Specifically, individualism and community, thrift and benevolence, and freedom and fairness are ideas that have a long-standing presence in political discourse, and therefore play a key role in how this populist debate about economic morality reaches the American people in the public sphere. Because each of these values comes to the fore in debates about Wal-Mart, these three pairs will form the analytical scaffold of the ensuing discourse analysis in this book, both because they are frequently referenced in the discourse, and because they resonate well with key aspects of Wal-Mart's history, its business model, and the practical questions raised about Wal-Mart's consequences. In the next section of the book, we turn to the way that key SMOs as well as Wal-Mart draw from these dialectics to support their claims, and how the significance of these ideas in their language reveals the deeper, symbolic dimensions of the discourse that progressives and conservatives alike bring to American debates about economic dilemmas.

# PART 2

# Competing Frameworks for Market Morality

# 3

## Individuals and Communities

We need to cut taxes so that our families can keep more of what they earn and produce, and our mom-and-pops then, our small businesses, can reinvest according to our own priorities, and hire more people and let the private sector grow and thrive and prosper.
—Former Alaska governor Sarah Palin

When Sarah Palin addressed a crowd of Americans who had assembled in Boston on April 14, 2010, she was preaching to the faithful. Marking the last stop of the Tea Party Express—a bus convoy that had traveled throughout the country to rally groups of Americans advocating smaller government, individual freedoms, and fiscal restraint—Palin's keynote speech concluded this vigil in the symbolic Boston Harbor venue on the day before Americans would be required to file their taxes. The audience itself was surely something to behold, but beyond the sound bites and images, Palin's language tells a deeper story about the symbolic roots of economic debates and how they address the American public. Looking closely at her words from that much-publicized event, Palin's rhetoric succeeds at being both inclusive and exclusive by referencing a resurgent form of populism that pits "our families" against the allegedly out-of-touch, elitist Washington establishment that would presumably take their taxes without representation. Palin's language about "our families"—which also references "our mom-and-pops" and "our own priorities"—communicates membership in an inclusive community of like-minded individuals who presumably know who "our families" are, along with what "our own priorities" might be. Moreover, this language constructs an in-group by positioning itself against outsiders—in this case, President

Obama and liberal members of Congress like Nancy Pelosi and Harry Reid. In other words, the "our" in the speech can only exist in contrast with the implicit category of "their," and the discourse implies that those who are listening know exactly who "we" and "they" are.

While the Tea Party movement represents a highly visible endeavor that is certainly fueled by ongoing cable news coverage and aided by the celebrity endorsement of speakers like Palin, the same rhetorical strategies that we see in this kind of public speech appear in other social movements centered on economic issues. Taxes invite criticism not only because most of us regret parting with our hard-earned money, but also because economic issues inevitably arouse sentiments concerning our identities as members of families as well as our different perceptions of the appropriate relationship between members of a democratic polity and the government. Therefore, leaders like Palin were quick to criticize then vice presidential candidate Joe Biden's statement that paying higher taxes was a patriotic duty for wealthier Americans; when Palin repeated this remark to her audience she received the expected shouts of disapproval and disdain. Biden, however, had intended this remark to appeal to middle-class Americans who could expect a tax cut under an Obama–Biden administration. Yet this emphasis was largely ignored and the McCain–Palin campaign continued to emphasize the tax increases that Americans might face if Obama were elected. In both kinds of political speech—McCain–Palin warning of exorbitant tax hikes, Obama–Biden describing taxes as a patriotic duty—the speakers are trying both to convince the undecided as well as to activate their political base. In other words, they intend to construct and communicate with specific and distinct audiences who can understand and appreciate their particular kind of message. This chapter considers how similar movements founded on economic populism construct separate audiences through the public rhetoric of social movement organizations.

All social movements face the challenge of convincing uninvolved individuals that their chosen cause is worthy of investing voluntary time and energy—and the language they choose to use in doing so is always important for their success. Sociologists call this process "framing" because social movement organizers are strategically crafting the terms through which they package their issue to the public, and thus the terms on which their audience receives the information. Framing does at least three things to invite individuals to find common cause in social activism: diagnosing blame for a problem, suggesting a solution, and motivating participants to become and stay involved.[1] Framing thus performs a kind of packaged interpretation that invites onlookers to evaluate a situation in a certain way. Such choices of

SMOs are not accidental or arbitrary; in framing issues for the public, movement organizers could pursue any number of strategies—for example, arguing that the issue at hand is a moral concern that threatens a large portion of the public, or perhaps appealing to more individualistic motivations, such as the personal gains that one could achieve by participating in the movement or enjoying the fruits of its outcomes.

Whatever form it takes, the framing process inevitably creates ties between individuals and larger groups—a process most visibly seen in the recent surge of "identity movements" that forge connections under broad identity categories such as gender, sexual orientation, or race.[2] In a modern world characterized by increasing complexity and fragmentation, groups such as these unite people through their common identities as men, women, activists, or citizens; individuals may presumably be spurred to act on another person's behalf if they share similar identity characteristics.[3] Yet even as they promise to join and unite, these identity ties may also create new conflicts, as people affiliate with unique and bounded identities that they believe deserve special recognition.[4] This represents one of the enduring ironies of community activism—even movements oriented around collective well-being and inclusion may have the unintended side effect of exacerbating divisions and other differences between groups that make true consensus and community-building deeply problematic. In fact, even using the phrase "our community" inevitably means acknowledging, however tacitly, the presence of others who exist outside of the community's inclusive bounds.[5]

Yet while identity movements can call on identities of gender, country, or sexual orientation to activate the loyalties of potential supporters, groups like Wal-Mart Watch face a tougher challenge in convincing onlookers that they should care about where they buy paper towels or laundry detergent. Thus groups concerned with economic issues must construct new categories through which they distinguish between "us" and "them" in their public debates, and offer their audience a choice of identities by which they can "divide up and make sense of the social world."[6] And even though most researchers who study social movements focus on tangible group identities—groups in which activists engage in face-to-face interaction with others, for example—movements that connect individuals to a larger collectivity may ultimately do so through a more ethereal, "imagined" community as well.[7] Thus the metaphors and images used by a group in their public talk turn out to be particularly important in activist campaigns waged primarily through the media, as in the debate over Wal-Mart conducted between groups like Working Families for Wal-Mart (WFWM) and Wal-Mart Watch (WMW).

For example, the pro-Wal-Mart advocacy group Working Families for Wal-Mart once explained on its website that "Wal-Mart contributes to working families in a variety of ways," and went on to frame the identity of movement participants as being a part of four different imagined communities:

- *As parents*, we're always on the way to pick the kids up from soccer practice, or taking them to dance lessons, or helping them with their homework. There's so much going on that saving time, energy and a few dollars is important. Wal-Mart allows working parents to do all those things. . . .
- *As community leaders*, we understand that Wal-Mart is a company that cares about its neighbors. Working Families for Wal-Mart will work to ensure that Wal-Mart's community involvement and generous donations to charitable organizations continues. . . .
- *As customers*, we at Working Families for Wal-Mart want to ensure the low prices Wal-Mart offers to working families remain available. Wal-Mart saves the average working family over $2,300 per year. . . .
- *As Americans*, we want to see our economy grow, and we want to see jobs created. We're involved with Working Families for Wal-Mart because of the 210,000 jobs in our economy last year because of Wal-Mart—and the many more it will continue to generate.[8]

By offering website visitors at least four different identities through which to imagine their participation in WFWM, the group communicates that its vision is connected to larger collectivities: that of parents seeking more time with their families amid hectic lives, community leaders who appreciate Wal-Mart's charitable contributions, customers who need the store's savings, and, finally, Americans who "want to see our economy grow." These collective groups are also particularly noteworthy because they are *imagined*—they provide a connection to collective groups that are as abstract and ephemeral as they are real and widespread. Unlike the local Masons or Elks lodge, for example, the community of parents in the United States doesn't have a local chapter and regular meetings with fellow group members; at the same time, the group is so broad that few people could feel excluded from its membership. Because groups like WFWM are made up primarily of email addresses as opposed to local chapter initiates, rhetoric is the bread and butter of these groups in the same way that community socials and membership drives might have been the staple recruitment techniques of voluntary community groups a generation ago.

But how do social movements centered on economic issues construct these relationships between individuals and larger collectives? What imagined communities of reference does each group of activists refer to in their efforts to motivate the uninvolved observers of their campaigns to become more invested? This chapter addresses these questions by arguing that important differences emerge when we consider how each movement connects its participants to a larger collective in terms of the audiences to which they refer and speak. In doing so, I argue that both sides of this controversy create separate audiences as their imagined communities of reference—for Wal-Mart's supporters this group is that of the average family, for Wal-Mart's critics it is the citizen and activist (and to a lesser extent, the taxpayer). Yet despite the populist dimensions of these categories, I argue that these reference groups are ultimately divisive because of the economic dimensions of the organizations' language, in which Wal-Mart frames its supporters as average families pursuing the American Dream, while its opponents are portrayed as out-of-touch elitists.

Yet despite their differences, both SMOs also use person-centered rhetoric that dramatizes Wal-Mart as a person who has a certain moral character, and imputes other moral characteristics to the company by virtue of its association with key individuals. Although this is a strategic metaphor designed to heighten their audience's emotions, it ultimately creates a kind of false consciousness that simplifies complex, multinational processes by using personal characteristics as a shorthand way of talking about the activities of a global corporation. Finally, although both groups do reference ideas of community and collective good, the notion of "community" invoked throughout is one with a decidedly local flair that ironically makes it something of a divisive and conflictual concept, in that the wishes and desires of some communities are inevitably prioritized over the needs of others. I conclude the chapter by placing these findings in the larger context of economic populism, paying attention to the ways these same ideas and concepts are mobilized by other social movements—most recently the Tea Party, with leaders like Sarah Palin at its helm.

Divisive Populism

For WFWM and Wal-Mart itself, the language of various actors—spokespersons for WFWM or Wal-Mart, as well as the personal narratives of various Wal-Mart supporters—refers most consistently to the "average working family" as the primary imagined community that unites their supporters. For instance, a WFWM webpage titled "What's at Stake?" announced, "Working families everywhere know what the unions won't acknowledge: Wal-Mart is good for America's working families. Working families continue to shop at Wal-Mart and line up by the thousands for jobs at Wal-Mart stores because

Wal-Mart continues to save working families money and provide good jobs with competitive pay and affordable health care." Similarly, former ambassador Andrew Young (then president of WFWM) issued an early press release about Wal-Mart's ILC application on February 27, 2006:

> A few months ago, when the FDIC was first considering Wal-Mart's request, I went and testified. I told the FDIC that Wal-Mart is a good company, and that I support the company's request for an ILC. I told them how important Wal-Mart is to working families, and how this step will help Wal-Mart ensure that it can keep prices low.

Similarly, testifying to the FDIC on behalf of Wal-Mart's ILC application, WFWM steering committee member Catherine Smith framed some of her arguments in favor of the retailer's petition in light of the potential savings that could be passed on to customers, who also come from working families: "For working mothers and fathers, something as arcane as an industrial bank may mean the difference between shame or pride in the clothes their children wear to school or church" (WFWM website).

Of course, some of this may stem from the company's purposeful naming of its short-lived advocacy group "Working Families for Wal-Mart," in which the retailer's PR firm, Edelman, intentionally crafted press releases and public statements that emphasized the store's appeal to families seeking to stretch their limited resources. Moreover, WFWM solicited more than three hundred narratives from (mostly) customers, as well as employees and suppliers, who offer their personal testimonies about Wal-Mart's benefits. This imagined community of the "average working family" appears throughout Wal-Mart's own press releases, as well as the remarks the store solicited from these supporters on WFWM's website (emphases added):

> "During our most recent open enrollment period, we signed up more than 70,000 associates who didn't have our health insurance before. Fifty thousand of those *working men and women* were previously uninsured. And this is just a start," Wal-Mart CEO Lee Scott will say. "In the weeks ahead, we're going to take significant steps to make our health benefits even more affordable and accessible to the *working families* we employ." (Wal-Mart press release, February 23, 2006)

> Wal-Mart Stores, Inc. today announced its 2005 charitable giving numbers, which total more than $245 million in financial and in-kind donations to various charitable organizations and causes. The figure represents a nearly

$38 million increase from 2004 and demonstrates Wal-Mart's commitment to making a difference in the lives of *working families*—its customers, associates and neighbors. (Wal-Mart press release, July 13, 2006)

"These are medicines for diabetes, cardiovascular disease, asthma, colds and infections—the kinds of medicines that *working families* need so they can treat illness, manage conditions and stay well," said Simon. "Rising healthcare costs are eating up more and more of families' budgets, so this program brings a lot of value to our customers, associates and communities." (Wal-Mart press release, September 21, 2006)

I just want to say thank you Walmart for the low prices. Your prices cannot be beat. I am anxiously waiting for the new Supercenter to open that is closer to my home. Not only will I be saving on all my shopping needs at Walmart but also on my gas bill. My *family* buys everything from food to tires on all of our vehicles at Walmart and we save a lot of money. Keep up the good work for us *hard working Americans* to be able to afford more things because of your low prices. Thanks. Lou. (WFWM website, personal story)

There are two kinds of Americans—those who work for a living and those who tax for a living. Wal*mart is for those who work for a living and without Wal*mart I would not have enough money to satisfy the greed of those who tax for a living. (WFWM website, personal story)

In all these examples, Wal-Mart's supporters frame their constituency as that of the "working family" that derives certain benefits from Wal-Mart's low prices, such that these "hardworking Americans" are "able to afford more things" by virtue of the store's cost-saving efforts.

As the final example above also suggests, the category of the "working family" also subtly addresses the populist dimensions of this appeal, which comprises not just families but also those who know what it means to be a "working family" (in the last speaker's words, this has to do with "two kinds of Americans"—those who "work for a living," and those who "tax for a living"). Thus this concept of the "working family" acquires a particular kind of significance within the context of economic populism. Elsewhere, other words and phrases such as "everyday Americans," the "common man," and "regular people" reiterate this emphasis on a message that appeals to a large (yet largely amorphous) majority in an economically stratified society (emphases added):

Just as Working Families for Wal-Mart is made up of *everyday Americans* from all walks of life, our leaders come from a diverse range of backgrounds and experiences. (WFWM website)

Wal-Mart is a must in my family. There is no way that I could possibly not shop there. The low prices on *every day items* of necessity and even nonnecessity make it possible for the *average working family* to actually buy that Dove soap, BBQ grill, new bath towels, DVDs and the list goes on and on. (WFWM website, personal story)

It has long been my observation that if one sets out to make a great contribution to helping the socalled *little people* help themselves, one can expect a lot of opposition from many of the socalled big people (really a minority . . . but they are always there to try and kick you down). (WFWM website, personal story)

There are few institutions in America that champion *regular people*— working men and women—more than Wal-Mart. This is a company that has created 240,000 jobs over the last three years, offers $23 per month health plans to both full-time and part-time associates, and saves the *average American household* more than $2,300 per year. (WFWM website, "Paid Critics" page)

"But at the end of the day, when someone builds a better mousetrap, it's not the American way to deny *average folks* the chance to use it to improve their lives," Scott said. "The horse and buggy industry wasn't permitted to crush the car. The candle lobby wasn't allowed to stop electric lights. Ultimately, that's what this debate is about." (Wal-Mart press release, February 23, 2005)

Throughout these and other similar excerpts, speakers' language emphasizes how Wal-Mart meets the needs of average families with modest economic means. The populist nature of this appeal is underscored by speakers' references to groups like the "socalled big people," who, the speaker adds, are "really a minority . . . but they are always there to try and kick you down." Just as most Americans tend to identify themselves as middle class, the notion of "regular people," "average folks," or "people like us" would seem to offer a broad-based, populist appeal.

Yet implicit in this discourse is the idea that the audience of these utterances is one that can sympathize with the perspective contained in these emails and press releases—not to mention the personal stories collected by WFWM. Thus the "working families" cultivated as an audience in this discourse actually creates an even more focused audience—for Wal-Mart's supporters, this audience is one that can identify with the perspective of average Americans who have to watch their household budgets:

> My mother and I appreciate Walmart! Like *a lot of people*, we struggle with our finances. We know that we can get about anything we need at Walmart and know that it will be quality and great priced. (WFWM website, personal story)

> *Us that are on fixed low income*s appreciate the convience [*sic*] and savings that we get from Walmart. Thank You Walmart. (WFWM website, personal story)

> Wal-Mart is the kind of company we can all be proud of. It grew up in small town America, the product of one man's dream. Now it makes a difference every week for millions of *working families across America.* (WFWM email, September 7, 2006)

For instance, in the first example, the speaker announces that she and her mother are "like a lot of people" in how they struggle with money; likewise, the second speaker presumes that other people in the audience are in the same group—"us that are on fixed incomes" appreciate Wal-Mart's bargains. And finally, in the WFWM email the official party line of Wal-Mart's advocacy group speaks from the perspective of inclusion—it is a "company we can all be proud of" that assists millions of "working families across America." Here, the imagined community of reference is one that presumably anyone could be familiar with—the "average man" or "working family"—but the way in which this category is constructed is necessarily exclusive because of its populist undertones.

One way that the pro-Wal-Mart activists construct this populist conception of the family among their audience is by referencing the concept of the American Dream. Although the American Dream is certainly a commonplace trope that invites widespread support and acceptance, Wal-Mart uses this concept with a stratified slant that emphasizes socioeconomic differences between those who support Wal-Mart and its better-heeled critics:

> I wish those down on Wal-Mart would visit Bentonville. They would see that Wal-Mart "is" small town America housed in a building that not one

other big US Corporation would ever consider suitable for a headquarters building. I wish they could hear my buyer at Wal-Mart state his enthusiasm for a company that gave him his first job stocking shelves and has given him the opportunity to grow in a manner he never thought possible. (WFWM website, personal story)

"We hope that by helping so many young people reach their dream of a higher education, we can help improve the standard of living for families, local communities and our national community," said Betsy Reithemeyer, vice president of Corporate Affairs over the Wal-Mart & Sam's Club Foundation at Wal-Mart Stores, Inc. (WFWM press release, June 2, 2005)

If many more companies were like Wal*Mart, maybe we would not need to have a discussion about the store. Are there issues that need to be improved at Wal*Mart . . . yes, any corporation can improve itself for its employees. However, let's give Wal*Mart some credit for being there for a lot of people when others are practicing what I call "Economic Snobbery" by not wanting poor people in their communities in housing or shops . . . they are more concerned about Starbucks and other high-end shops . . . give some credit to a man's dream being fulfilled. (WFWM website, personal story)

Incorporating the trope of the American Dream in the pro-Wal-Mart discourse represents yet another way that Wal-Mart's supporters are rhetorically connected to the larger community of "average Americans"—that is, those who work hard to do their best, stretch their dollars, and achieve their dreams. Thus Sam Walton was frequently mentioned for his own pursuit of an entrepreneurial dream to create a company "we can all be proud of," which offers opportunities for economic mobility, and doesn't practice "economic snobbery" by eschewing low prices in favor of "high-end shops" like Starbucks.

If Wal-Mart's supporters are the "regular people," then it follows that their critics must be elitist. Indeed, this explains why Wal-Mart frames its opponents—be they critics like Wal-Mart Watch, unions, or politicians who have publicly questioned the store—as elites and hypocrites. Thus WFWM steering committee member Catherine Smith criticized John Edwards for shopping at Wal-Mart and once owning Wal-Mart stock even as he criticized the company for its provision of employee benefits: "Now he and other political candidates are telling working men and women that they can't save money or take jobs at Wal-Mart? This is all about special interest politics" (WFWM press release, August 4, 2006). Elsewhere, WFWM juxtaposed Edwards's statement that "I want to be a champion for the people I have fought for all my life—regular people" with its claim that "there are few institutions in America that champion regular people—working men and women—more than Wal-Mart" (WFWM website, "Paid Critics" page). Similarly, WFWM wasted little time highlighting allegations of hypocrisy among opposing groups like Wal-Mart Watch, which had posted a job advertisement noting that successful candidates should be willing to work long hours, including weekends. WFWM went on to allege that WMW had used paid picketers to protest a local Wal-Mart—and paid them less than the average wages of the Wal-Mart workers employed inside.

The essence of this strategy thus serves to link Wal-Mart supporters and potential advocates with a larger imagined community of "regular people," who are primarily part of "working families," while their opponents and detractors are simultaneously portrayed as inauthentic hypocrites concerned only with special interests. Further, the "average" or "common" people referenced throughout the pro-Wal-Mart discourse is a group defined largely in populist, economic terms: these families are such because they need Wal-Mart's low prices, and thus can't afford the luxury of criticizing the retailer on high-minded grounds and perhaps choosing to shop elsewhere. The backdrop against which this exchange takes place is one with a decidedly stratified slant: the world contains just a handful of elites for whom money isn't a concern, while "the rest of us" and our families have to watch our pennies. Just as the speaker quoted above referenced the "socalled big people" who were "really a minority," another supporter explained:

> I have always been an advocate of Walmart and I have the utmost respect for Mr. Walton who is someone who built a tremendous company thru hardwork and intelligence unlike other companies who have grown thru nothing but mergers. Mergers help only the top-level executives and the workers suffer layoffs. Walmart helps millions and millions of people thru the lower prices which is something only the Unions can dream about. Unions only help the union members and that's it. Society is stuck with paying for it. (WFWM website, personal story)

Wal-Mart's low prices, then, are the means by which "millions and millions" of people receive assistance, while unions "only help the union members and that's it." By virtue of its massive appeal, Wal-Mart's imagined community of reference becomes an inclusive collectivity in which membership is achieved simply by defining oneself as a "regular person" or a member of an "average American family."

Citizens and Activists in WMW

In contrast to the family-centered appeals of Wal-Mart and WFWM, the imagined community of reference for the progressive organization Wal-Mart Watch centers on a cluster of categories that I argue are connected to the larger concept of citizenship, such as other activists and taxpayers. WMW also frames this appeal in the language of populism, arguing that "it takes a village to beat a Wal-Mart" (WMW website, "Battlemart" page), and reminding its supporters and potential allies that "Wal-Mart's business practices affect us all in many ways" (WMW website).[9] At the end of a series of issue-based pages detailing Wal-Mart's alleged grievances, WMW tells website visitors "What You Can Do," suggesting that the uninitiated can "join thousands in signing the Handshake with Sam agreement" and "tell friends and family" about Wal-Mart's shortcomings "and how that affects our communities" (WMW website). Throughout, the community of reference is others who are fighting Wal-Mart—other citizens' groups, other "citizens like you," the "thousands" you can join in this campaign, and so on. In fact, the very structure of the WMW website sets up its appeals in this manner, offering visitors resources and connections created for other like-minded activists under the heading of "Networks"—other elected officials, other communities battling Wal-Mart locally, other people in faith communities, and so on.

Any appeal in a social movement of this sort is designed, at least initially, to empower people in grassroots activism. Accordingly, WMW emphasizes broad-based notions of empowerment in a series of emails sent to those who had already signed up as partners with the organization (emphases added):

And while Wal-Mart has added hundreds of new marketing experts, high-powered lobbyists and expensive lawyers to their team since our campaign started last April, *we've added you.* (WMW email, March 9, 2006)

Over the past year, Wal-Mart Watch and our partners nationwide have been quietly building networks of activists, community leaders and elected officials who together represent an unstoppable force for change. This is not just another political campaign. This is a call for reform that requires thoughtful dialogue and bipartisan state-and-community-specific partnerships. Above all, *this fight requires you, your support, your willingness to stand up for what's right for your hometown.* (WMW email, January 13, 2006)

You stopped Wal-Mart from sneaking its bank through the process, and now it's *time for you to weigh in* on these hearings. We've found the email address to send comments to the FDIC—take a moment to compose your own thoughts and tell them why the Bank of Wal-Mart is a bad idea. (WMW email, April 5, 2006)

By framing appeals for activism in terms of participants' existing membership in a community of activists—while also crediting them for past successes against big business—WMW attempts to empower these supporters by connecting them to the larger collectivity of other anti-Wal-Mart activists. Such a move is particularly important in a large virtual movement such as this one, when many of WMW's supporters may do little more than check the organization's website or occasionally forward a web link to a friend.

Although its correspondence to the converted may take the form of appeals like those above, Wal-Mart Watch constructs a slightly different, but related, imagined community for the broader public—those who might only read about the organization in a passing visit to the website, or in press releases cited in the larger media. In these cases, the community of reference created by WMW is most consistently framed as taxpayers, another identity that is closely linked to the larger ideal of citizenship. This category is created most obviously via the organization's criticism of the public support of Wal-Mart created through corporate tax breaks and Medicaid for Wal-Mart's uninsured workers (emphases added):

Now your state senator needs to hear from you. If you agree that Wal-Mart, a company with $10 billion in profit, run by a family worth $90 billion and growing, should *not be getting welfare from you*, speak out today! (WMW email, February 7, 2006)

Despite numerous tweaks to their health plan, Wal-Mart simply cannot offer an affordable plan to cover its workers. Lagging behind industry averages, Wal-Mart's employees are subjected to unnecessary charges and fees, wait longer for coverage eligibility, and are *forced to seek out public health programs to fulfill their health care needs*. (WMW website)

Right now, when health care coverage fails, everyone ends up paying the cost. That includes individuals and small businesses. When people are uninsured, we all pay for non-emergency visits to emergency rooms, which is how the uninsured most often get care. The visits translate into higher insurance premiums. When people go on Medicaid as a last resort, *our taxes pay to cover their health care.* (WMW website)

The Fair Share Health Care Act is being supported by a broad coalition of organizations including business, faith-based, union, and community groups who are demanding that Wal-Mart pay its fair share. We will no longer accept Wal-Mart's unfair tactic of *shifting health care costs to the taxpayer.* (WMW press release, January 9, 2006)

Wal-Mart's failure to provide healthcare to their employees is costing American taxpayers over 1.5 billion dollars every year and leaves an estimated 46% of the children of Wal-Mart employees on publicly-funded healthcare programs. *How much does it cost your state?* (WMW website)

In recent months Wal-Mart, America's largest corporation and private employer, has been exposed and shamed for shifting the responsibility of its employees' health care costs onto Medicaid, and, consequently, foisting billions of dollars onto the *backs of local taxpayers like us.* (WMW press release, January 9, 2006)

Partly because WMW had organized ballot initiatives proposing that Wal-Mart pay some remunerations for the costs of its workers who use state public assistance, the economistic language of taxpayers' financial interests comes to the fore when considering imagined communities of reference. It thus makes sense that WMW would want to motivate those on the sidelines to take action by reminding them of their economic self-interest in this issue—if Wal-Mart's workers use public tax dollars to fund their health care needs, the public arguably has an economic interest in holding Wal-Mart accountable for the way it cares for its employees.

Yet the irony of creating this kind of imagined community is that it is actually a rhetorically fracturing move. If motivating the public toward engagement requires reminding them of how Wal-Mart shifts "its responsibilities" onto "the backs of local taxpayers like us," and thus "our taxes pay to cover their health care," this inevitably creates not one imagined community but two: those who are unfairly made responsible for the medical care of uninsured workers, and those dependent, uninsured workers themselves. In inviting onlookers toward engagement in this way, WMW may have created a discursive universe in which its language leaves open to question just whom the movement aims to benefit: the workers who are poorly compensated, or the "public" who, as a result, assumes the cost of their care? Therefore, much in the same way that Working Families for Wal-Mart creates divisions in its imagined community by emphasizing economically stratified concepts like the "average working family," WMW also divides its audience by emphasizing the financial self-interest that audience has in reforming Wal-Mart. In both cases, these populist appeals have the subtle but unavoidable side effect of addressing separate audiences and constructing a divided public.

## A Darker Side of Community?

In like manner, a closer examination of the use of the word "community" by both SMOs suggests that the rhetorical construct of community—at least as expressed here—has a more subtle, divisive meaning. Both Wal-Mart/WFWM and WMW use the word frequently—to talk about topics ranging from "Wal-Mart's positive impact on our communities" (WFWM press release, November 1, 2006), to WMW's stated goal of "real change—transparent and lasting—to benefit Wal-Mart communities" (WMW website). A closer examination of "community" in context, however, suggests that the meaning of the word is really a synonym for "local" or, conversely, "*not* national."

Thus Wal-Mart frequently refers to "the communities we serve" and the arguably vague notion of "helping the community," but the "community" referenced here is most often a local grouping or regional area. Thus customers tell stories of how "Wal-Mart is continually helping in the community, whether it be sponsoring local groups or providing a place for groups to sell their cookies or whatever" (WFWM website, personal story), and argue that "Wal-Mart is a great community-oriented company" because it allowed that particular speaker's civic group to sell Christmas trees on the store lot, donated supplies to a pancake breakfast, and supported other local nonprofits (WFWM website, personal story). Similarly, Wal-Mart's own statements affirm that "Wal-Mart is committed to community stewardship and service" (Wal-Mart press release, March 5, 2005) through efforts such as preserving national parks and the Sam Walton Community Scholarship program, which awards scholarships to outstanding students recognized at local stores. This localized notion of "community" has been at the heart of Wal-Mart's ethos from the beginning, as Sam Walton's initial goal was to seek out underserved small towns and provide them with more varied merchandise. (In its modern-day form, Don Soderquist, former Wal-Mart executive, referred to the "store of the community" to describe the ways that Wal-Mart uses technology to tailor its merchandise offerings to local needs and tastes.)

But Wal-Mart Watch also used "community" in much the same manner. Describing itself early on as an organization that will "bridge the gap between ordinary citizens and community organizations" (WMW website), WMW offered citizens concerned about Wal-Mart's expansion a collection of resources to fight a proposed Wal-Mart in their "community," and published a research report in 2005 titled "Shameless: How Wal-Mart Bullies Its Way into Communities across America." Here, as in Wal-Mart's own discourse, "community" bespeaks the concept of a local town or regional center—presumably one that is able to practice self-determination and should be safe from intrusions from "outside" entities. Thus, in excerpts such as the examples below, WMW also used community in a similarly local manner (emphases added):

> Whether it is accepting unnecessary subsidies, driving local stores out of business, pressuring local town officials or encouraging workers to join state health rolls, Wal-Mart has a negative impact on *local communities.* (WMW website)

> Wal-Mart's efforts in Flagstaff serve as a warning to communities nationwide that the world's largest corporation will stop at nothing in its attempts to force-feed *local communities* its own brand of greed. (WMW press release, May 18, 2005)

> Wal-Mart Watch executive director Andrew Grossman today urged Wal-Mart to heed the words of its founder, Sam Walton. Grossman said, "Sam Walton wrote that Wal-Mart should 'not go where we're not wanted.' Walton also said 'if some *community,* for whatever reason, doesn't want us in there, we aren't interested in *going in* and creating a fuss.' We urge Wal-Mart to adopt the principles of Mr. Sam and reconsider their decisions in California and Florida." (WMW press release, May 24, 2006)

Framed in such ways, "community" also has an exclusionary undertone. Thus, when Wal-Mart speaks of "the communities we serve" or "giving back to the community," it implies that Wal-Mart is not itself a *member* of the community, but more of an interloper whose identity remains separate, even removed, from the local store's surrounding area. Thus, in one instance where Wal-Mart mentions "our own community," it does so in reference to a contribution the corporation made to expanding preschool education in the company headquarters town of Bentonville, Arkansas (emphasis added):

"Education is always a smart investment," said Betsy Reithemeyer, vice president of corporate affairs at Wal-Mart and executive director of the Wal-Mart & Sam's Club Foundation. "Wal-Mart has an ongoing commitment to education, and I can't think of a better way to demonstrate that commitment than by helping children and families in *our own community*." (Wal-Mart press release, February 8, 2006)

In marked contrast, when the same spokesperson issued a comment on Wal-Mart's charitable contribution of $2.5 million toward Gulf Coast reconstruction after Katrina, she explained, "Wal-Mart remains committed to helping the people of the Gulf Coast region restore *their* lives and communities" (Wal-Mart press release, January 12, 2006, emphasis added). Here the concrete adjective "their" reinforces the sense of a divided public audience, in contrast to the more inclusive dimensions inherent in the concept of community.

For Wal-Mart Watch, many mentions of "community" serve to underline a similarly divisive, even exclusionary message. When "Battlemart" pages describe how local activists fight "to keep the unwanted mega-store from intruding upon their community" or proclaim that "thanks to the community's efforts, Turlock, not Wal-Mart, can decide what's best for its residents" (WMW website, "Battlemart" page), the notion of community invoked is parochial and protectionist. In keeping with this theme, one local organization highlighted on the site adopted the name "Our Community First." Much as some critiques of communitarianism would expect, the use of this concept in the discourse of both groups of activists may actually serve to underscore existing divisions between towns and other municipalities, and between different groups of activists themselves.[10]

Accordingly, notable social scientists in recent years have expressed reservations about the potential of community-focused discourse to successfully motivate widespread moral concern about economic issues. Wuthnow, for example, suggests that moral language that invites individuals to examine their own economic decisions more easily resonates with the strains of individualism that are deeply entrenched in American culture; as a result, it's much easier to imagine economic reforms being successful when they work within that individualistic paradigm rather than against it. Yet Wuthnow also cautions that such individualistic discourses have their limits, especially because moral language that prioritizes individualism is not always separated from the assumptions that dominate economic spheres of discourse—such as ideals of consumerism that promise low prices, good values, and the opportunity to define oneself expressively through material purchases.[11] Further, economic issues may prove especially problematic for activists who hope to knit together both individualistic and communitarian rhetoric in motivating collective concerns. Whereas one could support immigrants' rights or environmentalism without experiencing any negative consequences, it may be more difficult to imagine how activists could support the kind of improvements that Wal-Mart Watch envisions for Wal-Mart without suffering some kind of individual hardship. Advocating for increased standards among workers in the "global community," for example, could well mean higher prices for everyone, activists included. Economic issues offer a particularly difficult challenge for individualistic kinds of language that seek to build movements that improve outcomes for large groups of people.

Strategies of Personhood

One way that SMOs can attempt to bridge this gap between individually and collectively desirable outcomes is by activating emotional sentiments in their language and arguments. Particularly in moral debates, activating emotions can build support for a group's chosen cause in ways not possible through rational debate. Experimental brain research, for instance, shows that people make moral decisions based on emotional reactions, not rational deliberation. In the classic "trolley experiment"—where individuals are first asked if they would sacrifice one life to save five others by flipping a switch, and then asked if they would do so if it required pushing a bystander in front of a train—the more personalized test setting (which involves physically initiating a stranger's death) activates the emotion centers of the brain as test subjects decide what they would do in this unenviable hypothetical situation.[12] Not surprisingly then, scholars of social movements argue that emotions can play very powerful roles in all phases of social movement motivation and execution—particularly in motivating the uninitiated to join with others in a collective response.[13] Therefore, person-based discursive strategies—for example, focusing on personal narratives, emphasizing the outcomes of economic policies for certain individuals, or adopting metaphors that conceptualize groups or institutions in person-based terms—may be particularly compelling both in their ability to resonate with individualistic impulses in our culture, and in their ability to activate emotions in ways that more abstract, collectively oriented language cannot.

The latter strategy, using person-based terms to talk about groups or institutions, is especially important in language about corporations like

Wal-Mart. In fact, the metaphor of an institution-as-person appears rather often in both colloquial and formal discourse about institutions and typically allows us to ascribe emotions or moral characteristics to otherwise large and impersonal bureaucracies. Personifying the federal government as "Uncle Sam," for instance, allows cartoonists to depict the U.S. government as alternatively aggressive, weak, sheepish, ailing, angry, or confused. Metaphors of personhood also appear frequently in discourse about the economy, such as when the entire economic system is dramatized as a sick or ailing hospital patient.[14] Moreover, the unconscious ease with which we think of corporations themselves as persons appears in the popular "corporate citizenship" rhetoric, which projects a set of personalistic values (those of democratic, community minded individuals) onto the corporation itself. Accordingly, long before the controversial 2010 Supreme Court ruling on campaign finance in *Citizens United v. Federal Election Commission*, the sociologist James Coleman observed that in the United States, corporations were generally treated legally as persons, in that they have many of the same rights as individuals even as their size and scale creates an asymmetry of power between corporations and individuals, or what Coleman terms "natural persons." Similarly, corporate actors in this "asymmetric society" threaten natural persons because corporate actors tend to be bigger, control more information, and give people more opportunities for malfeasance, since corporations are rarely monitored as carefully as "natural persons" are.[15] In this way, the rallying cry against such corporate personhood in movements such as Occupy Wall Street represents only the most recent expression of backlash against this form of corporate power and influence.

Not surprisingly, then, Coleman and others warn that the imbalance between corporations and persons is so great that only other large-scale actors, such as the state, can effectively direct their activities toward community-minded pursuits (with often ambiguous results, since the state is also a kind of corporate actor).[16] Wal-Mart, for example, tends to focus its corporate citizenship activities on small-scale, local communities and specific "do-good" initiatives rather than large-scale projects; as a result, such initiatives are often short-term in duration and offer little in the way of lasting benefits.[17] Examining how a corporation like Wal-Mart embodies a metaphor of personhood in a divisive public debate offers important clues to understanding how different social movements in the democratic polity ground their claims on a company's moral obligations to the common good. In particular, looking at personhood in discourse about corporations may help shed light on why Americans experience no small amount of difficulty in holding corporations to higher standards (one need think only of recent corporate disasters such as the BP oil spill, the Enron accounting scandal, or the long-standing allegations against the tobacco industry), as well as the cultural challenges we face in sustaining more broad-based, lasting forms of public-spirited collective action.

Consistent with Coleman's observation that corporations in the United States bear the same legal status as natural persons, the most common strategy of personhood observed in both groups of texts concerned framing Wal-Mart as a person, particularly by invoking physical metaphors to describe the corporation. For example, physical attributions to Wal-Mart were common in both groups. A WFWM representative claimed that "working families pour into Wal-Mart because they know that Wal-Mart pours its heart out for them," and the WFWM website mentioned how "Wal-Mart touches the lives of hundreds of millions of Americans." Giving Wal-Mart a heart, and describing the company as something that "touches the lives" of Americans, adds to this image of a corporation having a physical body with moral dimensions. Likewise, on its webpage WMW asked its supporters to "join thousands in signing the 'Handshake with Sam' agreement and calling on Wal-Mart to wean itself from public dollars," and argued that "Wal-Mart can have a massive impact by taking positive steps to improve its environmental practices or can continue to leave a negative footprint across the globe." Implicitly framing Wal-Mart as a company that needs to "wean itself" from public subsidies and "take steps" that reduce its "footprint" gesture to metaphors of the body that give the company a corporeal existence, and by extension, a moral dimension that can and must be redirected.

Using the metaphor of personhood to frame Wal-Mart's contributions and opportunities for action serves at least two main functions. First, despite the backlash against corporate personhood that has become more common in recent years, this metaphor of personhood actually attempts to embody Wal-Mart with a kind of moral character: the company that "touches the lives" of working families who benefit from low prices, or "pours its heart out" for people in need. These strategies of personification underscore these interpretations because they imply that Wal-Mart indeed acts as a *person*, rather than as a diverse group of individuals in a corporate hierarchy whose actions are only loosely coordinated, at best. If Wal-Mart is a person, not a complex organization, then its true character might be more easily distilled and examined. Second, constructing Wal-Mart in such physical terms often frames the corporation as one that stands at a crossroads: Wal-Mart in this view can either "take positive steps" for the environment or "continue to leave a negative footprint," or could choose to "extend its hand" to those who challenge it to embrace higher standards of operation. In a slightly different way, this rhetorical strategy also creates a false picture of the complexities of change for a multinational corporation like Wal-Mart: deciding to be more environmentally responsible becomes as simple as turning a corner or taking a new direction. As a person, Wal-Mart could simply *choose* to act differently and thus change.

Accordingly, both Wal-Mart and its critics projected character traits that we typically associate with individuals onto the larger corporation itself. For Wal-Mart and WFWM, personalizing Wal-Mart in these ways alternately frames Wal-Mart as either a caring hero or, ironically, as a "little guy" who needs defending. In this way, both activist groups capitalize on a political culture that tends to invoke binary images to frame political candidates in the public eye. As Jeffrey Alexander has summarized, "Making oneself pure, polluting one's opponent—this is the stuff of which political victory is made."[18] In the case of Wal-Mart's proponents, this means that Wal-Mart itself is framed as a hero that stands out among the landscape of similar corporations, for Wal-Mart is a corporation that truly cares about the people who work and shop inside its doors. As one Wal-Mart employee explained, Wal-Mart is different from other corporations, which must rely on unions to keep them committed to their employees:

> I have told many people about how Wal-Mart has allowed me to trans-
> form from a typical college student to a business professional able to suc-
> cessfully deal with difficult situations. I have been given opportunities to
> grow, learn, and mature and have been compensated fairly. . . . My father
> is a member of a union because he has no realistic choice. Otherwise, no
> one would be looking out for him and he wouldn't have a voice. Wal-Mart
> gives associates that voice without the need for union dues—which drives
> down prices and saves American families thousands. (WFWM website,
> personal story)

Just as this speaker emphasized Wal-Mart's gifts of "opportunities to grow, learn, and mature," in other places Wal-Mart's own rhetoric also frames the corporation as something of a virtuous "little guy" being attacked by mean, bullying critics from all sides—a dubious claim in light of the company's size, scale, and influence. Thus this discourse turns to other physical images to urge activists to come to Wal-Mart's rescue and "stand up" or "speak out" for their company in the name of populism. Similarly, other narratives express their wish that Wal-Mart be "left alone," much in the same way that a parent might hope their child would be ignored by the playground bullies (empha-ses added):

That's why civic and community leaders from all over have joined together to form Working Families for Wal-Mart—an organization that will talk with friends, neighbors, and people in our communities about the positive contributions Wal-Mart makes every day. Join us, and *speak up* for Wal-Mart and working families everywhere. (WFWM website)

Now Working Families for Wal-Mart is *standing up* to support Wal-Mart and help the company continue making positive contributions for families and communities across the country. (WFWM website)

*We can't let them get away with it.* We need to send a clear message to Wal-Mart and the paid critics. Wal-Mart needs to know that we support and appreciate their move to lower prices on generic prescription drugs. The paid critics need to know that we're not overlooking their hypocrisy. (WFWM email, September 25, 2006)

*I wish that Wal-mart could be left alone.* People shop where they want to shop regardless. If Wal-Mart's competitors is where people want to shop they will. I personally want and very much need to shop at Wal-Mart. (WFWM website, personal story)

Keep it [Wal-Mart] free from a union it is better that way. They never wanted a union. So *please leave them alone.* They work too hard to have to worry about this. (WFWM website, personal story)

Framing Wal-Mart as a kind of David in a battle with Goliath is no accidental move—Wal-Mart, of course, has worn the nickname of the "retail giant" in the national media for over a decade, and has even been tagged with the alliterative epithet "the bully from Bentonville." Attempts to turn the tables on this metaphor challenge the person-based language that otherwise frames Wal-Mart as a behemoth bent on expansion at all costs. And indeed, this is a typical outcome of the kind of physical imagery applied to the retailer by Wal-Mart Watch (emphases added):

We all need to be on-watch against Wal-Mart. Put simply, their sheer size, market share and irresponsible business practices *threaten* you and your family, regardless of where you live. (WMW website)

Since 1962, the Wal-Mart Dust Machine has done damage in every state in the country. Wal-Mart has *cannibalized* mom and pop shops on the bottom, to the mid-level regional chains, to the very top national chains. Local businesses are known for their better service and higher quality merchandise, but too often cannot compete against Wal-Mart's harmful low-pricing scheme. (WMW website, "Battlemart" page)

The *retail giant's* self-interest sunk to a new low in the Flagstaff campaign. We certainly commend the citizens of Flagstaff for standing up to Wal-Mart's vicious tactics, resulting in the narrowest vote margin of just one percent. But Wal-Mart's efforts in Flagstaff serve as a warning to communities nationwide that the world's largest corporation will stop at nothing in its attempts to *force-feed local communities* its own brand of greed. (WMW press release, May 18, 2005)

A Wal-Mart Bank would *dwarf* the banks of other retail stores. Target's FY 2006 revenues of $52 billion were only one-sixth the size of Wal-Mart's. Other large companies with ILCs—like General Electric and General Motors—are only approximately half the size of Wal-Mart. (WMW website)

In sum, although Wal-Mart's supporters' rhetoric and that of its critics use physical imagery to different ends—to render Wal-Mart a hero or weakling, or a bully with an insatiable appetite—both use this metaphor of personhood to ascribe a certain character to Wal-Mart. The kind of imagery used—caring or bellicose—mitigates the ultimate characterization, but in both instances personalizing Wal-Mart in such a manner serves to construct a kind of false consciousness that simplifies the debate's more complex contours, reducing the ethos of a gigantic corporation to the kind of character traits we more typically associate with individual persons.

Both groups also render their language more person-based by identifying individuals who exemplify the different controversial issues involved in the Wal-Mart debate. This strategy singles out specific persons—former executives of Wal-Mart, union leaders, paid lobbyists, and the like—for criticism and then uses their individual failings to illustrate principles ascribed to larger, collective groups. Again, this strategy was invoked among both pro-Wal-Mart and anti-Wal-Mart actors:

Our organization was saddened and greatly disappointed to learn of the alleged rampant corruption of New York Assemblyman Brian McLaughlin, a close union leader ally and one of the nation's most vocal anti-Wal-Mart officials. We were sad because the victims of this anti-Wal-Mart associate's alleged theft include taxpayers, dues-paying union members, and even Little Leaguers. We were also disappointed because the union-supported leaders responsible for spending millions of hard-earned union dues to demand transparency, accountability and change from Wal-Mart appear incapable of holding their own allies and associates to the same standard. (WFWM press release, October 19, 2006)

Wal-Mart Watch commends the Maryland legislature for recently passing a bill that would compel Wal-Mart to increase its health care spending for the more than 10,000 employees in that state. But Maryland Governor Robert Ehrlich has threatened to veto the bill, saying that protecting the retail giant trumps the health care concerns of his constituents. (Ehrlich has also been the beneficiary of political donations from Wal-Mart, including a Wal-Mart-hosted fundraiser in December 2004 and a donation in January 2005). (WMW press release, May 2, 2005)

Remember Susan Chambers? At the same time Wal-Mart was trying to convince us that it offered suitable healthcare to its employees, she authored last year's infamous "secret" memo. In it, she recommended that the company increase physical activity in associates' jobs as a way to discourage unhealthy employees and lower Wal-Mart's healthcare expenditures. Well, last week, Wal-Mart promoted Ms. Chambers to Executive Vice President of Human Resources. (WMW email, April 12, 2006)

The common thread in these strategies concerns singling out a single person—anti-Wal-Mart activist Brian McLaughlin, Maryland governor Mark Ehrlich, or Wal-Mart VP Susan Chambers—to illustrate how that individual's actions are indicative of the skewed values or hypocrisy of the larger organization he or she represents. In terms of the ensuring discourse, the purity of the larger organization becomes polluted as a result.[19] The importance of such associations was underscored by former ambassador Andrew Young's statement of his resignation as the chairman of WFWM after making comments about shop owners in minority neighborhoods that many interpreted as being culturally offensive:

I took on the position of chairman of Working Families for Wal-Mart because I believe so strongly in the good that Wal-Mart does to lift up the lives of the working poor. The last thing I would want to do would be to distract from that good. Therefore, effective immediately, I am resigning the chairmanship of Working Families for Wal-Mart. (WFWM press release, August 17, 2006)

Of course, we see similar actions in the field of political campaigns regularly. Republican congressional candidates took pains to avoid being seen with an unpopular Republican president during their 2006 campaigns; some pundits considered Al Gore morally "tainted" by his association with President Clinton; Rudy Giuliani faced accusations of impropriety due to his previous relationship with Bernard Kerik, the former New York City Police Department commissioner indicted on numerous charges of fraud and conspiracy. But the significance of this rhetorical strategy accomplishes more than simply tarnishing the associated party's reputation: in a debate such as the one over Wal-Mart, this kind of person-based rhetoric shifts the moral focus of the language onto *individual* rather than *collective* actors. Focusing on the alleged hypocrisy of individuals associated with groups like WMW or WFWM gives participants a concrete individual identity on which to attach their moral censure—thus, using Susan Chambers to highlight the larger corporation's alleged mistreatment of employees draws rhetorical attention to a person, not a process.[20]

These strategies are arguably successful and thus represent a conscious PR tactic—questioning an individual's character, however officially decried in political campaigns, does bring results (witness the "Swift Boat" campaign of 2004 against presidential nominee John Kerry). But rhetorically it has a darker side as well—if individuals become the scapegoats of larger collectivities' failings, the logical corollary is that individuals should be the primary agents of their solutions. In Coleman's terms, the "asymmetric society" endures because we turn to individuals to solve corporation's problems, too often neglecting the complex organizational and political realities that contextualize the actions of a multinational corporation like Wal-Mart. Thus it's not surprising that Wal-Mart Watch made a personal appeal to Lee Scott via a pleading letter from faith-based leaders:

> As people of faith, we are asking you to commit in writing to the principles of "A Handshake with Sam," a proposed agreement which outlines Wal-Mart's moral responsibility to employees, customers and communities. . . . Because Sam Walton was a man of faith, we hope that you will not follow the path that leads to corporate plantations and move to a higher, moral ground. (WMW website, faith-based community letter)

Of course, in reality, Wal-Mart Watch has pursued numerous collective actions to challenge Wal-Mart's hegemony—the campaigns in Maryland and elsewhere for Faith Share for Health Care, and vigils for workers it argues have suffered under Wal-Mart's influence. Particularly when considered alongside such collectively oriented social movement strategies, the organization's *rhetorical* emphases on individual dimensions of change within Wal-Mart itself are particularly striking.

## Conclusion

Examining the public talk produced by activist groups involved in the Wal-Mart debate offers an important opportunity to examine how groups on both the political right and political left appeal to their perceived or potential audiences through their public discourse, illustrating how social activists can create linkages to larger communities of identity in their public talk. Focusing on the discourse of Wal-Mart and its supporters, as well as the retailer's main critic, Wal-Mart Watch, this chapter has argued that each group constructs a certain audience through its language—speaking to those who think of themselves as "average working families" in the case of Wal-Mart, and grassroots activists or taxpaying citizens in the case of Wal-Mart Watch. On the one hand, this is not entirely surprising—a store that encourages consumption would logically appeal to the families in which such consumption occurs, while an SMO involved in criticizing Wal-Mart would naturally address its constituency of potential activists as citizens. What's interesting, however, is how each group uses these categories to emphasize their separation from the other side, even though America's working families could hardly be considered an exclusive group, and "citizen" is itself a collective category. Rather, the economistic focus of this language emphasizes the divisions of this debate, such that the populist discourse ultimately constructs the separate reference groups to which each side refers and speaks.

This chapter has also argued that both of these SMOs adopt language that is heavily person-centered—for instance, framing Wal-Mart as a person and focusing criticisms on individuals instead of organizations. To some extent, this emphasis on individuals stems from Wal-Mart's decision to make personal stories a centerpiece of its Working Families for Wal-Mart website, whereas no comparable presentation appears in Wal-Mart Watch's public materials—people writing stories about their own responses to Wal-Mart will surely emphasize personal and individual experience. Likewise, because Wal-Mart Watch is orchestrating a massive campaign to educate the public about Wal-Mart and its alleged negative effect on Americans, we would almost certainly expect that its discourse would more prominently feature a consideration of the common good as it references a collective vision of economic justice. But despite these different organizational and rhetorical strategies, both groups prove remarkably similar in the way ideas of individualism and community appear throughout their public statements. Both discourses invoke person-based strategies throughout their rhetoric, and numerous examples from both groups of texts point to the difficulties inherent in using more community-focused rhetoric to create a broader discourse of inclusion.

While these findings focus on the case study of recent debates over Wal-Mart, the patterns observed here also surface in other forms of resurgent populism, most recently the Tea Party movement. Although it draws mostly from middle-class, white Americans, the Tea Party's discourse carries a thoroughly populist, "protect the little guy" rhetorical slant. Thus astute observers of the movement find that while the smaller government, fewer taxes rhetoric of the Tea Partiers has been around for decades, the movement also carries a decidedly anti-elitist tone that has created new rifts within the GOP itself.[21] In this instance, the justification for lower taxes lies not in the benefits of "trickle-down" economics, in which big businesses are induced to invest tax savings in economic development, but rather in the sanctity of smaller units of social life to determine their own economic values. As Sarah Palin herself explained, "We need to cut taxes so that our families can keep more of what they earn and produce, and our mom-and-pops then, our small businesses, can reinvest according to our own priorities, and hire more people and let the private sector grow and thrive and prosper."[22] Therefore, the movement is not merely a front for tax-cutting in the name of corporate welfare, or an outlet for the rage of middle-class Americans who have seen their economic fortunes decline steadily over the past thirty years. Rather, the movement has a potentially wide appeal among middle-class Americans precisely because it finds its rhetorical foundations in a much longer and deeper tradition that sees the rejuvenation of civil society as primarily the work of smaller social units, or "mediating structures," such as family, local communities, and small business.[23] These smaller forms of social organization pale in size and strength when compared to the perceived steady encroachment of big government, labor unions, and multinational corporations, which make them perfectly situated for an us-against-them rhetoric of conflict. For this reason, Wal-Mart can become the "little guy" despite the corporation's massive economic power, as its symbolic importance is perceived as being part of a larger ideological struggle in which the store is a key piece of the daily survival strategies that families use to make ends meet. In the context of resurgent populism, movements like these unify the "little platoons" of families and local communities precisely because these categories of reference take on a particular significance when juxtaposed against an "other"—in the case of both Wal-Mart's supporters and the Tea Party faithful, these are the out-of-touch elitists who spend wastefully to shore up the well-being of larger collective groups, such as labor unions, who usurp the free will of average, hardworking American families.

Understood within this economic context, the community-focused rhetoric of such populist movements can hardly be anything *but* divisive. In this way, focusing on the rhetoric of populism illustrates some of the most enduring fault lines of the current culture war debate. Most important, the divisions here are not rooted in orthodoxy and liberalism, or in different understandings of family and sexuality. Rather, the source of the divisions within this rhetoric stems from the ways the ideal of the family is situated in a larger discourse of economic scarcity, a frontier of the culture wars that has for the most part escaped the notice of most scholars who study ideological polarization. Although the Tea Party has taken pains not to make social issues a centerpiece of its platform,[24] the centrality of the "average working family" to the movement's ideology lurks just beneath the surface. This is but one of the reasons why Sarah Palin was such an effective early personification of the movement's public presentation. Not only does she blur class boundaries in her appeal to both suburban, middle-class mothers as well as working-class, rural American men (after all, her husband, Todd, was a member of the United Steelworkers), but Palin also made her familial identity as the mother of five children an effective component of her political appeal as a vice presidential candidate.[25] Referencing her identity as a "hockey mom" in her acceptance speech at the Republican National Convention, Palin continued to use familial tropes to describe her approach to politics, as when she framed her thinking about foreign policy: "As the mother of one of those troops, [John McCain] is exactly the kind of man I want as commander-in-chief. I'm just one of many moms who will say a prayer every night for our sons and daughters, our men in uniform."[26]

The subtle dimensions of this us-against-them rhetoric was partly what made Sarah Palin's speech at the RNC in September 2008 so electrifying for conservatives—and on the other hand, so alarming to progressives. Palin continued:

> A writer observed: "We grow good people in our small towns, with honesty, sincerity, and dignity." I know just the kind of people that writer had in mind when he praised Harry Truman. I grew up with those people. They are the ones who do some of the hardest work in America . . . who grow our food, run our factories, and fight our wars. They love their country, in good times and bad, and they're always proud of America.[27]

Having established just who "those people" are—the ones who "grow our food, run our factories, and fight our wars"—Palin continued moments later not only to cultivate the audience to whom she was speaking, but also to establish her credentials as a reliable member of that imagined community: "Before I became governor of the great state of Alaska, I was mayor of my hometown. And since our opponents in this presidential election seem to look down on that experience, let me explain to them what the job involves." Then, in perhaps the most controversial moment of the speech, Palin delivered just what her audience was hoping for:

> I guess a small-town mayor is sort of like a "community organizer," except that you have actual responsibilities. I might add that in small towns, we don't quite know what to make of a candidate who lavishes praise on working people when they are listening, and then talks about how bitterly they cling to their religion and guns when those people aren't listening. We tend to prefer candidates who don't talk about us one way in Scranton and another way in San Francisco.

Moving through the speech, Palin had described "those people" who make America great, and only moments later established herself as a true insider among an audience who was prepared to detect imposters. "Those people" that she praised for their quiet resolve and unfailing patriotism, the "working people" who don't like to be talked down to, become "we" as the speech unfolds: "*We* tend to prefer candidates who don't talk about *us* one way in Scranton and another way in San Francisco." The implication is clear: Palin carefully treads the path at the beginning, referencing her credentials as a mother, her respect for hardworking people, and eventually her disdain for politicians who seek the votes of working people in one context, then insult them in another. The message is subtle but unmistakable: you know who "they" are, and I am not one of "them." I know who you are, and I am one of you.

The reference to "working people" so early in Palin's speech was telling. As a key early figurehead of the Tea Party movement, Palin effectively injected the movement's populist rhetoric with the trope of the family in ways that emphasize not sexuality and reproduction, but economic survival and self-determination. Accordingly, Freedom Works (the grassroots organization behind much of the Tea Party's on-the-ground success at recruiting supporters for local events and rallies) includes school choice as one of its key platform issues alongside other economic priorities, such as tax reform, repealing health care reform, and regulating immigrant workers.[28] Palin

herself personalizes the movement, just as calling health care reform "Obamacare" personalizes the debate by marking the health care reform legislation
with the image of a president many conservative activists see as representative of all that they find deplorable about progressivism, most importantly
an emphasis of collective forms of redress for large-scale inequalities, promoted by an elite spokesman. The historian Lisa McGirr has observed that
conservatism has appealed as a remarkably coherent ideological movement
because it has "provided a total set of explanations for what they believe is
wrong with America, focusing specifically on the dangers of federal power
and control along with liberal efforts to distribute power more equitably in
society."[29] Obama, as a key personification of these forces, offers a powerful rallying cry against which Tea Partiers can construct a common, collective identity that grows out of their rage over a host of economic issues, such
as tax policy, health care reform, and looming budget deficits. In contrast,
Sarah Palin becomes a hero, representing an opposing personal identity that
signifies everything that Obama is not.

Focusing on the significance of the family and the citizen as potentially
opposing rhetorical categories helps to demonstrate how economic divisions
lurk beneath the surface of much of the culture war rhetoric and give these
debates such potential for division. Consistent with the economic topic of
focus, these communities of reference on both sides of the debate are defined
almost exclusively by their economic parameters—"average Americans"
are those who can't afford not to shop at Wal-Mart, and citizens are those
whose tax dollars go to support a corporation that critics allege has failed
to properly care for its employees. In different ways, then, the strategies of
both Wal-Mart activists and Tea Party participants reference potential movement members' economic well-being in their attempt to motivate participation on different sides of a social movement. With these economic categories
at the heart of their rhetorical strategies, movements organized around economic populism face steep challenges in creating compelling discourses that
can successfully tie these individualistic economic concerns to large-scale
changes, be they consumption practices or national tax policy. In the case of
Wal-Mart, the store's critics will eventually need to convince individuals that
they will need to spend a bit more on groceries; likewise, the Tea Party will
eventually face a reckoning concerning Social Security and Medicare—programs that benefit its middle-class supporters even as they create the very
same looming budget deficits that the group decries. In each case, an effective economic solution will demand that activists think not just as individuals, but also as members of a collectivity. In each case, however, activists have
yet to create a discourse that effectively frames relevant issues in this way.

Why does the rhetoric of such groups really matter? After all, one could argue, what really matters are the concrete techniques that SMOs such as these employ to advance their causes—including organized rallies, media campaigns, or consumer boycotts. Although social action may be the ultimate means by which any change is effected, economic debates such as this one are primarily being waged in the national media. Because a corporation like Wal-Mart is so ubiquitous and powerful, the best hopes of its critics lie in tarnishing Wal-Mart's public persona so that negative press hits the retailer where it matters most—store sales declines, decreasing stock value, and other negative indicators of economic performance. The Tea Party's tactics have similarly relied on grassroots methods of turning out supporters who can increase the visibility of the movement's platform and successfully convince the Republican establishment to acknowledge the movement's growing national presence. The media is the primary tool by which most SMOs advance their message; therefore, in these campaigns the primary currency is language—either in the group's own publications and statements, or in the media coverage it may generate in print and in broadcast sources like television and radio. Thus language is essential because it is the main venue by which these activists make their case to the public. Language also represents the means by which groups like the Tea Party can legitimize their cause by justifying it within in the larger traditions of American political culture, particularly constitutionalism. The multivocality of the narratives of America's founding, for instance, allows Tea Partiers to frame their claims for less government and more freedom within the context of the national identity, as a powerful symbolic beacon of both past and future hope.[30] These rhetorical strategies carry so much power precisely because they draw on shared meanings and narratives, however subtly, that sample from common American traditions about individualism, freedom, and the family.[31]

Further, all social movements rely on language to mediate their concerns for both the uninitiated and their core loyalists, which is why social movement scholars have placed so much emphasis on the concept of framing. Understood in this way, the significance of framing suggests another reason why the individualistic or person-based nature of a movement's rhetoric remains of particular interest to analyses such as this one. If the categories used to frame a problem are largely personal/individualistic, then it stands to reason that individual persons will similarly be the units of analysis targeted for action in return. In this case, if Wal-Mart is framed in person-based ways—either by emphasizing its moral failings in ways that we typically associate with individuals, or by describing the questionable actions of individuals associated with the corporation—then it follows that those problems might be solved by simply amending the character of the company itself, or by bringing in different individuals to participate in its leadership. Either way, such person-based terms of a debate make it more difficult for SMOs like Wal-Mart Watch to motivate observers to think in the collective-based terms required to challenge the individual-based economic rhetoric that privileges Wal-Mart's low prices and consumer savings.

The sociologist Karen Cerulo has argued that Americans are remarkably optimistic, and thus often fail to think about the worst thing that might happen. As a result, we often need what Cerulo calls "emancipating structures" to prod us toward preparation for disasters like September 11 or Hurricane Katrina.[32] Likewise, rhetorical structures that place economic problems in a larger web of systemic and institutional processes may be required to help people think outside the parochial economic box that leads many of us to simply not question Wal-Mart's benefits for the country, or the potential downsides of tax cuts. If my own, individual grocery bill is significantly lower because of Wal-Mart's low prices, it becomes difficult to imagine how other people or aspects of society could be suffering in order to bring those savings to me and my household. Rhetoric that relies largely on similarly individualistic themes—as in WMW's pleas to website visitors to consider how Wal-Mart may negatively affect their community, or how Wal-Mart's corporate welfare misspends "your" tax dollars—may be effective in motivating involvement among the uninitiated, but may prove somewhat less potent in prompting deeper consideration of the systemic and institutional factors that are also at work in such economic dilemmas. Rhetoric, in this way, shapes our perception of who has power to effect change, and just how much influence they wield. Moreover, the implied audiences in public debates such as this one also affect how its moral dimensions are received and interpreted among those divergent publics. The next chapter demonstrates that these different reference groups shape how the moral values of thrift and benevolence acquire such different meanings in the public debate about Wal-Mart.

# 4

## Thrift and Benevolence

Back in 1751, Franklin and like-minded citizens saw a need and put their money and resources together—yes, private funds—to open America's first public hospital: Pennsylvania Hospital. It's still in operation today. Franklin saw that there really were, at that time, sick people wandering the streets of Philadelphia without any-where to go. But he didn't expect the government to fix the prob-lem. In fact, he refused money from the politicians and instead went to friends to secure the funding. . . . The Founders could have written it in the original Constitution—they had health care prob-lems back then too—but they knew the answer was private, not the government.
—Media personality Glenn Beck, December 15, 2009

Americans' debates over health care reform raise a host of issues invit-ing moral reflection from the American people. Is health care a right or a privilege? Who should make decisions about costly end-of-life procedures? And perhaps most important, how much will health care reform ultimately cost? Aside from the ethical issues involved in health care decisions (the crazed panic about "death panels" notwithstanding), the debate over what would eventually become the Patient Protection and Affordable Care Act was unavoidably one about how much of a public entitlement program the United States could actually *afford*. At the same time, this politically charged controversy also forced Americans to consider where the responsibility for funding health care appropriately resides: with the state (as Obama initially suggested with the short-lived "public option" proposal), or with private citi-zens, as the conservative talk show host Glenn Beck argued to his viewers by appealing to the legacy of Benjamin Franklin. Referencing Franklin served more than one purpose in Beck's remarks, most notably to frame the health care debate as one relevant to an individual's interpretation of the Constitu-tion. Yet Beck's reference to Franklin also connects the health care debate to a larger moral concept with deep and lasting symbolic power: the moral value of thrift. Regardless of how supporters or opponents of health care reform attempted to look at the issue, there was no way around the cold, hard truth that insuring the American public was going to be very expensive.

Beck's appeal to Franklin reminds us that even the recent health care debate is tied to a long cultural tradition of moralizing thrift in public discourse about economic issues. In his famous *Poor Richard's Almanac*, Benjamin Franklin offered such memorable aphorisms as "A penny saved is two pence clear" and "Pay what you owe, and what you're worth you'll know."[1] It was, of course, this characterization of Franklin's ascetic restraint that prompted Max Weber to offer excerpts of Franklin's writing as an example of the spirit of capitalism that so famously captured his attention in *The Protestant Ethic*. Yet Franklin's own life choices also illustrate the importance of philanthropy and volunteerism, as he retired early and proceeded to devote much of the latter part of his life to supporting the arts, community issues, and politics.[2] Accordingly, Franklin warned of the perils of unchecked thrift, which could degenerate into the kind of rampant greed that undermines relationships and calls out for voluntary self-restraint. "Avarice and happiness never saw each other; how then should they become acquainted?" he asked, while additional proverbs from the *Almanac* note the risks of unrestrained greed, such as "A wise man will desire no more than he can get justly, use soberly, distribute cheerfully, and leave contentedly." Understood in this way, the pennies saved over one's lifetime will serve their master well only if they are used responsibly, shared willingly, and protected for the well-being—and presumably prudent usages—of others. Thrift, when properly apprehended in Franklin's writings, is merely one part of a continuum by which resources are saved but also shared, connecting it to its companion virtue of benevolence.

This edifying vision of thrift stands in marked contrast to another, much more negative historical characterization of thrift: the character Ebenezer Scrooge in Charles Dickens's 1843 classic novella *A Christmas Carol*. Initially described as a "tight-fisted" miser who doesn't mind keeping his house cold and poorly lit because "darkness is cheap," Scrooge undergoes a profound transformation that renders him the picture of cheerful benevolence by the end of the story. Central to Scrooge's transformation are, of course, the three spirits of Christmas past, present, and future who visit him during the evening. But the scenes these spirits show him say even more about the larger context of his rampant greed: Scrooge's avarice is explained in the story as a vice rooted in his own ruptured familial bonds—specifically, a father's cruelty and the death of his kind and loving sister. Similarly, Scrooge's redemption is found in witnessing scenes of kinship (Bob Cratchit's meager but happy home and his cheerful but disabled son Tim) and culminates in his surprising decision to join his nephew's family for Christmas dinner. If, for Franklin, thrift resulted in the virtues desired on behalf of a worthy citizen, Dickens's portrait of avarice turned benevolence finds its greatest fulfillment and expression in care of the family.

These time-honored literary portrayals of thrift and benevolence are significant not only because they exemplify both the best and the worst conceptions of thrift—the responsible Poor Richard and the greedy, selfish Scrooge—but also because they illustrate well the moral values placed on thrift and benevolence in our broader culture, as well as the potential difficulty inherent in reconciling them. Simply put, thrift and benevolence take on moral relevance because they proscribe some manner in which one is to live a good life. How people spend or share their material resources has some bearing on the well-being of others, as well as the character of the individual herself (think, for example, of Scrooge's potentially atrophied soul and Poor Richard's warning that avarice and happiness are incompatible). Further, thrift—defined simply as the frugal use of one's material resources—need not be estranged from its companion virtue of benevolence. In Franklin's conception, thrift and benevolence are almost two sides of the same coin—thrift itself is an example of the kind of moderation and restraint that leads one to share her wealth instead of hoarding it, which will ultimately bring the greatest happiness and contentment. But when we consider the meaning of benevolence more broadly—for example, as generous acts or concern for the welfare of others—we can understand why Dickens's portrayal of Scrooge confers a much harsher sentence on thrift, as he comes quite close to pronouncing its complete abandonment as the only way to redeem oneself in generosity and goodwill toward the less fortunate. Thus finding the right balance between frugality and benevolence is not necessarily an easy project.

This tension between thrift and benevolence emerges in a very clear way in economic debates—about taxes, health care reform, government bailouts, or Wal-Mart—precisely because both sides of these controversies refer to these ideas through their language, although I will argue throughout this chapter that they do so in profoundly different ways. Focusing specifically on the debate over Wal-Mart, I argue that the store and its supporters emphasize thrift as the more important moral virtue, while the store's critics tend to emphasize benevolence. Yet the most important differences between the two groups have more to do with the *contexts* in which they invoke these moral virtues. Wal-Mart and its supporters in WFWM consistently reference thrift as a moral virtue practiced primarily within the context of the family; with this frame of reference, thrift can be easily reconciled with benevolence because Wal-Mart's low prices help individuals and families be more generous to others. In contrast, Wal-Mart Watch (as the store's leading critic) frames its arguments as being primarily about thrift and benevolence as they affect larger social groups, especially workers, citizens, and taxpayers. These different referents—which create different contexts for the use of these moral values—lead the two sides to construct radically different moral frameworks, even though they do so by referencing common values.

This chapter also reveals that when conservative economic activists speak of the importance of thrift, they do so largely without reference to the larger economic forces that make it more difficult for their families to make ends meet, focusing instead on coincidental explanations and family disruption as the root causes of economic hardship. As a result of this familial context of discourse, many of the Americans whose manufacturing jobs have arguably been eliminated due to the outsourcing of big-box retailers speak of a store like Wal-Mart as a lifeline for their family, rather than a threat to their economic well-being. On the other side, Wal-Mart Watch, in focusing on the store's relationship with its workers and the broader ramifications of its employee policies, situates its construction of the market within the broader category of economic systems. In this context, Wal-Mart becomes a greedy corporation that need only show a little less thrift by acting more benevolently to their employees. At the conclusion of this chapter, I extend this argument to other recent national debates, most importantly the debate over health care reform that led Glenn Beck to invoke Benjamin Franklin's legacy of economic privatization as well as ascetic restraint. In both cases, we find common themes in political language, especially a conservative rhetorical worldview that places the family and thrift at its center, as opposed to a more progressive conception of benevolence that emphasizes the needs of the citizen within the context of larger webs of social groups.

## Thrift and Benevolence, Families and Citizens

As noted earlier, the examples of Poor Richard and Scrooge exemplify the best and worst potential of thrift and benevolence, as well as some of the challenges that may arise when we attempt to reconcile such potentially competing values. But these literary illustrations are also noteworthy because they point to ways in which thrift and benevolence have long been connected to other key concepts, such as the citizen and the family. For example, Franklin connects both thrift and benevolence to the virtues of citizenship, while Dickens roots both Scrooge's avarice and transformed generosity in the transcendent bonds of kin. Accordingly, these categories still prove relevant in our present day—findings in the social sciences, for example, emphasize how families view thrift as a moral virtue. The anthropologist Daniel Miller demonstrates this in his study of women's discourse about shopping. When wives and mothers talk about their grocery shopping, they celebrate their ability to save money while also buying special items for their loved ones. Any "treats" purchased alongside the necessities only underscore the centrality of thrift in the process of buying household necessities.[3]

Yet consumers often struggle to reconcile household thrift and larger concerns for the welfare of others; even as they render shopping a moral activity, similar work suggests that consumers are unlikely to view purchasing behavior as a primary place to take ethical or moral stands.[4] Union label campaigns in the early twentieth century, for example, faced steep challenges from union housewives whose predominant concern was frugality,[5] and even individuals whose family-run businesses have cratered due to Wal-Mart still buy groceries there because of its irresistibly low prices.[6] Miller's explanation for this kind of mismatch may be particularly relevant for understanding how shoppers construct a moral framework that incorporates both thrift and benevolence in the Wal-Mart debate. He concludes that while "thrift expresses the larger significance of working on behalf of the household as a moral enterprise," it is often "incompatible" with ethical alternatives, like buying fair trade coffee or organic produce. He continues to argue that

> ethical shopping is a means by which the immediate interests of the household are subsumed in the larger concern for others. These others may be the social welfare of producers or a general sense of the global environment, but they are defined as large and global in contradistinction to the parochialism of the household as a focus. The incompatibility of these two agendas is particularly clear when it comes to the question of price, since, at present, ethical shopping is almost always regarded as more expensive than ordinary shopping.[7]

Put another way, the conflict becomes one in which family meets society, or what the nineteenth-century social theorist Ferdinand Tönnies called *Gemeinschaft* and *Gesellschaft*. Tönnies was referring to two different means by which societies may be organized— *Gemeinschaft* (which means "community") bonds of family and group ties, which are contrasted with *Gesellschaft*, or the more rationalized bonds of modern society. In close communal ties, people are satisfied with relationships themselves as a source of meaning, while members of more modern social groups generally seek to have their needs met through a series of contractual regulations.[8] These distinctions can also help to explain why thrift and benevolence are not always easily reconciled: while the ethic of thrift may serve well the moral bonds of family and household, shoppers may find that acting as an ethical citizen on behalf of the larger society—for example, by paying higher prices for goods made in sweatshop-free factories—is incompatible with this ethic.

Given Wal-Mart's long-standing emphasis on thrift, it should come as no surprise that a central trope in the Wal-Mart debate concerns the family, particularly for Wal-Mart's supporters. Don Soderquist, former vice chairman and COO of Wal-Mart, emphasizes the family in his description of the "Wal-Mart way": "We are a family store. We want to supply the everyday needs of every member of the family. Furthermore, we want to offer merchandise that every family in the country needs, regardless of the socioeconomic level."[9] Similarly, as the historian Bethany Moreton has observed in her historical analysis of Wal-Mart's ascendancy, the company's agrarian and evangelical roots created a culture in which workers voluntarily accepted low wages, long hours, and dead-end futures in exchange for the folksy feeling associated with being part of the Wal-Mart "family."[10] Given the power of relationships and relational norms to imbue market relationships with meaning, as well as their centrality in our everyday lives, using the trope of "family" is a key rhetorical tool in any contentious debate. The magnitude of Wal-Mart's wages means something different depending on whether those wages support a "family" or simply provide pocket money to consumption-hungry teenagers.

But the family is more than merely a linguistic construct. Roger Friedland, for example, has argued that modern nationalist movements that center on religion often place the family—and its defense against the corrupting influences of capitalism—at the very center of their ideology.[11] Given the Enlightenment's legacy of creating modern individuals to be the building blocks of a rationalized society, a return to the discourse of family and an affinity for its filial ties as "the social space through which society should be conceived and composed,"[12] both challenges the Enlightenment paradigm and connects with earlier strains of socialist ideology that defended the family via campaigns for "living wages," the elimination of child labor, and the establishment of protections for those who might be unable to support their families due to disability, age, or economic recessions.[13]

Of course, supporters of Wal-Mart are not religious nationalists, but this argument offers valuable insight into the way that activists might use the concept of the family as a defense against the perceived encroachment of a destructive capitalist marketplace. Even as empirical research on the relationship between social ties and the capitalist market exposes the shortcomings of this "hostile worlds" approach to market society,[14] analysis of discourse often suggests that hostile worlds *talk* is alive and well.[15] Invoking the theme of family—as Wal-Mart itself has done by establishing the group called "Working Families for Wal-Mart"—is a powerful rhetorical device that highlights simultaneously the messy intermingling of economic and intimate rhetoric along with some of the difficulties this may create for envisioning social change. In families, for example, people do not usually ask for raises or demand promotions. Families call to mind norms of altruism and self-sacrifice that may not be compatible with economic solutions to inequality, such as organized labor or consumer boycotts.

The previous chapter argued that Wal-Mart consciously constructs the "average working family" as the core audience in its discourse, but Wal-Mart is not alone in invoking the theme of family. Large corporations have long encouraged employees to think of their commitment to the company and their co-workers in familial terms, and workers often talk about work in narrative forms that emphasize its human dimensions.[16] Some progressive organizations have begun using familial terminology as well, perhaps recognizing the rhetorical appeal and political success of social movements organized around these strategies.[17] In 2000, Al Gore initially adopted the campaign theme "Change That Works for Working Families,"[18] and Wal-Mart's critics have similarly begun to critique the company on the grounds that its wages do not allow workers to "provide for their families." Yet the way that both groups conceive of and use "the family" as a rhetorical construct in their discourse proves an important way of distinguishing the moral worldview of Wal-Mart from that of its critics—a disjuncture I will discuss later on in this chapter.

Noting the potential conflict between conceptions of thrift that emphasize the family and the larger, ethical concerns that call for benevolent citizens, Christine Williams concludes that the best hopes for addressing the inequalities wrought by the retail industry will be those that break down the dichotomy between worker and consumer, and that between economy and household.[19] If people can think more deeply and systematically about their purchasing decisions (e.g., did other people's children in a Bangladesh sweatshop make the clothes I buy for my children at Wal-Mart?), then the moral consequences of thrift and opportunities for benevolence may be more readily apprehended. In this regard, Miller's argument about the micro- and macro- foundations of moral criticism offers an important clue for understanding some aspects of the rhetoric in the Wal-Mart debate: when we speak about families, thrift seems the more fitting moral priority, but when we speak of citizens and the larger society, benevolence more easily comes to mind. Therefore, bringing concerns rooted in the family to bear on larger concerns regarding the labor market and commercial sector might represent a useful strategy for connecting these two frameworks, and thus a useful source of critique. However, the analysis discussed in this chapter suggests that so far Wal-Mart's critics are not employing such strategies.

## The Morality of Thrift for Wal-Mart's Supporters

When compared alongside the other moral concepts considered in this book—for instance, freedom and fairness, individual and communities—the values of thrift and benevolence are far and away the most prevalent in representative samples of language drawn from the Wal-Mart debate. Even so, this is primarily because these values are so frequently mentioned in the documents produced by WFWM and Wal-Mart Inc. Of 402 separate references to thrift in these documents, for example, 353 of them occur in documents related to Wal-Mart and its chief advocates. Benevolence is almost as frequent, with 309 references coded as such—most of them (279) in Wal-Mart supporters' materials. Additionally, when Wal-Mart and its supporters speak of thrift in particular, they do so with reference to the family at least a quarter of the time—89 instances out of 353. And while some might argue that excessive thrift undermines benevolence (think, for example, of the pre-Christmas Scrooge), the discursive universe of Wal-Mart and its proponents do not understand thrift and benevolence to be at odds with each other. Quite the contrary, they are complementary, with one furthering the other.

One document that exemplifies all these themes is an email I received from Working Families for Wal-Mart's board member Courtney Lynch upon signing up as a supporter of the group via the website.[20] Titled "Thanks for Joining Working Families for Wal-Mart," the first portion of the email began:

It starts with $2,300.

That's how much Wal-Mart saves the average working family each year. But that's just one way to measure the good that Wal-Mart does for working families and communities like yours every day. You know, because you've seen them yourself.

- The senior citizen who's able to earn extra income thanks to an opportunity with Wal-Mart.
- The student working her first job and cashing her first paycheck.
- The family that can finally afford a portrait for the mantle or glasses for their youngest thanks to Wal-Mart's low prices.

- The local charity that's able to help more people thanks to Wal-Mart's generosity.
- The small business that makes it big after Wal-Mart begins carrying its product.

This email represents many of the key themes in WFWM's discourse about thrift and benevolence: most important, the centrality of the family, not the citizen or the worker, as the main referent in their language. The words "family" or "families," for example, are mentioned fourteen times in the entire email—not only by reiterating the group's name, "Working Families for Wal-Mart," throughout, but also by calling attention to Wal-Mart's savings for families and (at the conclusion of the appeal) asking the reader to share this positive message with "friends and family." But more than just cohering around familial categories, both here and elsewhere WFWM constructs a moral universe in which thrift and benevolence are complementary, not conflicting, moral goods. Below I explore these themes more fully.

*Thrift and the Family*

It is no accident that my email from Courtney Lynch began by explaining "Wal-Mart's positive message" with a reference to thrift—"It starts with $2,300" a year—or that this value of thrift would be immediately tied to the concept of a family—"That's how much Wal-Mart saves the average working family each year." The letter goes on to reference positive stories about Wal-Mart that the reader has likely seen firsthand: a senior citizen who is able to earn extra money working for Wal-Mart, or a family who can purchase necessities for its children because of Wal-Mart's low prices. Although it also contains press releases not unlike those found on Wal-Mart's company website, the centerpiece of Working Families for Wal-Mart's website highlights personal stories of this nature. The significance of thrift for this demographic takes on even more significance when we consider that in a recent survey 56% of Wal-Mart's regular shoppers come from families making less than $50,000 a year. Similarly, only 27% of the store's regular shoppers have household incomes that exceed $75,000.[21] The store's shoppers are not primarily poor people, but rather Americans who are solidly middle and working class, seeking to stretch their wages a bit further to support their families.

Understood in this context, thrift acquires a particular moral significance in the larger discursive setting of the family, particularly in the following personal stories showcased on the WFWM website. The central role of thrift and family in these narratives becomes clear after reading the opening lines of just a few of these testimonials:

My husband is a police officer in a nearby city and I am a stay at home mom of three small children so needless to say we don't have a lot of money.

My husband recently decided to go back to school to finish his degree. This has definitely had an impact on our finances. We have two small boys and it has been really hard to make ends meet.

WalMart is great! We call it "Wally World" in our family because you get so much for my money when I go there, especially since they put in the grocery store.

I am a mother of 3 teenage children and are proud to say that I love to shop in Walmart. It saves us a lot of money towards groceries and I also support taking our yearly pictures at Walmart studios.

I am a married mother of three school age children and Walmart's low prices are the only way I can survive.

I am a mother of three, ages 8, 4, and 2. It can be hard at times to take everyone places I need to go. Wal-Mart supercenter makes it alot easier on me by having just about everything I need in one place.

My family and I do appreciate the low prices at Wal-Mart. Because of Wal-Mart's low prices we are able to stretch an already stretched budget!

We recently had our first child, a little girl. Having a baby is very expensive but Wal-Mart prices make it a little easier.

My name is Kourtenay and I am a single mother of three. That should be the whole story as to why I shop at Walmart but theres [sic] so much more . . .

As a mother of a growing teenager and recently gaining custody of my niece, it's nice to have a store where I can shop for just about everything and still save money.

In these examples, and the countless others like them solicited by WFWM, the speakers almost always begin by referencing their membership in a family—their role as a mother, or a wife, for example—or by designating their family as the unit that shops at Wal-Mart. In other cases, shopping at Wal-Mart allows not only thrift of money but thrift of time, which enables the shopper to get home more quickly and spend precious time with loved ones. The consistency of this narrative formula certainly raises suspicions that Wal-Mart's PR firm, Edelman, might have crafted these stories itself, although the variety and diversity of the stories would require seemingly endless creativity. Either way—whether these narratives are genuine or counterfeit—their central place in Wal-Mart's chief advocacy group underscores the intentionality with which Wal-Mart presents a message emphasizing thrift and its connection to the family.

In addition to their prominent focus on family, these narratives make a number of consistent assumptions about the referents of this discourse and its intended audience. Most important, they refer to a worldview in which women are presumed responsible for managing the family's budget, and the speaker's associated familial identity emerges early in the author's story—as the wife of a hardworking breadwinner, the mother of consumption-hungry teenagers, or the single head of household with numerous mouths to feed. Consistent with accounts that emphasize women's roles as the chief mediators of their families' consumption,[22] the narratives offered here consistently refer to women as the family members who most often acknowledge the daily sacrifices demanded for frugal living, and who take it upon themselves to help the family live within its means.

The pro-Wal-Mart discourse also presumes a familiarity among the audience with the "average working family" discussed in chapter 3. In some instances, Wal-Mart and WFWM issued press releases that emphasized their allegiance to the country's working classes—for example, one advocate explained in a WFWM press release from August 2006 that "Wal-Mart gives the poor and working class people the opportunity to live like they are middle class, at a working class cost." Similarly, Wal-Mart frequently mentioned providing jobs to "those who need them most," and WFWM criticized its detractors for being elitist, as in a WFWM press release dated October 19, 2006: "Sadly, the critics who are paid to attack this company no matter what it does, fail to face the fact that perhaps more than any single company in America, Wal-Mart is providing the opportunity for a better life for poor and working families."

In the WFWM personal stories, allusions to class were quite frequent but also more understated. Unlike the speaker who said straight out, "We're on the lower end of the Middle Class scale," most speakers referenced their lower-middle-class status in ways designed to obliquely communicate their need for savings alongside their determination to remain self-sufficient. Words indicating class included the ubiquitous "afford," as well as references to the financial challenges involved when "we have to juggle our bills every month" or the hardship of working two jobs. One writer referred to "my family of eight, income of one," and how Wal-Mart has "made basic household needs and recreational wants readily affordable." Thus, over and over again, social class is communicated in largely economic terms. Even a reference to "hardworking people" serves to communicate both the speaker's pride and his or her seemingly precarious economic position:

> I have just retired at age 66 and lost B/C–B/S. Cobra was too expensive for me so I had to join Humana's PPO. Cost of prescriptions for me now is from $7.00 to $70.00, which I can't afford, plus a fee every month which i [sic] didn't expect. If Wal-Mart charges $4.00 I will change over my medication to them. Thanks for thinking of us hard working people who live on a fixed income.

To be sure, in some cases speakers speak of thrift as an absolute essential for survival (e.g., "Walmart's low prices are the only way I can survive," as one woman wrote), but in many cases speakers describe thrift as a virtue that helps them achieve upward mobility—or at least the illusion of it. For example, one speaker—echoing the reference to "average working families" in WFWM's initial email—said simply, "I am an 'average' American. I earn an average income. Walmart helps me to be more than average." Others emphasized how Wal-Mart's savings helped them provide more of the "extras" they wanted for their family:

> In September 2005, we had a wonderful addition to our family. A grandson whose father was in Iraq. Mom & baby moved in with us. Then came the increased expenses. I shopped at Walmart and found everything we needed for the baby at very reasonable prices. The lower costs allowed us to purchase extra little things for the baby, as well as develop pictures to send to Dad. I've found shopping there to be economical and a great benefit to our family.

> Our daughter recently got married (June 24), and she chose Wal-Mart for her gift registry. This has helped her new husband and her start their new home together by saving hundreds of dollars on appliances, bedding, and other household items. She also bought some of their wedding decorations

there—such as the wedding cake topper and guest book pen. This was at a big savings as well as we compared these prices to many others around.

As far as I'm concerned, Wal-Mart is one of those factors that makes it possile [sic] for us to raise our children in relative prosperity, yet allowing us to spend more time with them to share the values, disciplines, and love that will help them grow into the sort individuals and citizens we can all be proud of.

In such examples, the formula is remarkably consistent: financial savings (thrift) allows family members to participate in the activities (consumption) that constitute decent living and upward social class mobility. Most important, the virtue and morality of thrift take shape within this core discursive context of the nuclear family.

### Gemeinschaft and Gesellschaft in the Wal-Mart World

In this discursive landscape, one must ask the question: Why would families need the opportunities for thrift that Wal-Mart offers—either to simply survive or to purchase "extras" such as a wedding cake topper? Why would children need parents to "spend more time with them" in order to bring them up with the proper values and discipline? In conjunction with the overarching emphasis on the relationship between thrift and family, the more common explanation for economic hardship in these personal stories has to do with familial disruption, not economic or social contract disruptions. Instead, the larger economic scene in which these individual family struggles are played out recedes into the background, rarely confronted head-on and almost never mentioned explicitly (although there are some exceptions).[23] The following excerpts from the WFWM website illustrate how speakers view economic disruption through the primary lens of the family:

I am single mom with three children. Two in college and one a sophomore in high school. I have worked for the Postal Service for over 20 years love my job. Working single mom's favorite store is WalMart, not just because they have great prices, but because they have everything from groceries to school supplies and are open 24 hours.

I am a widowed, handicapped senior on a fixed income, so I am limited in my ability to get around. I am very pleased to be able to shop at Wal-Mart because I can make my money go farther with their low prices.

Wal-mart gave me a job when others wouldn't. I had been looking for a job for about two months but kept getting turned down because I was pregnant. By the time I interviewed at wal-mart I was seven months pregnant. I went to the interview and it went well and as I had [with] all the others I made them aware that i [sic] would need time off when the baby was due. I got the call an hour after I left the interview. The department I worked with gave me a baby shower and covered my position without complaint. When I had the baby they were the first to send flowers and cards. You become like a family.

In these three examples, women describe the difficulties of making ends meet without the financial support of a household breadwinner. As in the first excerpt above, the refrain of being a single mom was frequently offered as a justification for needing Wal-Mart's low prices. In examples such as these, the speaker's status as a single woman—whether divorced or widowed—is offered as enough of a reason for financial hardship. For the widowed retiree mentioned in the second excerpt, it is notable that she references her family disruption—in other words, her status as a widow—before listing other conditions that are understandably associated with financial difficulties, including being handicapped and living on a fixed income. Finally, the woman who was employed at Wal-Mart in the latter months of her pregnancy even goes so far as to name her Wal-Mart coworkers as "like a family," since they gave her a baby shower and sent immediate congratulatory gifts and cards after the birth of the baby. Her initial difficulties were rooted in her family situation—being an undesirable employee because she was pregnant—but by the end of the narrative she has found both employment and a new kind of family in her Wal-Mart coworkers. Further, when she speaks of her new job, she emphasizes not the wages, but her relationships with employees—"When I had the baby they were the first to send flowers and cards."

Some narratives that reference economic disruption do attribute their difficulties to the economic cause—a spouse's illness that renders her unable to work, or a husband being laid off. Yet in the following examples, even when the family is intact and economic hardship occurs, the speaker scarcely considers the larger context of the wage earner's difficulty, but focuses instead on the experience of hardship for the family:

As a long time cutomer [sic] I would like to thank you for giving my family and I a chance to survive in tough times. My husband was just layed [sic] off from his job that he had for over 10 years. Lets [sic] keep it simple.

Without your prices, we would not be able to eat and clothe ourselves with just my income.

My name is Danielle Hodge and, like many people, our family has experienced the transition from two incomes to one. My husband was laid off in October of 2005 and has had a very hard time finding work. He finally accepted a position not too long ago but is only making 1/4 the salary he once made. Since he was the primary source of income, I found myself having to cut corners anywhere possible. I love WalMart, because not only am I able to save on groceries but I save on other necessities, as well. . .

My husband and I have no money and now live week to week since my husband's diabetes was discovered about two years ago. We went from living on a happy medium to a very low medium because his medication does not allow him to continue his occupation which was roofing. We are about to lose our vehicles and our roof over our head, but, WalMart has made it possible to keep food on our table by continuing with their low prices.

Several years ago my sister-in-law experienced major health problems and many resulting surgeries. My brother had a very good supplemental insurance policy with the company he retired from, still his deductibles and co-pays was more than their budget could afford. He applied for and was hired by Wal-Mart in Semi, California. He has now worked there as a senior greeter for almost ten years. He will be eighty next January (2007). His pay not only helps them pay for the out-of-pocket expense of her many medical bills but also gives him such a sense of pride and well being.

The first speaker, for example, begins the narrative by thanking Wal-Mart "for giving my family and I a chance to survive during tough times." This declaration precedes the explanation for hardship—her husband being laid off. In the next two examples, the male breadwinner has been unable to continue contributing to the household as he once did, either by forced layoffs or illness. In response, the narrator explains the hardship as the family has experienced it, glossing over any explanation that could be found in larger economic processes, such as corporate downsizing or inadequate preventive health care. Instead, the speaker, Danielle Hodge, frames the hardship as one borne by the family, not the wage earner, and describes her contributions to the family's survival strategies. In a similar manner, the third speaker frames her husband's difficulties—he "could not continue his occupation" due to his medication—as one experienced by the family: "*We* went from living on a happy medium to a very low medium," and "*We* are about to lose *our* vehicles and *our* roof over our head" (emphasis added). The speaker takes little time to explore how these hardships are potentially rooted in forces outside the individual and the family unit in which they are most pointedly experienced—even while the agent that comes to the family's rescue is Wal-Mart, a corporate giant that arguably plays a role in the very economic system responsible for recessions that prompt layoffs, or corporate cost-cutting that reduces available funds for comprehensive medical care. In C. Wright Mills's terms, these "troubles" remain just that—private troubles that have yet to be transformed into the public "issues" worthy of collective concern.[24]

Perhaps because Wal-Mart's help in these tough times is experienced at the level of the family, there's little cognitive dissonance involved in simultaneously ignoring the "issues" of the economic system for their causal role in private "troubles"—thus Wal-Mart itself couldn't be a part of the external economic system that forced someone into early retirement. Much as Daniel Miller's research would portend, the centrality of the family as the referent of this language may obscure the larger social concerns that linger behind the low prices that enable families to partake of Wal-Mart's thrift. In the same way that large corporations encourage "local" and familial thinking to augment employees' perceptions of their own personal influence,[25] the WFWM speakers' locus of control is likely relevant as well—the larger systemic forces of the economy are well outside the realm of one's individual manipulation, while the family budget can be directed and controlled at will. This may also lead supporters to speak more concretely about the family and the way that Wal-Mart's savings have been experienced in their personal household, than they do about the comparatively distant and chaotic economic system.

A potential source of this familial lens for discussing thrift might also lie in the genre of these utterances—personal narratives or testimonials are more likely to lie in the realm of personal or family experience simply by definition. Yet even beyond the narratives solicited by WFWM—which rely on individuals' perceptions of these issues—Wal-Mart Inc.'s own corporate statements frame the family as the unit under attack by these larger economic forces, and emphasize the role of Wal-Mart in facilitating thrift. As declared in a Wal-Mart press release on September 21, 2006:

> "Each day in our pharmacies we see customers struggle with the cost of prescription drugs," said Wal-Mart CEO H. Lee Scott, Jr. "By cutting the

cost of many generics to $4, we are helping to ensure that our customers and associates get the medicines they need at a price they can afford. That's a real solution for our nation's working families."

The "customers" who struggle with the cost of prescriptions at the beginning of Scott's statement are framed as "our nation's working families" at its conclusion. Similarly, elsewhere Scott called the store's low prices "a lifeline for millions of middle and lower-income families who live from payday to payday" and a WFWM email sent out around Christmas of 2006 explained that "Wal-Mart is working hard this Christmas to help American families in need." Although common sense tells us that that living "from payday to payday" or needing assistance at Christmas is inextricably linked to being a worker in the paid economy (or perhaps unemployed or underemployed), the workers here are nearly invisible, replaced by the collective family unit. In Tönnies's terms, the familial bonds of Gemeinschaft triumph as the discursive terms in which Wal-Mart and its supporters speak of the economy and its ramifications; the worker who claims his role in the Gesellschaft of modern society is mentioned only in passing, eclipsed by that worker's experience in a network of kinship ties.

This discursive preference for Gemeinschaft over Gesellschaft also helps to explain why unions are so often vilified in these narratives. For example, as one WFWM supporter declared, "People need the low prices and we don't need the unions." Underscoring this point further, a WFWM press release issuing a statement from a member of the WFWM steering committee explained, "It's just plain wrong for union leaders to waste the hard-earned money of their members attacking a store where the vast majority of those members shop to save money," concluding, "If union leaders aren't on the side of their members and America's working families, whose side are they on?" (WFWM press release, January 4, 2006). Elsewhere, another WFWM spokesperson explains, "Working families everywhere support Wal-Mart—and that includes the people of New York City [site of recent Wal-Mart opposition] and those in union households, who are working families too" (WFWM press release, February 3, 2006).

The choice of the word "members" in statements such as these describes a critical feature of this discursive context—union membership is voluntary, contractual. People choose to join or leave unions in ways that they don't choose to become members of families—although, as WFWM argues, union households "are working families too." Thus the categories of union member and working family have an interesting relationship in this discourse— on the one hand, union membership is distinct from working families, as indicated by the construction "union members and America's working families." However, the category of working families is sufficiently broad to encompass union households as well. In this discursive landscape, the context of "family"—one rooted in deeper, transcendent bonds—trumps other rationalistic, society-created categories like "worker" or "union member." As WFWM explained in the wake of Wal-Mart's announcement of a four-dollar generic prescription drug program:

> It is beyond explanation that union leaders claiming to advocate on behalf of working families are attacking a program that will not only make prescription drugs more affordable, but will also make sure those who haven't been able to afford their medicines now have the opportunity for better health. Only a failing campaign would attack an initiative that makes prescription drugs more affordable for working families. (WFWM press release, September 22, 2006)

Union leaders, then, err by focusing their attention on the wrong targets: corporations, atomized workers, or morally bankrupt political campaigns. The proper focus—and the one in which thrift takes on the fullest expression of moral relevance—is the family.

### Reconciling Thrift and Benevolence

Thrift need not be opposed to its companion value of benevolence; in fact, they are often linked, as in the proverbs of Ben Franklin mentioned earlier. And to be sure, for Wal-Mart and its supporters the two values find little conflict with each other. This is explained by three primary reasons. First, the language of Wal-Mart's supporters tends to frame both thrift and benevolence largely at an individual level. For example, one shopper almost perfectly echoed Franklin's suggestion to balance thrift with charity, writing:

> As a private individual I have shopped at Walmart since they first opened in my area. I try very hard to be a good steward of the money God has given to my family. I realized early on that the savings I realized at Walmart would allow me more philanthropic opportunities. (WFWM website, personal story)

In other cases, Wal-Mart itself references the benevolent actions of its employees, framing benevolence in terms of the actions of individuals, as in the following: "With more than a million Wal-Mart Stores associates nationwide serving 138 million customers per week, the ability to help thousands of children through their efforts is quite amazing . . . even just collecting donations through the purchase of balloons, one dollar at a time" (Wal-Mart press release, April 15, 2005). In other instances, Wal-Mart's benevolence comes through in stories about how customers were able to use Wal-Mart's premises for fund-raising, or the way that Wal-Mart made a financial contribution to an organization with which the speaker was affiliated. But because these benevolences are framed in individual terms by the speaker who experienced them—for example, "I was at our Boy Scout Troop meeting and one of the parents reported that the East Meadow Walmart made a $1000 donation to our troop" (WFWM website, personal story)— they pose little challenge to the ethic of thrift that simultaneously pervades these narratives. The same person who witnesses or benefits from a benevolent act can subsequently exercise thrift on her own without reconsidering its potentially negative consequences.

A second strategy through which thrift and benevolence are rendered complementary among Wal-Mart and its supporters is the way that Wal-Mart Inc. frames its corporate benevolence in press releases and related materials. In many instances, Wal-Mart's generosity is designed to encourage thrift itself—to help students who are stretching their family resources to go to college, to further environmental conservation, or to reward elementary school students for exemplary recycling programs. Further, unlike the stories of individual kindness between employees and customers, these press releases stress the magnitude of Wal-Mart's charitable contributions and consistently emphasize their large size and local ramifications—in other words, the company's external effects on communities as opposed to its internal dealings with employees. Thus statements like "As the largest corporate cash contributor in the country with a presence in more than 3,800 communities nationwide, Wal-Mart makes 90 percent of its charitable contributions at the local level, where they can have the most impact" (WFWM website), reiterate themes heralding the size and scale of Wal-Mart's philanthropy. By focusing attention on the corporation's benevolence *outside* of the company's internal practices, much of the potential tension between thrift and benevolence is averted. Accordingly, little discourse within the pro-Wal-Mart writings considers the internal workings of the corporation. And even if it did, the logical conclusion might be that it is actually *because* Wal-Mart cuts costs within its business operation that it can give so much money away.

Even more important, a final strategy by which Wal-Mart and its supporters reconcile thrift and benevolence concerns the way Wal-Mart itself

is framed as a benevolent and helpful entity, which has less to do with traditional conceptions of benevolence—for example, as when a corporation
gives away charitable donations of cash—and more to do with the way its
supporters frame Wal-Mart as an entity that goes out of its way to truly help
people. By hiring those who are hard to employ, making others feel needed,
or offering low prices to those who need them most, Wal-Mart's supporters
paradoxically portray the company as an entity that is actually anticapitalist
and thus has chosen principles of benevolence instead of the market-driven
values of greed and accumulation. One excerpt from the WFWM website
makes this point most compellingly:

> It sought out low prices for its customers—by way of low margins for
> itself—and brought affordable goods to working families, often in rural
> and underserved communities, by offering a high volume of those goods
> at a high number of stores.

The Wal-Mart presented in the above account, and Wal-Mart's business
model itself (in which thrift and low margins are central) is portrayed as
a selfless act of benevolence on behalf of working families in underserved
rural locations.

As in the above example, the verbs used to describe Wal-Mart's actions are
most illustrative; in the examples that follow, Wal-Mart alternately provides,
gives, serves, helps, offers, supports, cares, and saves (emphases added):

> Wal-Mart *provides* communities with good jobs, opportunity for growth,
> affordable health care and huge savings for working families. (WFWM
> press release, September 11, 2006)

> What other company ever went into small town America and *gave* us a
> store we could buy anything we need. They are the best. (WFWM website,
> personal story)

> Community leaders discussed how this underscores a need for the good
> jobs Wal-Mart *offers* in the Chicagoland area, as well as considerable sav-
> ings and philanthropic grants to the Evergreen Park community. (Wal-
> Mart press release, January 26, 2006)

> Wal-Mart *saves* working families money, creates quality jobs in areas
> where they are needed most and is a corporate leader on environmental
> sustainability efforts. (WFWM press release, November 15, 2006)

We think it is great that they *give* older people and those just starting out a place that will hire them and give them a chance. (WFWM website, personal story)

Wal Mart is the only store in my eighty years that ever really *cared* about their customers. (WFWM website, personal story)

Wal-Mart Wheat Ridge (CO) has *given* willingly to Wheat Ridge Rotary Club year after year. (WFWM website, personal story)

Walmart has really *helped* our community with all types of charitable giving. (WFWM website, personal story)

Wal Mart has *provided* opportunities for many of my friends' children and may be a place for my dad to work someday. (WFWM website, personal story)

By using such terms to describe Wal-Mart's actions, Wal-Mart's supporters frame Wal-Mart as a benevolent entity in and of itself. As a result, Wal-Mart's benevolence becomes almost taken for granted, as if woven into the very fabric of the corporation. Understood in this way, how could this kind and caring entity be anything like the miserly Scrooge who revels in the stacks of gold piled up in his counting house? Within this frame, Wal-Mart's ethic of thrift poses little threat to its image as a benevolent store-of-the-people.

In addition to framing Wal-Mart as the kind of entity that engages in benevolent behavior through the verbs detailed above, many of the narratives mention Wal-Mart in ways that imply reciprocity, thanking Wal-Mart for its contributions. The curious thing about these rhetorical moves is that by thanking Wal-Mart for things like job opportunities and low prices, the narratives imply that Wal-Mart has made the decision to engage in these activities *voluntarily*. Just as Scrooge made a choice to end his miserly ways and show care and concern for his fellow men, Wal-Mart has chosen—at least from this perspective—to ignore some of the most basic rules of market capitalism. Time and again, speakers concluded their narratives about Wal-Mart with a simple "Thanks, Wal-Mart." One particularly enthusiastic speaker went so far as to proclaim, "It feels wonderful, to let you finally know how I feel about your Fantastic (low prices) store. I loveeeeeeeeeeeeeeeeeeee Wal-Mart and I thank you, for your great store" (WFWM website, personal story). When speakers thank Wal-Mart for doing the things one might typically expect of a corporation—offering goods at competitive prices, hiring workers to represent it to the public—they imply that these activities are being understood as benevolent choices rather than expected requirements of the capitalistic marketplace.

The Discursive Landscape of Wal-Mart's Critics

In contrast to the materials produced by Wal-Mart and WFWM, the discursive landscape of Wal-Mart Watch focuses less on thrift and more on benevolence. However, the conception of benevolence presented here is quite different from both the externally oriented benevolence touted by those who laud Wal-Mart's charitable contributions, and the individualistic conception of benevolence presented in narratives that focus on how Wal-Mart has helped them personally. Instead, when Wal-Mart Watch speaks of benevolence it tend to do so in an entirely different context: focusing on the company's actions toward its workers, and challenging Wal-Mart to provide more generous wages and benefits for its employees because the company could afford to do so. In other places, Wal-Mart Watch suggests that Wal-Mart could help workers simply by raising its prices by pennies on each item—a suggestion that, by definition, directly challenges a strict ethic of thrift. For this reason, benevolence and thrift are more often seen as oppositional in this group of texts, which represents another central difference between the moral worldview created in the language of Wal-Mart's supporters and that of its opponents. Finally, although Wal-Mart Watch does mention families, the vast majority of this discourse concerns the categories of worker and citizen. In this way, Wal-Mart Watch uses the common symbolic language of thrift and benevolence, but applies these moral ideas to a very different central category. Moreover, this differential focus leads to a radically different conclusion: far from being a benevolent store of the people, Wal-Mart's critics construct it as a morally bankrupt, greedy exploiter of both workers and taxpayers.

All these themes are illustrated in a *New York Times* ad on April 20, 2005 that announced the group's formation and mission. The advertisement featured the headline "How much does Wal-Mart cost American taxpayers every year?" and included text alleging that "Wal-Mart's low pay and meager employee benefits force hundreds of thousands of employees to resort to Medicaid, food stamps, and public housing. Call it the 'Wal-Mart Tax.' And it costs you $1.5 billion in federal tax dollars every year." A press release[26] announcing the ad (and issued the same day) explained:

The ad highlights the "Wal-Mart Tax"—the more than one-and-a-half billion dollars in federal taxpayer dollars that flow to the company each year on top of its annual profits of over ten billion dollars. And millions more in corporate welfare from state and local governments further add to the company's bottom line.

Wal-Mart Watch Executive Director Andy Grossman said, "Wal-Mart may say 'low prices' but we're here to ask 'at what cost?' As the biggest corporation in the world, Wal-Mart is also one of the biggest recipients of corporate welfare in the world. They greedily use American taxpayers' hard-earned dollars to enrich themselves at the expense of smaller businesses that don't get corporate welfare. Shameful."

Key features of this press release point out some of the more pronounced differences between the discursive context of Wal-Mart Watch and that of Wal-Mart's supporters. Most important, WMW eschews much talk of thrift in favor of an emphasis on benevolence, particularly in light of Wal-Mart's purported corporate greed. Because this benevolence is understood in largely comparative terms—Wal-Mart can and should do more because it has so much in comparison to its low-wage workers—WMW frames thrift as oppositional to the moral value of benevolence. Finally, unlike WFWM and Wal-Mart, which use the family as their primary referent, WMW conducts much of its discussion of both thrift and benevolence with reference to the categories of worker, taxpayer, and citizen. Using the above press release as a starting point, I discuss all these strategies below.

*Benevolence, Not Greed*

As illustrated in this press release, Wal-Mart Watch fundamentally rejects thrift as a primary moral value: "Wal-Mart may say 'low prices' but we're here to ask 'at what cost?'" The characterization of Wal-Mart offered here is more like the unreformed Scrooge, as Wal-Mart "greedily use[s] American taxpayers' hard-earned dollars to enrich [itself] at the expense of smaller businesses that don't get corporate welfare." The presumed reprehensibility of this practice is further underscored by the addition of the word "shameful" at the conclusion of this statement. The press release also implies that Wal-Mart's profits are already sufficient without the support provided by public revenues, contributing to the company "on top of" its existing profits exceeding $10 billion.

Wal-Mart Watch's rejection of thrift as a guiding principle—and the difference this creates between it and Wal-Mart's supporters—is further illustrated by examining the way Wal-Mart Watch talks about the store's environmental impacts. While Wal-Mart was unabashed in explaining how good environmental practices were also good business, Wal-Mart Watch maintains that saving money is not a good enough reason to embrace conservation. The organization's statement on environmental issues briefly acknowledges Wal-Mart's initial steps toward waste reduction before arguing that the retailer still needs to atone for its past grievances:

> Wal-Mart has made a name for itself over the past year by highlighting various environmental initiatives, which it sees as an easy way to improve its image. While reducing packaging on food products and selling more energy efficient light bulbs are important steps that Wal-Mart should be applauded for, they must do much more to make amends for an environmentally unfriendly past. In the past, Wal-Mart has been guilty of air pollution, storm-water violations, and improper storage of hazardous materials. With millions in fines resulting from these violations, Wal-Mart's environmental record has been blemished. (WMW website)

Saving the environment in the name of thrift—note that the two examples mentioned above are "reducing" food packaging and marketing energy-saving light bulbs—is only part of the issue. Other environmental concerns, presumably those that might cost money and not save it, must be addressed for Wal-Mart's environmental reforms to be interpreted as genuine.

By focusing on thrift in a context that emphasizes employees, Wal-Mart Watch frames the value as something negative when it's what the company does at the expense of its workers. As Andrew Grossman (who was then WMW's executive director) argued in another press release in the fall of 2006:

> Their corporate headquarters pressures managers to reduce wage costs on the store level, and the store managers shift the burden onto the hourly workers. They're exploiting their workers and passing it off as efficiency. Wal-Mart employees deserve far better from America's largest corporation. (WMW press release, October 12, 2006)

In this statement, words like "reduce" connote thrift—Wal-Mart is attempting to cut down on labor costs, through which store managers end up "exploiting" their workers. Note that this statement doesn't imply that "efficiency" itself is morally questionable; what's wrong in this case is that the purported efficiency requires asking workers to assume extra burdens. Workers are again at issue in WMW's denouncements of a well-publicized leaked memo, in which (then) Wal-Mart VP for employee benefits Susan Chambers suggested that among other ways to control health care costs would be to add physical requirements to all jobs in order to discourage less healthy workers from staying with the company. This earned vocal renunciations from the company's critics; in press releases and emails from that week WMW claimed that Chambers had "detailed cutthroat measures to maximize savings—at terrible costs to their front line workers." When "savings" (thrift) comes at "terrible costs" to workers, WMW argues that it is immoral and thus indefensible.

At the heart of Wal-Mart Watch's moral worldview is a scalar understanding of justice that argues that those who have more resources should have greater responsibilities. Thus WMW used the theme "To Whom Much Has Been Given, Much Is Expected" to christen a "Higher Expectations" week in November 2005 that challenged faith communities to consider the effects of Wal-Mart on their communities and the larger society. Simply put, this understanding of justice argues that the Scrooges of the world have more responsibility than the Bob Cratchits to act with benevolence simply because they can afford to do so. Wal-Mart Watch reiterated this argument time and again:

Even though the company makes billions in profits, you and your family are stuck paying the "Wal-Mart Tax" because the retail giant fails to provide adequate health care for its workers and does not pay enough to keep its employees and their children off of New Jersey's public health care programs. (WMW email, February 7, 2006)

It is unacceptable that America's largest employer, a company with annual profits of $10 billion, has a health care plan that covers less than half of its employees. (WMW email, January 13, 2006)

A study released today by the Economic Policy Institute (EPI) asserts that Wal-Mart, the world's largest retailer, can offer better wages to its employees while keeping profit margins nearly 50 percent greater than key competitors. . . . The authors' analysis also shows that Wal-Mart could provide workers sizable increases in wages and compensation without affecting prices if the store accepted the same profit margins as some of its competitors or even accepted the same profit margins that characterized its own operations in the recent past. (WMW press release, June 15, 2006)

Wal-Mart's portion of the BadgerCare tab is four times as large as any other Wisconsin employer. It's unacceptable that Wisconsin taxpayers are paying over $2.7 million to provide health care for Wal-Mart's employees. Wal-Mart profited $10 billion dollars last year, yet 1,200 of its workers and their children are forced to rely on BadgerCare health care to make ends meet. (WMW press release, January 17, 2006)

Just as Wal-Mart Watch prominently mentioned Wal-Mart's $10 billion in profits in the initial press releases noted earlier, this figure is used again and again to explain why Wal-Mart has failed by not providing more for its employees. Accordingly, this discrepancy is repeatedly called "unacceptable"; benevolence here is almost a mathematical proposition. And as such, it can't be entirely reconciled with the practice of thrift, which is also portrayed as a largely mathematical calculation on the part of the company. Thus Wal-Mart "does not pay enough," could "provide increases in wages," and its health care falls short in that it "covers less than half" of its employees.

Most of the discussion of thrift and benevolence thus far has focused on the relationship between Wal-Mart and its workers. But Wal-Mart Watch, like WFWM, also made some attempts to frame benevolence in individual terms. Most notably, WMW seized on the opportunity to compare heiress Alice Walton's personal wealth—and expensive art acquisitions on behalf of a new museum in Bentonville—to the needs of Wal-Mart's workers. In one instance, WMW noted that Alice Walton could have provided health care for ten thousand Wal-Mart workers for the $68 million she spent on a painting from the New York Public Library. And taking the opportunity to hammer away at the most notorious of Walton's conquests—the historic, Philadelphia-housed painting *The Gross Clinic* by Thomas Eakins—WMW actually invoked the theme of "A Real-Life Christmas Carol" to frame her spending. Particularly since the subject of the painting in question was a young child receiving medical care, WMW wasted no time in drawing connections intended to highlight Walton's alleged personal greediness, and urging her toward benevolence instead: "This holiday season, while Wal-Mart continues to deny nearly half of its employees' children health care, Sam Walton's daughter Alice—a billionaire heiress—is going art shopping. And guess what she has her eyes on? A $68,000,000 painting of a doctor treating a young boy." The email sent shortly before Christmas in 2006 went on to explain that "we're doing this for all the Tiny Tim's out there—sons and daughters of janitors, associates and drivers who can't afford to see a doctor," and concluded that "truth may be stranger than fiction, but sometimes it can have the same ending. Right now, an out-of-touch billionaire cares more about a $68 million painting than the welfare of millions of children who's [*sic*] parents depend on her company. . . . It's time for a real-life Christmas Carol" (WMW email, December 21, 2006).

As opposed to the largely family-centered conception of morality created by WFWM (one that focuses on the practice of thrift as a moral enterprise), the conception of morality here is one that fundamentally relies on large-scale, societal comparisons: it is wrong for one person like Alice Walton to have so much disposable income when the workers who support her source of income are not adequately provided for by the company that generates her wealth. The cost of the painting—$68 million—is mentioned several times in the email, underlining this comparative, scalar conception of justice. On this scale, WMW implies, Alice Walton is simply greedy. The morality of her actions is not affirmed by their connection to a larger institution—as in WFWM's conception of thrift as a moral enterprise and its ties to the family—but framed in a comparative context. When she has so much, and has not shared it benevolently, WMW invokes the trope of Scrooge to hold her accountable.

### Workers, Not Families

In its initial statement of its mission, Wal-Mart Watch says that it aims to "improve Wal-Mart as a neighbor, employer, and corporate citizen" and encourage it to act "more responsibly toward its neighbors, its employees, our environment, and the American business community." Any mentions of family—families who are presumably paying taxes, families who depend on a Wal-Mart employee for health care, or families who shop at Wal-Mart—are conspicuously absent. Similarly, in the larger text of the previous email about Alice Walton, "families" is mentioned only once—and this is when quoting a leaked Wal-Mart memo admitting that the company's health insurance is "expensive for low-income families." And while the email does mention family ties—"the sons and daughters of janitors, associates and drivers" and the "children of employees"—these family members are referenced in conjunction with a *worker's* identity—a janitor, driver, employee, and so forth. WMW's initial press release makes similar rhetorical shifts, mentioning "taxpayers" as the victims of Wal-Mart's greedy exploitation of public revenues and listing among its goals facilitating networks between the "activists and citizens" who are already involved in fighting Wal-Mart in some way. The Gemeinschaft category of family, in this discursive context, has been superseded by Gesellschaft categories such as workers, taxpayer, and citizen. These are the key categories that animate the discourse surrounding thrift and benevolence produced by Wal-Mart Watch.

Of course, it would be an overstatement to claim that Wal-Mart Watch does not ever speak of families in its effort to reform Wal-Mart. Wal-Mart does sometimes refer to "working families" as well as "workers and their families" or "employees and their children." Unlike WFWM, however, Wal-Mart Watch devotes scant attention to individual narratives that report a family's experience with Wal-Mart. Further, when Wal-Mart Watch does speak of "working families" it is almost always in reference to a systemic economic issue—health care, wages, cost of living—and not to activities that are constitutive of the family itself, such as helping workers with erratic schedules find more time to spend with their children. The following are particularly illustrative examples (emphases added):

They have the power to raise the bar for millions of hourly employees rather than *nickel and dime* working families at every turn. (WMW email, October 26, 2006)

"Working families need *higher wages* to keep up with the *rising prices* of gas and housing," said co-author Josh Bivens. "*Rent or mortgage,* utilities, medical services and transportation—these are what take up the *largest portion* of a family's *income*—not goods bought at Wal-Mart." (WMW press release, June 15, 2006)

We continue to work with our broad coalition to illuminate the harmful impact of Wal-Mart's *business model* on America's working families. (WMW press release, June 22, 2005)

Union leaders across the country want working families to benefit from Wal-Mart. Unfortunately, Wal-Mart blocks every attempt by local employees to organize for *fair wages,* health care benefits and equal employment opportunities—silencing those who stand up for their rights. (WMW website)

Of course, Wal-Mart and WFWM connect families to economic processes, too—most notably to the economy of thrift within the household. Yet the difference between WFWM and WMW is that the latter more often connects these economic processes to identities such as "workers" or "employees" who deserve "fair wages" and face the challenges wrought by the larger economic system—harmful "business models" and "rising prices" on things like fuel and housing.

Thus the difference in referring to families on both sides of the debate is not so much one of *frequency*—by which I mean the presence or absence of certain words or constructions—but one of *context*. For progressive activists constructing discourse for Wal-Mart Watch, these examples suggest that the referential category of "worker" (along with larger, systematic economic processes) are central to WMW's moral worldview in much the same way that the more localized bonds of kin and community were fundamental in Wal-Mart's. Accordingly, Wal-Mart Watch would surely insist that families are an important unit of consideration in this public debate, but at the same time WMW consistently adopts rhetorical constructions that subsume the family under the larger category of "worker" or "employee"—speaking of "employees and their children" or an employee's economic ability to "sustain a family." For example, in the foundational "Handshake with Sam" document—in which WMW uses Sam Walton's own words as a challenge to the company to live up to its "moral responsibilities" in areas such as wages, supplier relationships, sustainability, and public relations—every mention of the family is tied to systemic, economic relationships: Wal-Mart will pay "a family-sustaining wage" that "will enable the associate to raise a family without having to rely on public assistance." Similarly, WMW demands that "Wal-Mart will set a national example by ensuring that all employees—salaried, hourly, full-time, and part-time—have quality affordable health insurance that fully covers the employee and their children."

In this discursive universe, the family ties of Gemeinschaft are eclipsed by the Gesellschaft of the rationalized economy, in which workers are the primary referent, not families. Other rationalized categories—such as consumers, citizens, and manufacturers—are similarly prioritized. This was affirmed when I received an email from WMW with the title "Wal-Mart Toys with Your Children's Health" (the email concerned large-scale toy recalls from Chinese manufacturers). Inside, the body of the email curiously contained only fleeting references to children or their safety, aside from an initial introductory sentence that declared, "Thousands of concerned parents are rushing to pediatricians' offices to have their children tested for lead poisoning," continuing:

> Mattel has taken responsibility for the safety of its products, but Wal-Mart has to be held accountable as well. As it stands, you can't trust that the toys Wal-Mart is selling you are safe. As the world's largest retailer, Wal-Mart sets the standard for product safety—and by bullying companies like Mattel to produce toys and other products at bottom dollar costs, it's pushing American companies into shady overseas operations. Tell Wal-Mart to care about its customers' health, and demand a higher quality for its products. (WMW email, August 21, 2007)

The text of the email then moves quickly to the importance of "product safety" and "labor violations" in China, which presumably allow factories to avoid restrictions on hazardous materials in the manufacturing of children's toys. While the beginning of the email referenced the family—specifically parents and children—the conclusion of the text had rendered readers as "customers" and framed their children's potential lead poisoning in terms of global labor violations and Wal-Mart's poor regulation of its suppliers. Here again, different categories entirely—customers and manufacturers—were of ultimate concern.

The centrality of rationalized categories such as "worker" or "manufacturer" help to further explain how Wal-Mart Watch appropriates the values of thrift and benevolence in this discourse. In the same way that Wal-Mart and its proponents repeatedly championed Wal-Mart's assistance to those who "can't afford" high drug costs, or the role of Wal-Mart's low prices in helping families "stretch their budgets" for more of life's extras, Wal-Mart Watch also considers "affordability," particularly in reference to Wal-Mart's health benefits (e.g., "Wal-Mart's new so-called 'Value Plan' remains a raw deal for its employees who can't afford the high deductibles and strict eligibility requirements" [WMW press release, February 23, 2006]). Thus, while Wal-Mart and WFWM focus overwhelmingly on thrift and families, WMW calls attention to the financial difficulties of individual workers by speaking of the difficulties of employees, not families. This dichotomy is interesting, because it would be quite simple for Wal-Mart Watch to substitute "families" for "employees" in excerpts such as the one above (or, alternatively, to say "employees and their families"), but this is not the case. Throughout, the dominant category considered in discussions of benevolence and thrift is that of the worker: Wal-Mart could afford to do more for its employees; similarly, it is workers, not families, who struggle to engage in enough thrift to take advantage of the benefits that Wal-Mart does offer.

## Systemic Conceptions of Economic Dislocation

Examining the rhetorical constructions surrounding the discussion of thrift and benevolence in Wal-Mart Watch's discourse also sheds light on another divergence between these texts and those produced by Wal-Mart and WFWM. While WFWM tended to construct the economic hardships that necessitated thrift in terms of family disruption (or conveyed economic difficulties primarily in light of their impact on the family), Wal-Mart Watch favors a more systemic view that faults larger-scale economic dislocation for the precarious predicaments of workers in the twenty-first century.

This difference in attribution also helps to explain why thrift and benevolence are seen as largely antithetical in the discursive universe of Wal-Mart Watch: WMW tends to consider the workings of thrift and benevolence on a macro-level as opposed to the micro-focus favored by Wal-Mart's proponents. In addition to WMW's focus on Wal-Mart's alleged lack of generosity to employees, WMW also renders thrift and benevolence as largely contradictory by emphasizing not family or individual hardship as the source of economic dislocation, but larger-scale problems in the broader capitalist marketplace.

The evidence for this conclusion comes in part from the warrants offered to support WMW's demand that Wal-Mart to be more benevolent toward its workers. One tactic used to support this point of view is comparative reasoning, particularly comparing Wal-Mart to similar corporations that have embraced more generous strategies of compensating their workers. The debate over the short-lived Fair Share for Health Care legislation (FSHC) in Maryland, in particular, embodied this argument. While the FSHC bill targeted all employers in the state that had more than ten thousand employees, only Wal-Mart was not spending the required 8% of payroll expenses on health care. If other big companies were able to do it, the argument goes, then the same can reasonably be expected of Wal-Mart. Similar reasoning has frequently prompted a comparison between Wal-Mart and Costco:

> For instance, Costco, a competitor in the large-market food business, had a net profit margin of 2 percent in 2005, and Wal-Mart's net profit margin grew from 2.9 percent in 1997 to 3.6 percent in 2005. Returning to its 1997 net profit margins would allow Wal-Mart to give its non-supervisory workers 13 percent pay increases without raising prices, while still maintaining higher profit margins than a main competitor. (WMW press release, June 15, 2006)

Turning the focus to how Wal-Mart's benevolence (or alleged lack thereof) compares to other retailers helps to place the context of this debate within the domain of larger economic systems affecting all retailers—and thus, by extension, other participants in the economy.

WMW's focus on larger economic systems is also underscored by the use of language that emphasizes the debate over Wal-Mart as one that carries with it the power to change other large and powerful actors in the American capitalist system. As the press release noted at the beginning of this section promised, "Reforms by Wal-Mart, the world's largest and perhaps most imitated business, will spawn improvements in corporate practices around the world." This theme was reiterated throughout the WMW literature (emphases added):

Because the [*Dukes v. Wal-Mart*] case seeks injunctive relief as well as monetary damages, a judgment in this matter would fundamentally alter the way in which Wal-Mart treats women at every level in its workplace, thereby *impacting how companies treat their women employees everywhere.* (WMW website)

"By bringing aboard Scalia, Wal-Mart has abandoned any pretense of even-handedness in its treatment of whistle-blowers," said Tracy Sefl, a spokesman for the Wal-Mart Watch activist group. "As the nation's largest private employer, Wal-Mart is *sending an ominous signal to millions of workers* that their rights may be even more imperiled." (WMW press release, June 20, 2005)

Companies across America are confronting the soaring cost of employee health care, and they are dealing with the problem in different ways. All of them *look to Wal-Mart, the nation's largest private employer and industry leader, to see how they manage health care costs* for their 1.3 million employees. (WMW press release, October 28, 2005)

We hope that as Lee Scott calls for a "new commitment from leaders in government and business," he will first acknowledge that his own corporation's woeful health benefits are a unique contributor to this nation's crisis. *As the world's largest company, Wal-Mart sets the standard for eco-friendly behavior that all other companies follow.* It's up to us to make sure they raise that standard and become a better corporate citizen. (WMW email, December 11, 2006)

WMW's focus on larger economic systems thus helps explain why so much of its rhetoric frames the controversy over Wal-Mart as a potential force for change among corporations everywhere. Its size, prominence, and role in economic processes such as globalization and the growth of service work all place Wal-Mart at the center of many economic questions plaguing Americans in the twenty-first century.

This systemic focus, then, also shapes how WMW talks about the values of thrift and benevolence—a large-scale system that emphasizes low prices for individual consumers or families proves ultimately incompatible with goals for worker protection, benefits, and long-term economic well-being. Put another way, WMW's systemic focus more closely approximates the macro-perspective of societal ethics that Miller identifies as a challenge to the micro-ethics of thrift rooted in the family. Thus the "mathematical" formula pitting thrift against benevolence discussed earlier makes it increasingly difficult to reconcile these two values. Prices cannot be continually lowered for consumers without neglecting some aspects of workers' economic well-being. Understood from this systemic vantage point, thrift and benevolence are fundamentally incompatible; further, it is benevolence—voluntary choices by a company to reject some of the price-cutting tenets inherent in free market capitalism—that emerges as the more worthy moral cause.

## Conclusion

I have argued that both Wal-Mart's advocates and critics employ a common symbolic language in their discourse about the company and its role in larger economic processes. Both Wal-Mart Watch and Wal-Mart Inc. (together with its advocacy group, Working Families for Wal-Mart) invoke the moral values of thrift and benevolence in their language about the store and its role in the larger economy. Yet the ways these values take shape in their discourse hinges on the very different reference groups that each side presumes in their public statements. For instance, Wal-Mart and its advocates build a discourse that centers on the family, and this familial focus colors both the store's and its supporters' evaluation of what they see as its largely positive effects. Understood within this discursive context of the family, Wal-Mart's low prices become a lifeline during tough times; accordingly, for Wal-Mart and its supporters, the value of thrift is closely linked to Gemeinschaft, personal narratives that explain economic difficulties either as a result of family disruption or as hardships experienced primarily via their expressions in the family. Conversely, Wal-Mart Watch creates a discourse surrounding thrift and benevolence that takes shape around a cluster of categories more closely linked to Gesellschaft. Here, the referential categories most emphasized by Wal-Mart Watch are workers, customers, taxpayers, and citizens. Again, activists use common moral ideas of thrift and benevolence to frame their arguments yet appropriate them very differently—Wal-Mart's critics create claims that primarily address the company's relationship with its employees, not the families that depend on the store for good bargains.

Another key difference in these discourses surrounding thrift and benevolence concerns the larger context in which the opposing referents of family and worker are located. Pro-Wal-Mart speakers—whether individual supporters or the company itself—tend to place their arguments in a context that looks most closely at individuals and individual-level experiences. This individual context allows the store's supporters to reconcile both thrift and benevolence when it comes to Wal-Mart because they focus primarily on how Wal-Mart's low prices can help individuals be more benevolent (such as when buying food or clothes for the needy) or because Wal-Mart has helped their own charitable cause in the past. Because Wal-Mart's supporters consider thrift and benevolence largely in individual terms, these moral dialectics are rarely contradictory. On the other hand, the store's detractors tend to focus on larger-scale economic systems, and thus benevolence is generally understood as something that is, in the final analysis, incompatible with large-scale thrift, particularly when focusing on the company's internal operations toward its employees. If Wal-Mart would just be less thrifty, the critics' argument goes, then the store could be more benevolent toward its workers. Again, both sides of the debate refer to the common moral values of thrift and benevolence, yet deploy these terms with reference to different core categories and within different contexts.

This analysis of thrift and benevolence is a particularly compelling way to understand the distinctive features of conservative and progressive activists' approach to the market and the dilemmas created by capitalism. While this chapter has argued this point by closely examining Wal-Mart debates, a brief examination of the discourse surrounding health care reform suggests that these patterns also appear in other economic conflicts. For instance, a close look at President Obama's speech to Congress on September 10, 2009, in which he first laid out his proposals for reforming the nation's health care system, provides a useful illustration of these same themes. In the opening moments of the president's address to Congress, he motivated his call for health care reform by saying:

> We are the only advanced democracy on Earth—the only wealthy nation— that allows such hardships for millions of its people. There are now more than thirty million American citizens who cannot get coverage. In just a two-year period, one in every three Americans goes without health care coverage at some point. And every day, 14,000 Americans lose their coverage. In other words, it can happen to anyone.[27]

Notably, the president's initial attempt to motivate reform places his arguments squarely within the context of citizenship—in an "advanced democracy" that is also a "wealthy nation," the president suggests that the hardships of being uninsured are simply not acceptable for the country's citizens. As he continues, he describes a litany of health insurance failures—such as a man refused surgery because of gallstones, and woman whose cancer doubled in size due to an insurance policy's fine print—as "heart-breaking," because "no one should be treated that way in the United States of America." Here it is *citizens* who deserve the right to health care coverage, particularly in light of the nation's comparative wealth and affluence. Throughout the speech, Obama returns to the concept of citizenship as a justification for the proposed reforms, as when he claims that "in the United States of America, no one should go broke because they get sick."

Similarly, Obama appeals to the audience not as working families, but as taxpaying citizens who are all stuck with the bill for other people's health care—most importantly, those workers whose health care costs are not shouldered by their employers:

> Now, even if we provide these affordable options, there may be those— particularly the young and healthy—who still want to take the risk and go without coverage. There may still be companies that refuse to do right by their workers. The problem is, such irresponsible behavior costs all the rest of us money. If there are affordable options and people still don't sign up for health insurance, it means we pay for those people's expensive emergency room visits. If some businesses don't provide workers health care, it forces the rest of us to pick up the tab when their workers get sick, and gives those businesses an unfair advantage over their competitors. And unless everybody does their part, many of the insurance reforms we seek—especially requiring insurance companies to cover pre-existing conditions—just can't be achieved.

Just as Wal-Mart's critics called on Wal-Mart to "use some of [its] profits to help some of [its] people," the president makes a similar appeal to benevolence among employers, who are expected to do "their part" so that "the rest of us" will be spared the burden of having to "pick up the tab when their workers get sick." Accordingly, Obama also emphasized benevolence within a collective system of economic activity when he later argued that "large-heartedness—that concern and regard for the plight of others—is not a partisan feeling. It is not a Republican or a Democratic feeling. It, too, is part of the American character. . . . A recognition that we are all in this together; that when fortune turns against one of us, others are there to lend a helping hand." Later in the speech, appeals to large-scale benevolence also surfaced when the president added that businesses that don't subsidize their workers' health care will be required to "chip in" to subsidize their workers' costs, because "we cannot have large businesses and individuals who can afford coverage game the system by avoiding responsibility to themselves or their employees. Improving our health care system only works if everybody does their part." Just as in the discourse produced by Wal-Mart's most outspoken critics, the progressive case for health insurance reform appeals to benevolence, along with the ideals of citizenship, as justification for seeing health care as a fundamental right for Americans.

Alongside these references to collective conceptions of citizenship, another notable feature of Obama's initial speech concerned what was absent—any mention of families. Here, the president might have motivated his calls for reform by appealing to families' need for affordable care, or difficulty in meeting health care costs in the wake of intermittent employment or prohibitively expensive premiums. But, in fact, the Gemeinschaft concept of "family" or "families" was referenced only three times in a speech that lasted nearly three-quarters of an hour. Instead, Obama's text referred primarily to the rationalized, Gesellschaft categories of Americans (mentioned thirty-one times), individuals (ten times), customers/consumers (nine times), workers/employees (eight times), citizens (two times), and taxpayers (two times). The progressive rhetoric prioritizes citizens and benevolence, appealing to collective norms that suggest that no American citizen, in a wealthy nation such as ours, should have to go without health care.

Not surprisingly, opposition to the reform package centered around two main objections: the cost of the bill, and the risks it posed to the autonomy of individuals in making health care decisions for themselves (for instance, as in the proposed provision in the bill that would require uninsured Americans to purchase health insurance). Put another way, opposition to the bill focused on the moral value of thrift and, however subtly, the prerogative of families to make decisions without government intervention. Even before the president's speech in September, Sarah Palin's Facebook page notoriously warned that the bill would be expensive while also usurping families' self-determination to make their own decisions about medical care:

> The Democrats promise that a government health care system will reduce the cost of health care, but as the economist Thomas Sowell has pointed out, government health care will not reduce the cost; it will simply refuse to pay the cost. And who will suffer the most when they ration care? The sick, the elderly, and the disabled, of course. The America I know and love is not one in which my parents or my baby with Down Syndrome will have to stand in front of Obama's "death panel" so his

bureaucrats can decide, based on a subjective judgment of their "level of productivity in society," whether they are worthy of health care. Such a system is downright evil.[28]

Not only does Palin render a moral judgment on the plan—"Such a system is downright evil"—but she also references both thrift (the substantial costs of the legislation, which might not be solvent) and the family—her parents or her disabled child. Most important, she juxtaposes the Gemeinschaft of family with the Gesellschaft of modern society, which would allow "bureaucrats" to make health care decisions based on individuals' "level of productivity" in the larger social order. Of course, both the president and rational observers everywhere decried the notion of "death panels" that would make such outrageous decisions, but the six months following the president's speech—which ultimately culminated in the passage of the Patient Protection and Affordable Care Act on March 23, 2010—did see a vigorous debate about the proposed costs of the bill in light of ballooning budget deficits, along with the rectitude of government intervention in the distribution of health coverage.

The day after the bill passed, Phil Gramm wrote the following in an editorial in the *Wall Street Journal* titled "Resistance Is Not Futile" (emphasis added):

Any real debate about health-care reform has to be centered on solving the problem of cost. Ultimately, there are only two ways of doing it. The first approach is to have government control costs through some form of rationing. The alternative is to empower families to make their own health-care decisions in a system where costs matter. The fundamental question is about who is going to do the controlling: *the family or the government.*[29]

Here, the former Republican senator frames opposition to the health care reform bill in terms of its larger ideological significance: the gulf between responsible cost management and out-of-control deficits, and the locus of control for Americans seeking to manage their health care. The government becomes a distant system that cannot be counted on to control costs, while families should be empowered to make responsible, close-to-home decisions and stay free of government meddling. The terms in which Obama and his opponents cast the debate resonate throughout the deliberative process precisely because they are drawn from a larger cultural and political context in which ideas about family and thrift, citizenship and benevolence, acquire meaning by virtue of their connection to older traditions in political culture.

These different referential categories of the family and the worker/citizen help to explain how it is that each side of these economic debates arrives at such different conclusions—either concerning the moral rectitude of health care reform, or the morality of Wal-Mart's low prices and their significance for Americans. The effects of these different discursive contexts in larger market processes—particularly those that concern the ideals of freedom and fairness—is the subject of the next chapter.

5

Freedom and Fairness

We cannot, and must not, and we will not let our auto industry
simply vanish. This industry is like no other—it's an emblem of the
American spirit; a once and future symbol of America's success. It's
what helped build the middle class and sustained it throughout the
twentieth century. It's a source of deep pride for the generations of
American workers whose hard work and imagination led to some
of the finest cars the world has ever known. It's a pillar of our economy that has held up the dreams of millions of our people. And
we cannot continue to excuse poor decisions. We cannot make the
survival of our auto industry dependent on an unending flow of
taxpayer dollars. These companies—and this industry—must ultimately stand on their own, not as wards of the state.
—President Obama's remarks on the American auto industry,
March 30, 2009

As Americans welcomed in the new year in 2009, most were still reeling
from the previous year's financial meltdown. Americans had lost substantial portions of their retirement savings in the fall's perilous stock market
decline, and watched the equity in their homes evaporate seemingly overnight. Economists forecast double-digit rates of unemployment, and cable
news was abuzz with talk about bailouts—both for distant Wall Street bankers, and for Main Street citizens facing foreclosure closer to home. As the
year progressed, more Americans prepared to lose their homes, and the
country watched helplessly as American car manufacturers filed for bankruptcy. The free market system and its promise of an "ownership society" had
been shaken to its core—along with the hidden streams of credit and finance
that were revealed to be essential for its continual prosperity. In the wake
of such destruction, one poll suggested that Americans' preference for capitalism over socialism had reached a historic low at only 53%.[1] Our market
system, once seemingly invincible, had shown itself to be vulnerable in ways
unthinkable only months before.

In such an environment, the public rescue of struggling banking and
financial companies appeared a necessary—indeed, vital—form of intervention in the global economy. Abiding faith in "free markets" was supplanted

with an urgent rush to intervention, as the United States Treasury and Federal Reserve infused faltering U.S. banks and insurance companies with the necessary capital to avoid complete and devastating collapse. President Bush, in his September 24, 2008, televised national address, had this to say about the proposed financial rescue package that would eventually become known as the Troubled Asset Relief Program:

> I'm a strong believer in free enterprise, so my natural instinct is to oppose government intervention. I believe companies that make bad decisions should be allowed to go out of business. Under normal circumstances, I would have followed this course. But these are not normal circumstances. The market is not functioning properly. There has been a widespread loss of confidence, and major sectors of America's financial system are at risk of shutting down. The government's top economic experts warn that, without immediate action by Congress, America could slip into a financial panic and a distressing scenario would unfold.[2]

In the wake of a widespread economic collapse more serious than any since the Great Depression, who would argue that an ideological commitment to free markets should trump immediate intervention that could potentially stave off another prolonged worldwide depression? In the months following the president's address, the United States government would commit $700 billion to save floundering U.S. banking and financial firms.

Of all the government-funded rescues that took place in response to the financial crisis of 2008, the bridge loan that the U.S. government provided American auto companies the following year was arguably the most controversial because it represented such a profound intervention in the free market processes that many believed should have permitted the struggling automakers to fail. As Michael Useem observed, the bailout signified "a new chapter in the history books on American capitalism," adding that "how we think about American free enterprise is really hanging in the balance."[3] President Obama and congressional Democrats justified the move in terms of preserving American automakers' place in the national economy, along with the industry's long legacy of manufacturing pride. Supporters also reasoned that assisting the struggling companies—specifically Chrysler and General Motors—would potentially avoid shouldering the massive unemployment costs that would surely come if the companies failed. At the same time, conservatives rallied against the intervention, arguing that it rewarded companies that had been poorly managed, produced inferior products that consumers didn't want, and had been dominated by unions whose over-the-top demands left the companies bloated and unable to compete against their streamlined counterparts in the open market. As a *Wall Street Journal* editorial declared after the automakers secured a bridge loan from the Obama administration, "From now on, GM and Chrysler are Mr. Obama's companies, and taxpayers should hold him accountable for every dollar they are forced to spend to save jobs for the UAW and to make cars that Americans don't necessarily want."[4] Viewed from this vantage point, American taxpayers had been forced to rescue a company that deserved failure—the market had spoken, and issued a death certificate for American auto companies. The Great Recession was a day of reckoning that was long overdue, and saving these companies was simply not fair to taxpayers or consumers. Understood from this perspective, the perversion of market forces was most offensive because GM and Chrysler *deserved* their dismal fate, only to have been saved by artificial tinkering with the purity of the market system.

The contentious discourse surrounding the controversial auto industry "bailouts" reveals how central the ideas of freedom and fairness are to public discourse about market processes. A closer look at how these concepts are appropriated in public talk offers important insights into how progressive and conservative activists view market systems more generally. While the previous two chapters have described how conservative and liberal activists use different referents in their language and come to different moral conclusions as a result, this chapter examines how each side of the Wal-Mart debate approaches the moral characteristics of the larger economic system of free market capitalism. In doing so, they tap into deep divisions inherent in the moral worldviews of the right and the left in political discourse. This chapter explores the language of both groups of activists, with particular attention paid to the way each group takes up these broader themes, and how they view the relationship between market freedom, individual freedoms, and larger concerns for fairness.

## Freedom and Markets in American Culture

Americans have had a long and often turbulent love affair with the theoretical idea of the free market, with roots that stretch back at least to the Boston Tea Party. As the historian Jill Lepore has observed, the modern Tea Party movement attempts to frame its current agenda for lower taxes by appealing to the Constitution as a document that represents the essential spirit of free market capitalism.[5] Accordingly FreedomWorks, the grassroots organization responsible for much of the Tea Party's on-the-ground turnout, describes its mission as fighting for "lower taxes, less government, and more economic freedom for all Americans." Free market ideology pervades public discourse, even in the very concept of a public "marketplace of ideas"—here the claim is that if left to compete on their own, without interference, the most compelling arguments voiced in the public sphere will naturally win out.

Yet while we often endorse market freedom in principle, practically speaking most of us approach market issues with no small amount of ambivalence. To wit, most Americans favor reducing the federal deficit but will likely still hope to claim their own Social Security and Medicare benefits. Survey data also reveal that most Americans are similarly conflicted in their thinking about market systems more generally. Robert Wuthnow, for example, reported that just over half of Americans think our economic system is in need of "fundamental changes," while only 6% think our economic system is superior to alternative arrangements.[6] And even a cursory survey of a century of American history reminds us that political movements concerned with economic equality have played key roles in the evolution of our financial policy. Key historical episodes such as the debate over the gold standard in the late nineteenth century, labor union struggles in the early twentieth, turn-of-the-century "trust busting," and New Deal economic interventions (to name only a few examples), were necessarily concerned with the fairness of various expressions of market freedom: the relationships between different actors in the economy (farmers and capitalists, wage laborers and factory owners), the appropriate limits that should be placed on market actors (the legality of the Standard Oil Company trust), and the viability of the free market itself (Keynesian economic policies in the early twentieth century). These examples also illustrate the many ways that Americans have sought to institute a growing set of controls on the "free" market, such that the very concept is something of a misnomer—witnessed, of course, most recently by the extraordinary amount of capital that the U.S. Treasury infused into American companies to ward off economic collapse during the financial crisis of 2008.

Even the libertarian economist Milton Friedman acknowledged the disconnect between Americans' vocal support for laissez-faire economics and the reality of government intervention. In the 1994 preface to F. A. Hayek's classic treatise *The Road to Serfdom*, for example, Friedman warned:

> Today, there is wide agreement that socialism is a failure, capitalism a success. Yet this apparent conversion of the intellectual community to what might be called a Hayekian view is deceptive. While the talk is about free

markets and private property—and it is more respectable than it was a few decades ago to defend near-complete laissez-faire—the bulk of the intellectual community almost automatically favors any expansion of government power so long as it is advertised as a way to protect individuals from big bad corporations, relieve poverty, protect the environment, or promote "equality."[7]

Friedman's observations highlight the difference between discourse (in this case, forms of "talk" that affirm the ideal of a free market) and popular support for government policies that emphasize the protection of the public and the egalitarian redistribution of resources. In reality, as Friedman astutely observed, Americans have traded a strict view of market freedom for a host of market interventions that seek to make the institution more altruistic, more manageable, and more equal—in short, more fair.

As a result, our public talk about markets inherently involves considerations of freedom and fairness—ideas that play key roles in other political debates as well. William Gamson, for instance, observes how the reciprocal themes of independence and equality continually surface in Americans' discussion of political issues. On the one hand, we might find the "self-made man" themes of Horatio Alger (in which hard work and perseverance reward individual effort and initiative); on the other, an emphasis on charity, mutual support, and the "Woodstock nation."[8] At a very deep level, this pair of themes has to do with freedom and fairness—the freedom of the individual to thrive in a world filled with opportunity, as well as the communal regard that may be necessary to ensure that everyone has the support they need to succeed. Such debates about freedom and fairness (or between procedural and distributive justice, as I argue further below) take on even more force when we consider their expressions in the domain of economic issues, because they necessarily concern the way people fare in a competitive economic marketplace. For instance, one of the issues that Gamson analyzes is affirmative action, in which supporters of affirmative action argue that such programs are necessary to create an equal playing field in the workforce, while its opponents vehemently oppose any attempts to tinker with a system that rewards people on the basis of their own independent efforts.

My examination of discourse about freedom and fairness suggests that despite our common ideological heritage in American political culture, liberals and conservatives talk about freedom and fairness with regard to the market in remarkably different ways. The different referents that both sides prioritize in their language have broader implications for how they evaluate the larger system of market capitalism. For instance, in this chapter I argue that Wal-Mart's proponents tend to prioritize procedural justice—in other words, "fairness in the means by which distributions or decisions are made."[9] In particular, these activists emphasize fairness as equal access for individuals—to the market system, to the labor market, and to market goods like employment and consumables. Because the market system itself is considered largely fair, conservatives emphasize procedural justice because it offers all individuals an equal chance out of the starting blocks. From this vantage point, if people put in enough effort, what they receive in return are the appropriate rewards. In contrast, Wal-Mart Watch tends to prioritize distributive justice, or "fairness in the distribution of a set of outcomes to a defined circle of recipients."[10] Procedural justice is necessary for just distributive outcomes, and therefore Wal-Mart's critics argue that the store limits market freedom through its monopolistic dominance of the global supply chain, which in turn creates unjust outcomes for various market players. Framing its arguments in terms of the rights of larger collective categories of people—workers, women, African Americans, and the disabled—WMW argues that the company needs to be more restrained precisely because it forces workers to rely on public assistance, drives small businesses out of the market, and usurps communities' right to self-determination.

Yet, despite their differences, both groups do endorse the free market—at least in principle. Even Wal-Mart Watch affirms the ideal of market freedom when it argues that Wal-Mart is so big it threatens that freedom with potential monopolistic dominance. But relying almost exclusively on these market-based warrants turns out to have a downside as well: when compared to the more extensive discussion of personal stories and individual narratives offered up by Wal-Mart's supporters, I argue that the vision of fairness offered by Wal-Mart's detractors is comparatively thin. Although Wal-Mart Watch makes some attempts to articulate a vision of fairness rooted in the family's economic sustainability, these remain ultimately underdeveloped. Instead, the warrants that WMW uses to ground its calls for fairness and equality come from the market itself, which makes it harder for progressive groups to criticize economic policies and market systems. Finally, as I have argued in the previous two chapters, these findings can also help us understand other contentious economic debates, in this instance the recent controversy over government subsidies for American automakers. I conclude by returning to this example with the goal of using the findings from my analysis of the Wal-Mart debate to enrich our understanding of economic debates more broadly.

Freedom and Fairness in Wal-Mart and WFWM

Overall, Wal-Mart and its advocate, WFWM, reference a relatively broad range of freedoms in their official discourse—although, interestingly, the word "freedom" itself is seldom used. Instead, these texts signal references to freedom with words like "choice," "choose," and "opportunity," alongside other terms that connote freedom lost, such as "mandate" "compelled," and "forced." In these terms, freedom is portrayed alternately as freedom of choice, expression, or opportunity, as well as personal empowerment. The common denominator here is that these freedoms, as a whole, are largely conceived of as individual-level attributes. Further, these individual freedoms are tightly linked to the idea of market freedom, which intersects with and complements individuals' own self-motivation, self-determination, and self-reliance. Because the free market rewards individual virtue in this moral framework, freedom and fairness are not at odds with each other; rather, they are largely coherent in much the same way that the discursive worldview of Wal-Mart and its supporters also created coherence between thrift and benevolence, as discussed in chapter 4.

*A Wide Range of Individual Freedoms*

The first interpretation of freedom found in the discursive universe of Wal-Mart and its advocates is personal freedom of choice. Thus Wal-Mart invokes the concept of freedom to portray its adversaries as committing a fundamental violation of individual self-determination, since Wal-Mart's employees choose to work there and Wal-Mart's shoppers choose to shop there:

> Working families choose to shop at their neighborhood Wal-Mart stores to save money, save time and to get everything they need in one convenient place. And associates choose to work at Wal-Mart because it offers good wages, solid benefits and a chance at a career. But some union leaders in Washington, D.C. don't want working families to benefit from Wal-Mart. These union leaders want to tell us—America's working families—where to shop and work. (WFWM website)

Similarly, Wal-Mart's customers offer a number of reasons for why they are loyal to the store, such as the way Wal-Mart allows them to select from a wide range of goods without sacrificing on price and quality:

I enjoy shopping at WalMart because they are accessible, in the neighborhood or near an interstate exit. Their prices are economical and their products are of good quality. Another reason I enjoy shopping at WalMart is because everything is in one store. I can shop for my gardening tools and plants, my exercise and weight training materials, my toiletries, underclothes, groceries, dishes, and tee shirts while having my car serviced as I shop. Parking is wonderful and seems to be quite safe. (WFWM website, personal story)

We are a retired couple (my husband was a noncom with 20 years in the Air Force) who now shop at Walmart for groceries and just about anything else we need (including Murphy gas). The low prices, high quality and wide variety of merchandise has made our retirement so much more enjoyable as it leaves us with money for other pursuits. (WFWM website, personal story)

In addition to allowing individuals to choose "where to shop and work," freedom of choice also helps individuals feel that they are self-sufficient, invoking themes of individual empowerment. This is particularly pronounced in the personal stories from the WFWM website. For example, a writer named Judy explains that "about 3 years ago because of a diabetic complication I became unable to walk without assistance from a 'walker.' But leave it to Wal-Mart to understand this and provide the electric carts to let disabled people shop" (WFWM website, personal story). For Judy, Wal-Mart offers the empowering experience of being able to shop for oneself without assistance. Similarly, other authors of the WFWM narratives stress how Wal-Mart helps them maintain self-sufficiency and dignity because they are able to get by without "government handouts." One customer explained Wal-Mart's ability to empower low-income shoppers in the following way:

I am a member of a resturant [sic] team and I am the manager, I am able to purchases [sic] things like prizes and gas cards for my team to help them strecth thir [sic] dollars and treat them to somthing [sic] extra when we have reached a goal. Walmart is the only store most of them shop at, because it is all that they can afford. If the gift card gets them food or shoes, I know that they are proud because they did it themselves, and that is important. To preserve one [sic] dignity, is most important, and enforces their self-respect. (WFWM website, personal story)

The low prices, then, allow people of meager incomes to purchase things "for themselves," which the author argues functions to preserve their self-respect. Finally, Wal-Mart and its supporters also create empowerment through providing jobs for hard-to-employ members of the labor force. As one couple explained, "We think it is great that they give older people and those just starting out to have a place that will hire them and give them a chance. It enables our mother to be more independent longer and be able to do all her shopping in one place" (WFWM website, personal story). This expression of freedom, then, emerges when individuals secure the means to provide for their economic needs on their own.

Such empowerment also echoes another kind of individual freedom, namely, freedom of self-expression. In this framework, Wal-Mart helps shoppers express themselves through the variety of consumables it renders more affordable. These goods, in turn, help consumers stand out in the way they present themselves and their homes to others. As one customer explained:

> I am an "average" American. I earn an average income. Walmart helps me to be more than average. With the great home furnishings and accessories—my home looks fantastic! I am constantly getting compliments from my friends and family on the way our home looks. I've even decorated our patio with my purchases from Walmart. In addition, I love the clothes and shoes—my co-workers make comments about my clothing and ask me where I get it—I always tell them—Walmart! (WFWM website, personal story)

Similarly, another Wal-Mart shopper simply stated, "Wal-Mart has the best prices and selection, period" (WFWM website, personal story).

This conception of freedom as self-expression also helps to explain why this side of the debate is so vehemently opposed to unions. For example, one speaker warned that the unionization of Wal-Mart would threaten employees' ability to do their jobs like they wanted to: "The last thing that Wal-Mart needs are employee unions and their rules and regulations that would prevent employees from serving the customer the way they want to and should" (WFWM website, personal story). Just as unions did not fare well in this moral universe because they are perceived as "wasting" members' "hard-earned dues" (violating the principle of thrift), unions are similarly vilified here because they violate these fundamental values of individual freedom of choice and expression, as in the statement noted earlier: "These union leaders want to tell us—America's working families—where to shop and work."

Another statement by WFWM similarly explained the pro-Wal-Mart results of a recent opinion poll as follows:

> "America's working families support Wal-Mart, because the company creates more than 100,000 jobs per year and offers health care for as little as $11 per month," said Working Families for Wal-Mart Steering Committee Member Courtney Lynch. "This poll shows that union families also support Wal-Mart. After all, they're working families too. The American people clearly want to decide for themselves where to shop and work." (WFWM press release, January 4, 2006)

In this view, unions should respect the choices that their members make with their feet. To try to sway their members away from a store that saves them money and offers affordable health care smacks of elitist control. Further, unions also violate the principle of freedom of choice in that membership is often mandatory and their activities typically directed by elites who are perceived as out of touch with the interests of their members. As one writer explained:

> I have worked for a few unionized companies and belonged to the unions whether I wanted to or not. I don't recall any benefits that I or my co-workers received which could not have been negotiated personally with management. I do recall the unions supporting political candidates which were not of my choosing using my union dues to do so. I also recall the union officers voting themselves salary increases beyond the percentages they obtained for their members in contract negotiations. (WFWM website, personal story)

In this particular narrative, the union's violations of freedom were twofold. Not only was the speaker's union membership compulsory—"whether I wanted to or not"—but its political advocacy used "my union dues" for purposes that were "not of my choosing." Being a member of a union was a fundamental violation of the speaker's self-determination.

Closely related to freedoms of choice and expression in the pro-Wal-Mart discourse is freedom of opportunity. Simply put, Wal-Mart helps individuals move up in the world by giving them jobs and helping them save money. In the words of a pro-Wal-Mart advocate who was also a union member, "Like millions of others, mine is a union family who shops at Wal-Mart and benefits from Wal-Mart's efficiencies. Wal-Mart puts money back in my family's pocket and creates jobs with unlimited opportunity for advancement for its associates. That is why I am speaking out" (WFWM press release, September 29, 2006). Personal narratives also illustrate some of the ways Wal-Mart offers opportunities to those who had previously experienced difficulty getting ahead in the capitalistic marketplace. One writer explained, "My son has a learning disability, and Wal-Mart gave him a job that has helped him finally get into work he can do with dignity" (WFWM website, personal story). Another similarly recounted, "I started with Wal-Mart in Searcy, Arkansas back in 1979, working in their distribution center there unloading trucks on a receiving dock. Wal-Mart gave me opportunities I had never imagined" (WFWM website, personal story).

Similar stories of Wal-Mart's offerings of economic advancement are commonplace in WFWM's online collection of personal stories, and likewise emphasize *individual* forms of opportunity. Throughout, the words used by the authors emphasize a highly individualistic and voluntaristic understanding of this kind of freedom (emphases added):

> I started at Wal-Mart October 13, 2004 as a cashier. . . . I'm now a department manager . . . . I do not know of many jobs that you can *climb the ladder* this quick with. *My goal* is to be on store set up. I have been *given the chance* to go to New Orleans and help with the stores that were hit with Katrina.

> OK, my point is Wal-mart has been great to me and my wife, they took us in treated us like family and *gave me all the opportunity that I wanted*. I worked for them 3 months and was moved to temp. department lead. I stayed that way until June 2006 and then took over the position full time. . . . Wal-mart is still treating me with great respect and *giving more training*. One day I'm looking to *try to join* the management team so I can give someone *the chance that I got*.

> While working for Wal-Mart with all the support I had from my co-workers each year *I grew stronger and more confident*. I went from Cashier to Department Manager to now an Assistant Manager and hope to *further my career*. Wal-Mart has made me who I am today. It brings tears to my eyes to think that a company cared that much for me and *believed in me*. I as an Assistant remember every day where I came from and share the lessons of compassion and caring and believe in associates the way Wal-Mart has *believed in me*. I love my family at Wal-Mart who has loved me.

> I am the coordinator for a small adult education program in rural Kansas. Many of our students come to our program lacking not only their high

school diploma, but decent job skills, and most of all *self-esteem*. We help them develop these skills, and Wal-Mart has been instrumental in *giving them the opportunity* to utilize them. Wal-Mart has been the *open door* to a new life for several of our students. Some of them have *opted to make* being a Wal-Mart employee their career!

I have been with Wal-Mart for over 7 years. I started when I was 17 as a cashier in West Burlington, Iowa. I was raised with the Wal-Mart culture, since my mom is a 21-year associate at the store in Galesburg, Illinois. *I worked my way up* in the company over the last 7 years to become a co-store manager. Wal-Mart has *given me the opportunity*, with almost no college education, to *make something out my life* and not to [*sic*] many other companies would do that. I owe a lot of thanks to this company for all of the wonderful experiences that they have *given me*.

My daughter, Vicki, has worked at our Super Walmart for approximately 7 years. Vicki received a closed-head injury in 1984 at age 16 and we didn't know if she could ever live a productive life after that. She was in a coma for 3 months & hospitals & a rehab center for 2 years after her coma. Her left side is affected like a stroke patient. She has no use of her left arm & cannot bend her left ankle. Walmart has been wonderful to her! She loves her job & has a real *feeling of accomplishment*.

Two main themes appear in these key phrases from the above personal stories and the numerous others like them. First, the narratives attest that Wal-Mart offers free and unlimited opportunities to those who have the drive to accept them—Wal-Mart "offers" and "gives" these chances away to willing recipients. Those who take advantage of this freedom are the people who are willing to "climb the ladder" or "make something out of [their lives]," those who have "goals" for advancement and "opt to" do what it takes to "further [their] careers" at Wal-Mart. In this way, the rhetoric surrounding the discussion of freedom of opportunity in this discursive framework presents it as one that is largely apprehended and experienced by individuals.

Of course, part of this emphasis on individual appropriations of freedom stems from WFWM's reliance on personal narratives to communicate key aspects of Wal-Mart's purported benefits—a strategy not pursued in like manner by its opponents. Yet individualistic frames of freedom also appear in other kinds of discourse associated with Wal-Mart's supporters, such as press releases issued by Wal-Mart Inc. For example, in a press release describing Wal-Mart's donations to the National Urban League, a representative of the

Urban League explained, "This grant will allow us to expand our workforce development initiatives and other programs, so that we can provide *individuals* in cities across the U.S. with the tools they need to secure economic self-reliance and power" (Wal-Mart press release, July 28, 2006, emphasis added). The perceived beneficiaries of Wal-Mart's benevolence—and those that Wal-Mart chose to highlight in such a public statement—are individuals who receive "tools" they need for "self-reliance." Similarly, Wal-Mart describes how its new Wal-Mart Discover card "shows our commitment to widen our services to help all our customers save money and improve their lives" (Wal-Mart press release, February 22, 2005). The customers can be offered the credit card only through Wal-Mart, but they may then choose to use it to save money and "improve their lives." Again, the individualistic and voluntaristic conception of freedom of opportunity remains paramount. And in a particularly telling example, Wal-Mart found ways to include personal narratives in its corporate press releases, most notably those highlighting its four-dollar prescription drug program:

> "In one pharmacy in Florida, our pharmacist told me that a woman broke down and started to cry as she told of how the $4 program was saving her $75 a month," said [Wal-Mart rep] Simon. "She said, 'It may not sound like a lot to you, but for the first time in a long time, I'll be able to buy my grandkids presents for Christmas. It has been a long time since I was able to do that.' This woman, and so many others like her, are what drive our commitment to ensure this program is available to as many Americans as possible." (Wal-Mart press release, October 19, 2006)

Here, Wal-Mart framed its decision to offer cheaper prescription drugs in terms that emphasize the empowerment of consumers—in this case, highlighting the way these savings translated into economic self-sufficiency for one particular individual, along with the freedom and empowerment that allowed that shopper to purchase presents for loved ones at Christmas.

To be sure, Wal-Mart also mentions groups in these texts, most notably as specific targets of empowerment. For example, Wal-Mart highlights partnerships with minority-owned businesses and ethnic activist groups with goals to empower groups such as Latinos and African Americans, who, due to historical legacies of discrimination, have been historically excluded from full participation in the benefits of market-based society. Wal-Mart also singles out military families as worthy of special acclaim, as in a program that partnered with Sesame Workshop to distribute interactive resources for families with a deployed parent:

"Wal-Mart has a long history of supporting our troops and their families. We are proud to be part of a program that will provide important resources to the children of our servicemen and servicewomen, who bravely serve our country and defend our freedom," said Ray Bracy, Vice President of Corporate Affairs, Wal-Mart Stores, Inc. (Wal-Mart press release, July 14, 2006)

Yet even though the statement is directed to the larger collective of "our troops and their families," Bracy also goes on to add, "At Wal-Mart, we are committed to honoring and supporting these *individuals* each and every day and we are proud to be part of a project that takes a holistic approach to helping the entire family" (emphasis added). Similarly, even when singling out groups for special consideration in press releases describing corporate benevolence, the emphasis is on empowerment, not carrying out any moral redress for past wrongs. And in some instances, as in the partnership with the Urban League "devoted to empowering African Americans economically and socially," Wal-Mart's donation still aims to "assist job seekers and program participants in meeting the requirements and performance standards of twenty-first century employers" (Wal-Mart press release, July 28, 2006). In other words, the empowerment of a group that has experienced discrimination is still to be accomplished through expressions of individual initiative—potential employees receive assistance for competing in the labor market.

### Centrality of Market Freedom

Another pattern in the discourse of Wal-Mart and its supporters concerns the way this range of individual freedoms—in particular, freedom of choice, expression, and opportunity—is tied to discourses about market freedom. (As noted earlier, even though ideal-typical laissez-faire capitalism does not really exist in the American economy, many of its subsidiary components do—such as open labor markets, consumer desire for choice and variety, and an emphasis on the ability of competition among both individuals and companies to bring enhanced benefits for the market's participants.) Just as chapter 4 argued that Wal-Mart's discourse rendered thrift and benevolence as a largely coherent, non-conflictual whole, the discursive worldview of Wal-Mart and its supporters emerges again as a largely consistent, tightly linked network of concepts: the individual freedoms of choice, expression, opportunity, and the like are all enhanced by the free market and its opportunities for fair play. As a result, this conception of freedom generates little conflict with its companion value of fairness. In particular, Wal-Mart's rhetoric emphasizes the virtues of individual freedoms largely because these freedoms are so compatible with—and indeed, find their fullest expression in—the free market economy.

For example, market freedom is tightly linked to freedoms of choice and expression because Wal-Mart's discourse suggests that the market brings more choices to consumers, enabling them to meet their needs and desires. Thus WFWM steering committee member Bishop Ira Combs proclaimed, "Let's start solving America's health care crisis by lowering the cost of health care to allow everyone access to it" (WFWM website). Here the market, not the state, can best assure that consumers' needs are met. Similarly, one woman wrote, "I love Walmart!!! My husband and I have a young family of 5 and I don't know what life would be like for us without Wal-Mart!!! From lower priced groceries to great savings for our everday [sic] needs. . . . Walmart makes me a smarter shopper in more ways than one" (WFWM website, personal story). For this Wal-Mart supporter, Wal-Mart's array of affordable choices helps the family participate in the consumption they desire. For another, Wal-Mart simply offers the goods consumers seek but can't attain elsewhere: "I just wish we could have [a Wal-Mart] here in Vallejo, but we will be forced to do all our shopping in the next community where they do have one" (WFWM website, personal story). Here, the narrative frames the lack of access to a local Wal-Mart as an absence of choice—"we will be *forced* to do all our shopping in the next community" where a Wal-Mart is available (emphasis added). Finally, other speakers simply explained, "I am able to buy things at Walmart that I could not afford to buy without their lower prices" (WFWM website, personal story). In all these cases, the savings afforded by Wal-Mart (a market mechanism) help facilitate individual freedom of choice and expression.

In addition to these personal narratives, Wal-Mart's own press releases often connect the purported benefits of the free market to the empowerment and advancement of lower-income consumers. For example, when a company like Wal-Mart has the freedom to lower prices on widely sought goods such as prescription medications, this brings new opportunities for low-income consumers who struggle to make ends meet. WFWM's "Paid Critics" section of its website, for example, lamented that "it is a sad day when a group that claims to advocate on behalf of working families attacks a program that will not only make prescription drugs more affordable, but will also make sure those who haven't been able to afford their medicine now have the opportunity to receive better health care." And just as the above excerpt references consumers' "opportunity" to improve their health care, in several instances Wal-Mart's press releases explicitly use words like "empower" and "access" to describe how market savings like the four-dollar prescription plan help consumers (emphasis added):

> "Wal-Mart has again stepped up and is accelerating the rollout of their $4 generic prescription program across the state," said Florida Gov. Jeb Bush. "This program *empowers* our people to talk to their doctors about accessing these more affordable medications, which can lead to higher compliance rates and better health. This program is good for Florida and even better for Floridians." (Wal-Mart press release, October 5, 2006)

> "We've received an amazing amount of positive feedback from the millions of seniors, working families and uninsured who are already *taking advantage* of this program," said Wal-Mart President and CEO Lee Scott. "We've added more medicines to our program so we can extend these significant savings to even more Americans. No one should be denied *access* to the medications they need, and this program is a big step in moving our customers and communities toward *access* to affordable medicines." (Wal-Mart press release, November 16, 2006)

In these examples, Wal-Mart's market offerings—which lower costs by virtue of the free market—help consumers expand their individual freedoms, as they are now "able" to spend money on other things, "take advantage" of this "opportunity," and "access" affordable medicines. Such verbal constructions underline the connection between the free market's offerings and individuals' own freedom of choice and expression.

Another way that discourse about the freedom of markets connects to discourse about the freedom of individuals appears in constructions that frame the free market as way of rewarding individuals who pull themselves up by their bootstraps through hard work. As one supplier explained, Wal-Mart's tough rules about cost-cutting and efficiency helped his company improve and prosper:

> Sure they [Wal-Mart] are tough and demanding but they have always treated us fairly. They are a major reason that William in production Bob in shipping, and JoAnn in the office were able to buy their first homes for their families in the last few years. . . . I'm not sure our company would exist today if Wal-Mart had not taken a chance on a 7 person firm 12 years ago. They have made us a far better company that provides 25 families with a decent living. We consider ourselves extremely fortunate to be a Wal-Mart supplier. (WFWM website, personal story)

In other examples, Wal-Mart offers essential job experience to individuals who transformed their opportunity into greater market success:

> A few years ago my neighbor's son who was quickly going nowhere took a job at Wal-Mart in the nursery. He was soon bringing home plants and landscaping his mom's yard. He scraped together enough money to buy a pickup truck and then a good lawn mower. He started working on neighbors' in his spare time. He said he found out at Wal-Mart that he wasn't worthless and he had a knack for landscaping. He now employs 4–6 people, has a big enclosed trailer [sic] and lots of equipment. He started with Wal-Mart where he discovered the value of hard work. (WFWM website, personal story)

Because Wal-Mart helped him "discover the value of hard work," the narrative suggests that the individual described above attained even greater economic and personal success.

## Fairness as Equal Opportunity

In large part because Wal-Mart and its proponents emphasize the centrality of market freedom and its close coupling with other, individual freedoms, the predominant vision of fairness that emerges in this discursive framework is one of procedural justice, or fairness as equal opportunity. Because little, if any, of this discourse questions the fairness of the market (any assumption to the contrary goes largely unspoken and thus unchallenged), the larger principles of fairness are achieved by giving everyone an equal chance out of the starting blocks. If people put in enough effort, then they get back an appropriate reward. Indeed, equality is referenced frequently in these materials, although Wal-Mart's supporters emphasize equal "access"—to a range of goods such as health care and market commodities—if not equal results. The outcome, then, does not indicate whether a certain situation is "fair"; instead, the idea of a "level playing field" takes center stage. In this way, freedom and fairness are tightly linked for Wal-Mart and its supporters, and fairness means giving everyone an equal chance to succeed or fail. Once they take their (presumably equal) places at the starting line, individuals are free to do their best, or if not, to fail. They are thus accountable for the outcome.

Because the market is generally assumed a "fair" institution in this discourse, individual rewards for effort receive significant emphasis. This provides yet another reason for rejecting unions in this moral worldview—workers give more to the unions than they receive in return. As one individual explained, "I do not wish to work for any union. I did not need a union while in the Army, and I do not need one now. I have seen how hard my dad & brother have worked under the union yoke with little or nothing to show from it" (WFWM website, personal story). Similarly, another described unions as simply "money paid out for nothing" (WFWM website, personal story). In another excerpt, the narrative describes Wal-Mart as a more "fair" employer than the grocery store where she worked previously:

> I recently in June left my job of 2 years with HEB and joined Wal-Mart at a new store in League City, Texas. As soon as I left, HEB gave my same job to a man and immediately gave him a 50-cent raise to do exactly what I was doing. Wal-Mart not only pays me more based on my abilities and experience and not my gender, but the rewards are greater. I have good insurance and the benefits are awesome. (WFWM website, personal story)

For this worker, Wal-Mart's compensation exemplifies the notion of fairness offered throughout this discourse: compensation based on "abilities and experience" and not the group-based category of gender. Similarly, in 2006 Wal-Mart Inc. emphasized merit-based pay increases "for those associates displaying excellent annual performance and customer service" (Wal-Mart press release, August 7, 2006).

With this understanding of justice in mind, it comes as no surprise that the following speaker concluded her narrative with the tidy aphorism "What you put into Wal-Mart is what you get out of Wal-Mart." Because individual effort is rewarded in the marketplace (just as lack of effort is presumably punished), the market becomes the institution charged with mediating one's inputs and one's just deserts. An extended personal narrative from the WFWM website argues just this point:

> I want to thank Wal-Mart for making my life better. Almost nine years ago we left Ohio and moved to Arizona for a job opportunity for myself with the State of Arizona. My husband had been working automotive retail for 10+ years. At the time we moved we assumed he'd be able to find employment in Phoenix in the same field. That wasn't to be; however, he applied and obtained a position as a night stocker at a Division I store.
>
> Since that time he has steadily received annual and merit raises at the maximum available rates. He has almost tripled his salary since he began working for Wal-Mart on October 6, 1997. He is now the Produce Lead in a SuperCenter and he enjoys working in the fresh areas of the SuperCenter.

I find it upsetting to hear the false and mis-leading information being dis-trbuted [*sic*] by the media. I know what Wal-Mart has provided for my family. As my husband tells people who ask him about Wal-Mart—"What you put into Wal-Mart is what you get out of Wal-Mart." I've seen it for myself. Thank you.

Most interestingly, in this excerpt the wife of the Wal-Mart employee pays little attention to her husband's difficulties in finding work in auto retail—an experience that might lead some observers to conclude that the market was indeed *not* rewarding individual effort and thus was an inherently *unfair* institution. This particular employee had over ten years of experience, and presumably worked hard to find employment in his previous field, since he ultimately accepted a position as a night stocker at Wal-Mart—almost certainly a demotion in any conception of the occupational hierarchy. Yet her husband's experience at Wal-Mart only affirmed that Wal-Mart is a fair employer—rewarding his effort with a tripled salary and promotions, and providing adequately for the speaker's family. By implication, this constructs the market as a fair institution overall.

Therefore, Wal-Mart itself emphasizes the ways the market can enhance fairness and equal access. Thus Wal-Mart's statements highlight ways in which the company is working to improve equality of opportunity and fur-ther access to the tools that individuals need to compete in the free market. A particularly telling group of examples appears in the company's state-ments on diversity and its description of charitable activities designed to help groups that have historically experienced market-based and other kinds of discrimination. For example, one agency recipient of Wal-Mart funds explained, "The Thurgood Marshall Scholarship Fund is extremely grateful to Wal-Mart for continuing to support the important work of the TMSF, and its ongoing work to prepare our best, brightest and most tal-ented students for the changing and challenging global marketplace" (Wal-Mart press release, October 24, 2006). Here, Wal-Mart presents its contri-butions to scholarships for outstanding black students as empowering them for market-based success. Similarly, Lee Scott explained why Wal-Mart hasn't been afraid to invest in stores in minority communities: "Wal-Mart has never been afraid to invest in communities that are overlooked by other retailers. Where those businesses see difficulty, we see opportunity. That is who Wal-Mart has always been, and that is who we remain today" (Wal-Mart press release, April 4, 2006). Here, Scott himself speaks of Wal-Mart's commitment to those whose position renders them precarious market players—"communities that are overlooked by other retailers"—and uses market-based terms like "invest" to describe Wal-Mart's interest in reaching these communities.

In fact, the bulk of Wal-Mart's prepared statements about corporate charity use similar language to present this market-friendly understanding of fairness as equal opportunity, as in the following examples (emphasis added):

> The first five years of a child's life are a time of great growth and learning. Yet many families struggle *to find an opening*—as well as the resources— for their child to participate in a pre-kindergarten program. Thanks to the Wal-Mart & Sam's Club Foundation, families in Bentonville will soon find hundreds of additional seats in classrooms for three- and four-year-old children. The company today announced a donation of $2.18 million to the Bentonville School District to fund significant expansion of its pre-kindergarten program. (Wal-Mart press release, February 8, 2006)

> "We firmly believe it is possible to increase diversity in newsrooms across the country," said Mona Williams, vice president for corporate communications, for Wal-Mart Stores, Inc. "This grant helps us demonstrate our strong commitment to both diversity and education by helping to ensure talented college students who aspire to be journalists will *have access to* practical training internships, and state of the art facilities." (Wal-Mart press release, February 25, 2005)

> "At Wal-Mart, we celebrate diversity 365 days a year," said Joy Wooden, a director of diversity relations with Wal-Mart. "We are proud to support a worthwhile organization like APIASF [Asian and Pacific Islander American Scholarship Fund], and we applaud the scholarship fund for its leadership in ensuring that Asian and Pacific Islander Americans *will be able* to pursue their dream of a higher education regardless of their financial situation" (Wal-Mart press release, May 18, 2005)

In all these examples, Wal-Mart implies that problems of inequality result not from disparities born of the market, but from unequal access to the tools that allow individuals to compete successfully in market institutions. Thus the appropriate form of redress concerns equipping these actors with the educational credentials they need to compete fairly in this market arena.

At the same time, these examples also point to an ironic disconnect within what is otherwise a largely coherent, unified understanding of various kinds of freedoms and their hospitable relationship with the principle of fairness: by addressing challenges to market access, and emphasizing ways that Wal-Mart helps empower those who would otherwise be left out of the labor market, much of the discourse simultaneously implies that some aspects of the market economy aren't entirely fair. Otherwise, such empowering programs of redress would be unnecessary, and supporters offering personal stories describing how Wal-Mart has helped individuals make something of their lives would not find this experience with employment so noteworthy. Yet these points of cognitive conflict are rarely, if ever, acknowledged, raising the question: how do Wal-Mart's supporters manage to avoid these pressing questions?

One strategy of avoidance concerns the language used by this group of activists. First, the texts produced by Wal-Mart and its supporters scarcely mention the words "equal" or "equality." This represents one way that the pro-Wal-Mart discourse effectively limits the range of meanings that could be ascribed to fairness in this group of texts. Thus, even in the texts where Wal-Mart acknowledges histories of discrimination against people of color, or describes its efforts to develop ties to minority-owned businesses, Wal-Mart frequently mentions "diversity" but not "equality." Although equality is certainly one expression of fairness that might be embraced in such statements, this interpretation is lacking in the pro-Wal-Mart texts. In this way, the discursive framework suggests it is "fair" to correct imbalances among market players by focusing on opportunity and "equal access," even as it simultaneously implies that changing the endgame to effect "equal results" is not fair.

Another discursive strategy that protects these contradictions from cognitive dissonance involves shifting the focus from the larger economic system to the experiences of isolated individuals. Even though Wal-Mart's supporters offer several anecdotes about Wal-Mart's willingness to employ "special needs" workers, such as learning disabled or mentally challenged persons, keeping the focus of these stories on isolated individuals again distracts attention from larger market systems. Although these individuals are often assumed to be largely unemployable by other companies ("There should be more companies like you that give everyone a chance at being successfully employed," wrote one speaker on the WFWM website), most speakers frame Wal-Mart as actually violating principles of market freedom by treating people as individuals, not as market commodities. As one Wal-Mart employee explained:

> Wal-mart is a great place to work and there are so many places to go with this company. My only regret is that I did not start when I was younger. Wal-mart does not look at your age or race when they hire you. They look at you as a person with the ability to work for Wal-mart, and to become part of the family. (WFWM website, personal story)

For instance, even as this narrative argues that Wal-Mart does not look at ascribed characteristics like age or race, but instead evaluates the potential employee "as a person with the ability to work for Wal-Mart," the terms in which she describes her experience with the company reinforce the broader conceptions of individual and market freedom emphasized elsewhere in these documents. Wal-Mart offers opportunity to those who would accept it, as "there are so many places to go with this company." Furthermore, research in social psychology affirms that, on the whole, an individual's sense of experiencing procedural justice enhances one's feeling of group loyalty and identification.[11] Therefore, placing these reflections within the context of the employee's own, largely positive individual experience also protects this account from any challenges that might result from considering whether the larger free market system is actually fair. Because the narrative frames Wal-Mart and its person-based opportunity for advancement positively, there seems little reason to challenge the broader principles of market fairness.

### Freedom and Fairness in Wal-Mart Watch

Given the centrality of the free market paradigm in American discourse, it comes as little surprise that Wal-Mart Watch, like its opponents, also affirms many aspects of this ideal. Yet WMW differs from its pro-Wal-Mart counterparts in two main respects. First, Wal-Mart Watch tends to argue that Wal-Mart restricts market and other freedoms, rather than enhancing them. Just as the pro-Wal-Mart contingency speaks of market freedoms in ways that are highly compatible with other, largely individual freedoms, WMW argues for placing limits on Wal-Mart's freedoms precisely because they hinder the freedom of other groups. In this way, both sides are operating within a shared moral framework, in which market freedom, in the best of all worlds, supports and enhances the freedoms of other kinds of social actors—they simply come to different conclusions about Wal-Mart's role in that process. The reason for this comprises the second main difference between the two groups, which concerns the primary referents for each side: whereas WFWM and Wal-Mart frame their arguments largely in terms of individuals and use individual stories to make points about providing opportunities to larger categories of workers (e.g., people of color), WMW focuses its attention on collective categories of communities, small business owners, and groups of disadvantaged workers. Similarly, WMW also endorses a conception of fairness as distributive justice; however, WMW attempts to connect this concept to a host of collective categories, not individuals. In this way, we might say that both groups are using similar blueprints for creating a coherent moral framework, but that they do so while focusing on different key components of the market system.

## Limiting (Wal-Mart's) Market Freedom

One refrain in Wal-Mart Watch's text materials, press releases, emails, and other communications is that the retailer's use of the free market must be restrained. For example, a WMW press release explained Wal-Mart's support for the Central American Free Trade Agreement (CAFTA):

> Wal-Mart Watch is not surprised that Wal-Mart is lobbying for CAFTA, since it could make it even more profitable for the retail giant to exploit Central American workers who lack basic labor rights. CAFTA would grant expanded access to the U.S. market without strengthening labor rights protections in that region. And by lifting trade barriers and granting increased protections to U.S. investors, CAFTA could increase the incentive for companies like Wal-Mart to undercut U.S. jobs by sourcing from these countries. (WMW press release, June 14, 2005)

Elsewhere, WMW similarly suggests that inequality itself lies at the root of the capitalistic market model, with statements such as "To keep prices low, Wal-Mart must source goods from areas of the world where employment standards are severely lacking" (WMW website).

At the same time, however, these instances in which WMW challenges the free market *itself* are comparatively rare. Instead, WMW's discourse more often speaks of "regulating" growth and cultivating "healthy" or "responsible" economic development instead of haphazard, unfettered capitalism. This was particularly pronounced in the "Battlemart" pages of WMW's website, in which local groups of activists shared their plans for restraining "unplanned and irresponsible growth" and endorsed such goals as furthering a city's "economic and cultural vitality . . . through thoughtful, socially and environmentally responsible growth." The common theme in these documents is that Wal-Mart's own brand of economic growth is reckless and poorly planned, and should be countered with more refined and responsible plans for economic development. In short, citizens and activists should take on the task of directing their local economies in positive ways—managing the market so that it meets normative goals for distribution and welfare among their citizens.

In particular, WMW argues that Wal-Mart's activities should be restrained in order to protect the free market itself. Accordingly, most statements concerning market freedom focus less on broader market inequalities and more on how Wal-Mart hinders other expressions of freedom, a rhetorical decision that can be interpreted as endorsing the larger principles of capitalism, warts and all. In this way, even though WMW differs from Wal-Mart's supporters in its policy positions, WMW has much in common with their endorsement of the free market as a taken-for-granted piece of a larger tapestry of freedoms.

The strongest expression of this perspective appeared in WMW statements and emails commenting on Wal-Mart's FDIC banking application, which warned that should the FDIC grant Wal-Mart's request for an Industrial Loan Corporation charter, the resultant "Wal-Mart Bank would create a dangerous concentration of commercial and financial power" (WMW website). Consumers should thus oppose Wal-Mart's application because it threatens the free market via a potential banking monopoly. Other WMW statements echoed similar concerns:

> Just like the "factory towns" of old, Wal-Mart wants to have its hand in every piece of the pie—and its next move is managing your money. Last September, Wal-Mart unveiled plans for the "Bank of Wal-Mart": an enormous power play to boost Wal-Mart's domination of our economy by creating one of the largest financial institutions in the country. (WMW email, April 5, 2006)

Accordingly, elsewhere the rhetoric surrounding the FDIC application warned of a "Wal-Bank" should activists and regulators not intervene: "Last September, Wal-Mart renewed its plans to create one of the largest financial institutions in the country—an enormous effort to boost the retailer's power in the marketplace. Wal-Mart execs thought they could breeze through the FDIC review process and quietly take control of the banking sector" (WMW email, July 31, 2006). In this view, Wal-Mart threatens to become a banking monopoly, which would undermine the very principles of market freedom that currently protect the best interests of consumers—as well as their freedom to find the best price and service among a multitude of financial providers in an open, competitive market.

In addition, WMW faults Wal-Mart's unparalleled ability to lower prices on large volume sales for putting smaller and local merchants out of business—in effect, interfering with a free market because these retailers are "forced" to close their doors as they are "driven" out of business. WMW's statement on Wal-Mart's "Community Impact," for example, explains, "Whether it is accepting unnecessary subsidies, driving local stores out of business, pressuring local town officials or encouraging workers to join state health rolls, Wal-Mart has a negative impact on local communities" (WMW website). Similarly, when Wal-Mart announced plans to explore markets in India, WMW warned that local Indian merchants would be at risk, because "small businesses, in particular, will be sacrificed at the expense of the global giant's business model" (WMW press release, July 18, 2005). And on a webpage titled "Why the Faith Community Must Get Involved," WMW portrayed the effects of Wal-Mart's business model as similarly exploitative of unregulated markets—and similarly injurious of freedom:

> Wal-Mart imported $15 billion worth of Chinese products last year, a result of pressuring its suppliers for costs so low they can only be achieved in an environment where human rights are violated at will. Its insatiable demand for cheap labor has crushed local competitors and driven thousands of American jobs overseas, leaving nothing but, you guessed it, Wal-Mart jobs, in their wake.

WMW similarly faults Wal-Mart for limiting consumer choice via market hegemony—in effect, using market dominance to subvert the freedom of choice that should accompany free and unregulated commerce. WMW statements about "Plan B" contraception prescriptions– which Wal-Mart had initially resisted stocking in its pharmacies—illustrate this perspective particularly well: "Wal-Mart is the only pharmacy in many of the rural markets it serves, and its corporate policy will determine whether women in these areas have access to the drug" (WMW press release, August 24, 2006). And, of course, WMW also accuses Wal-Mart of trampling on workers' rights by not allowing the freedom to organize: "Union leaders across the country want working families to benefit from Wal-Mart. Unfortunately, Wal-Mart blocks every attempt by local employees to organize for fair wages, health care benefits and equal employment opportunities—silencing those who stand up for their rights" (WMW newsletter, November 17, 2006).

Similarly, Wal-Mart Watch also turns its attention to the way the company is allegedly undermining freedoms for its workers by compelling them to rely on public assistance and take on additional jobs to make ends meet. In the following excerpts, the word "force" repeatedly emphasizes the nonvoluntary nature of these decisions (emphases added):

> Lagging behind industry averages, Wal-Mart's employees are subjected to unnecessary charges and fees, wait longer for coverage eligibility, and are

*forced* to seek out public health programs to fulfill their health care needs. (WMW website)

We are in a vigil because of thousand of reported and unreported workers who have been *forced* to work off the clock with no pay. (WMW website)

Wal-Mart profited $10 billion dollars last year, yet 1,200 of its workers and their children are *forced* to rely on BadgerCare health care to make ends meet. (WMW press release, January 17, 2006)

WMW also alleges that Wal-Mart violates fundamental freedoms by "forcing" the public—via its taxpayers—to fund these expenditures for the health care and other public assistance needs of workers who are not adequately compensated by their Wal-Mart jobs: "Wal-Mart Watch credits Wal-Mart for recognizing that their employee health plan is inadequate for their employees and unfair to taxpayers *forced* to support their use of Medicaid" (WMW press release, October 24, 2005). In this conception, Wal-Mart's relentless pursuit of profits in the free market means that its workers paradoxically lose some of their freedoms, either by working compulsory long hours or by being forced to access public assistance programs.

## Freedom and Fairness for Collectivities

The preceding section argued that, on the whole, WMW does not dispute the connection between a capitalist market and other expressions of freedom and self-determination: like its opponents, WMW consistently affirms the existence of a relationship between market institutions and the rights of communities, other retailers, workers, and consumers. However, WMW largely finds that the relationship between Wal-Mart's freedom and these other, related freedoms is a negative one—that is, the unrestricted market activity of Wal-Mart itself threatens these other freedoms, whereas Wal-Mart and WFWM would find that the retailer encourages them. In this section, I argue that the reason for this disconnect can be explained in at least two ways, both of which are useful for explaining public market discourse more generally. First, WMW tends to focus its language on the effects of Wal-Mart's unrestricted market activity on collectivities rather than individuals. This collective focus serves to highlight patterns of inequality that are obscured in the more individualistic-focused narratives and statements of groups like WFWM and Wal-Mart Inc. In addition, WMW largely conceives of fairness not as equal access but as just rewards. Together, these two patterns help explain why WMW and WFWM reach such different conclusions evaluating Wal-Mart's role in the free market.

The predominant collectivity that WMW emphasizes in this discourse concerns certain kinds of workers—particularly broad categories of workers who have been disadvantaged by Wal-Mart's alleged discrimination, particularly women, African Americans, and the disabled. As WMW simply summarizes:

> Wal-Mart has been accused of every type of discrimination imaginable. African American employees and customers have both filed lawsuits against the retail giant. Disabled workers have sued Wal-Mart for passing them over for promotions. And Wal-Mart is the subject of the largest class action lawsuit ever, based on evidence that Wal-Mart systematically pays women less than their male counterparts, and offers them fewer opportunities for promotion. (WMW website)

Instead of appealing to individual stories of bias, WMW relies on the media, legal proceedings, and the like to make this case.[12] To illustrate, on its main page detailing the key issue of "Discrimination," WMW cites such sources as the *Dukes v. Wal-Mart Stores* complaint, the NAACP, and numerous journalistic articles to allege Wal-Mart's systematic pattern of unequal treatment of these three categories of employees. WMW also introduces the issue itself in ways that highlight the equality of workers as a single class, emphasizing Wal-Mart's unequal treatment of particular *kinds* of employees, not individual employees themselves:

> As America's largest company, Wal-Mart has a duty to treat all employees and suppliers with respect. However, this is not always the case. Wal-Mart is currently facing the largest workplace-bias lawsuit in U.S. history for widespread discrimination against women employees; a class action lawsuit filed by African-American truck drivers; and numerous other cases involving discrimination against workers with disabilities. For example, in 2001, Wal-Mart paid $6 million dollars to settle 13 lawsuits, which alleged widespread discrimination and violations of the Americans with Disabilities Act. (WMW website)

The paragraph above begins by emphasizing equality across categories— "Wal-Mart has a duty to treat all employees and suppliers with respect"— yet closes by highlighting the legal injunctions that Wal-Mart faces for not upholding these principles of equal respect through bias, discrimination, and violations of the law.

In addition to WMW's focus on categories as compared to WFWM's focus on individuals, another difference between the two groups has to do with the way WMW conceives of fairness. In contrast to Wal-Mart supporters' dominant portrayal of fairness as equal opportunity, WMW emphasizes fairness as just rewards. To be sure, WFWM and Wal-Mart itself would likely agree that fairness is exemplified by getting what one deserves, either positively (promotions earned for hard work) or negatively (market difficulties due to laziness). However, WMW emphasizes fairness primarily in the context of "fair wages" or "fair compensation" for Wal-Mart's employees along with "fair competition" for small businesses. For instance, a telephone campaign commissioned by WMW used the following script:

> Hello, I'm calling with a special message for anyone who works for Wal-Mart. As you know, Wal-Mart has had a number of serious legal and ethical problems. To help make Wal-Mart a better and more fair place to work, the Center for Community and Corporate Ethics is seeking anyone who knows of wrongdoing within Wal-Mart. You will be treated with complete confidentiality. (WMW press release, June 3, 2005)

The common implication here is that when people or entities try hard, they should be rewarded, although even WMW stops short of advocating equal rewards or distribution of resources.

Yet how does the progressive side justify its claims for fairness in these instances? While WMW attempts to develop some moral grounding for these claims by drawing connections between fair wages and family sustenance, its discourse about fairness—and particularly about the level playing field that small businesses deserve alongside Wal-Mart—ultimately relies most heavily on market-based warrants. To be sure, there are instances where Wal-Mart Watch begins to offer a conception of fairness grounded in concern for the family, particularly in WMW's consideration of the relationship between compensation in the labor market and the well-being of the family. Just as WFWM and Wal-Mart emphasized the family primarily in relation to the moral value of thrift, WMW makes some attempts to connect the family to fairness, as when WMW challenged Wal-Mart to "justly compensate each associate with a family-sustaining wage" and to provide "affordable health insurance that fully covers the employee and their children" ("Handshake with Sam," WMW website).

Similarly, in a May 19, 2005, press release concerning Maryland's Fair Share Health Care debate, Wal-Mart Watch executive director Andrew Grossman stated, "I'm saddened, but hardly surprised, that Governor Ehrlich today chose the interests of his massive campaign contributor over the health and welfare of the hardest working Marylanders and their families." The implication of this statement is that Maryland's governor acted unfairly when siding with big businesses (and Wal-Mart's campaign contributions) in vetoing the FSHC legislation that would have compelled Wal-Mart to spend more money on its employees' health care. However, WMW stops short of explicitly declaring this unjust or unfair, and only loosely connects this alleged grievance to the interests and well-being of the family. The potential conception of fairness as a family-sustaining economic policy is only partially articulated.

Instead, the only place in WMW's discourse where a more grounded conception of fairness is repeatedly and consistently set forth is in its discourse about the tax subsidies that allegedly fund Wal-Mart's bottom line by providing public benefits for its shortchanged workers. In this framework, tax breaks for big corporations like Wal-Mart are unfair because they erode the ability of smaller merchants to compete on a level playing field. At the root of this argument is the contention that Wal-Mart is not playing fair, or contributing its fair share toward state Medicaid coffers. To this end, a host of verbal constructions emphasize fair play and fair distribution of responsibility throughout (emphases added):

Wal-Mart's profits have long been subsidized by taxpayers—from corporate welfare to Medicaid spending to *special treatment* from federal investigators. (WMW press release, October 31, 2005)

This new study rightly focuses further attention on Wal-Mart's effect on local communities. We already know that when Wal-Mart moves into a community, its small businesses and residents are hit with the "Wal-Mart tax," *picking up the tab* for store driveways, public aid for children of Wal-Mart employees, and a host of other hidden costs. (WMW press release, November 3, 2005)

"As small business owners, we pay our *fair share* for our employees' health care," said Robert Dickerson, owner of Work Printing & Graphics in Baltimore. "In most cases, we have not received government support to start our operations or maintain them. Moreover, we *carry our weight*, we pay our taxes, and we contribute back to our local host communities," added Dickerson. (WMW press release, January 9, 2006)

The Fair Share Health Care Act is being supported by a broad coalition of organizations including business, faith-based, union, and community groups who are demanding that Wal-Mart pay its *fair share*. We will no longer accept Wal-Mart's *unfair* tactic of *shifting* health care costs to the taxpayer. (WMW press release, January 9, 2006)

More than any other employer, Wal-Mart *shifts* its health care costs onto taxpayers—in all 21 states that have disclosed this data, Wal-Mart is by far the leader. Wal-Mart simply doesn't pay its *fair share*. (WMW email, July 20, 2006)

On the one hand, these objections on grounds of fairness are quite consistent in the way they appropriate this value: the underlying premise is that all businesses have a shared responsibility to contribute to their employees' well-being by funding quality health care programs. When employers fail in his regard, they "shirk" their responsibilities and "shift" those costs onto other businesses, public programs, and, by extension, taxpayers themselves. Small businesses, for instance, are not avoiding this responsibility, so Wal-Mart's actions are even more reprehensible—particularly because Wal-Mart's profits could well allow the company to do more. At the same time, this presentation of fairness (or unfairness, as the case may be) is somewhat curtailed in that it doesn't reach very deep to ground this claim of fairness in other moral discourses or ethical values. Instead, the grounds on which WMW urges fairness are rooted in the market itself (you should pay your share of required costs), and in the comparisons that may be drawn between Wal-Mart and other market institutions (if small business owners can afford to do it, so can Wal-Mart). Again, the progressive discourse is ultimately limited by referring to the market itself as a source of positive change. This rhetorical move may ultimately limit the organization's ability to challenge more fundamental premises of the market itself. For example, statements such as "[Wal-Mart's] medical coverage rates lag far behind those of other large employers" (WMW press release, December 5, 2005) place the burden of proof on comparisons with other corporations—alongside which Wal-Mart is found lacking—but not on deeper principles of ethical responsibility. More expansive possibilities for the discourse are not adopted, and the discourse does not make any further consideration of how such demands might be justified.

## Conclusion

This analysis of the ways in which various SMOs involved in the Wal-Mart debate appropriate themes of freedom and fairness suggests several main conclusions. First, both liberal and conservative activists acknowledge, to varying degrees, the centrality of the (theoretically) free market. Although Wal-Mart's critics urge that some limits be placed on market forces writ large—such as those that allow for sweatshop labor in developing countries—they are more likely to advocate limiting *Wal-Mart's* market activity so that the procedural justice of the free market might actually be preserved. For WMW, this kind of market freedom ensures that other forms of distributive justice for collective groups persevere: small businesses remain vibrant, communities may decide for themselves the kinds of stores they wish to build, and workers from groups that have experienced discrimination are appropriately compensated in the labor market. In contrast, Wal-Mart's proponents focus more on procedural justice alone—freedom of choice, expression, and empowerment—all of which find even fuller expression in the free market because the market can be trusted to best distribute a variety of goods, lower prices to help consumers express themselves, and reward the efforts of those who work hardest. Even though some aspects of the pro-Wal-Mart rhetoric implicitly challenge the notion that the market itself is fair, strategies of avoidance, including limited use of words like "equality" and an emphasis on individual narratives and experiences, serve to distract attention from some of these potential challenges of larger notions of fairness in the market and its institutions.[13] This analysis has also suggested that progressives' discourse about these themes is more limited than that of their critics, although it is difficult to specify fully whether this potential shortcoming inheres in the discourse itself or is an artifact of the David versus Goliath nature of the struggle between a small advocacy group like Wal-Mart Watch and a multibillion-dollar corporation like Wal-Mart. The power of a corporation to shape both the debate and the wider culture are formidable obstacles, to say the least.

Even alongside the centrality of various expressions of the free market in this framework, we do find some significant differences in the ways that conservative and liberal activists talk about the market as a moral system. For instance, Wal-Mart's supporters emphasize fairness as meaning equal access for individuals to the market and its institutions, while WMW frames fairness as just rewards and emphasizes how workers in particular should receive compensation that allows their families to be self-sufficient and avoid public assistance. Moreover, Wal-Mart's critics tend to focus more on collective groups—workers, women, and African Americans—instead of the individuals who receive paramount attention from Wal-Mart and WFWM. This helps explain why unions are praised by WMW and vilified by WFWM: unions may reward collective effort but overlook the varying abilities and contributions of specific individuals. For this reason, unions are suspect because they fail to endorse a key feature of the moral worldview articulated by Wal-Mart and its proponents.

The significance of unions proves similarly important in understanding why the government intervention in American auto companies was so controversial. For instance, in reflecting on the auto companies' bailout, one national commentator argued, "The trouble with General Motors is not that it went bankrupt. The trouble is that it didn't. It's still there, not going bankrupt and not going out of business. Instead, along with Chrysler, GM is sliding through a government-backed reorganization and emerging as part of the same old whining, subsidy-seeking, protectionist, union-locked North American auto industry."[14] Much like pro-Wal-Mart activists who endorse the sanctity of the free market system, Terry Corcoran sees the main problem with the GM bailout as having to do with it rewarding a set of bad practices that should have been punished. The perception that the American auto industries are "union-locked" only adds to their problems of performance. Similarly, other national newspapers' reporting of the events emphasized that Obama's intervention was designed to intervene with the workings of the economy to ensure a favorable outcome. Just as in the Wal-Mart debate, observers characterized the president's actions as using government intervention to maintain the sanctity of market competition—measuring the validity of a procedural system by virtue of its distributive outcomes. As the *New York Times* summarized early that summer, "President Obama will push General Motors into bankruptcy protection . . . making a risky bet that by temporarily nationalizing the onetime icon of American capitalism, he can save at least a diminished automaker that is competitive."[15]

One phrase that found its way into the public discourse during the bailout era was "moral hazard"—the idea that excusing some people or institutions from the consequences of their actions would lead other people to act in similarly irresponsible ways. This was a theme that reached beyond the auto industry loans and into the realm of homeowner assistance, mortgage modification, and even the TARP funds themselves. The conservative columnist David Brooks echoed many of the same themes that animate the discourse of pro-Wal-Mart activists when he wrote:

> Our moral and economic system is based on individual responsibility. It's based on the idea that people have to live with the consequences of their decisions. This makes them more careful deciders. This means that society tends toward justice—people get what they deserve as much as possible. Over the last few months, we've made a hash of all that. The Bush and

Obama administrations have compensated foolishness and irresponsibility. The financial bailouts reward bankers who took insane risks. The auto bailouts subsidize companies and unions that made self-indulgent decisions a few decades ago that drove their industry into the ground. The stimulus package handed tens of billions of dollars to states that spent profligately during the prosperity years. The Obama housing plan will force people who bought sensible homes to subsidize the mortgages of people who bought houses they could not afford. It will almost certainly force people who were honest on their loan forms to subsidize people who were dishonest on theirs.[16]

Here again, we see the same themes emerge in discourse about markets—the conservative perception of the foundation of a moral market lies fundamentally with individual persons who should act responsibly and then receive their just reward. Thus the larger economic system is just so long as it rewards the moral actions of individuals, so that those who suffer in its wake are receiving only what is fair—their deserved rewards in the larger scheme of procedural justice.

To be sure, President Obama also warned of the dangers of moral hazard in potentially rewarding American auto manufacturers' legacy of poor leadership by conceding that "these companies—and this industry—must ultimately stand on their own, not as wards of the state."[17] But he did so only after framing the impending government assistance in terms of larger, collective categories, particularly images of the nation and its legacy of manufacturing workers:

> This industry is like no other—it's an emblem of the American spirit; a once and future symbol of America's success. It's what helped build the middle class and sustained it throughout the twentieth century. It's a source of deep pride for the generations of American workers whose hard work and imagination led to some of the finest cars the world has ever known. It's a pillar of our economy that has held up the dreams of millions of our people.

In Obama's words, the reasons for assisting the struggling General Motors and Chrysler corporations have to do with the collective contributions of manufacturing workers to American "pride" that has been felt by "generations of American workers." The auto industry is significant for its role in a larger economic system, for it is "a pillar of our economy that has held up the dreams of millions of our people."

Obama's language is arguably inspiring, but I wish to suggest that the appeal of this rhetoric is ultimately less powerful than that of his conservative opponents because it draws on comparatively "thinner" moral warrants than does the language of a conservative spokesperson like David Brooks. Stephen Hart's work on progressive social movements provides a particularly helpful rubric for differentiating between thick or "expansive" discourse and its comparatively thin or "constrained" counterparts. Hart argues that three characteristics denote the difference: temperature, issue links, and civil-societal links. In temperature, expansive discourse is passionate and focuses on transcendent concerns rather than procedural ends. In terms of issue links, expansive discourse ties various issues together rather than focusing on one particular topic, and expansive civil-societal links connect concrete political issues to the existing cultural traditions of civil society. Hart argues that social movement activists cannot simply apply the language of values or rights to economic issues without doing cultural work to ground those claims in a framework that helps people interpret them alongside other values that might be conflicting.[18] To claim that a government bailout of General Motors is moral, for example, requires that progressives engage in deliberate cultural work to ground this claim in more transcendent concerns and to connect the issue to other similar causes and relevant institutions in civil society. President Obama, for instance, might be attempting do just this through his appeal to the auto industry's significance as an "emblem of the American spirit; a once and future symbol of America's success" that is simultaneously a "pillar of our economy." Yet such appeals to economic symbols and the American spirit may be less powerful than those rooted in a richer, more institutional moral discourse, such as that which revolves around the institution of the family. The abstract and ephemeral institutions of "the economy" and "the American spirit" may not carry the same emotional punch as rhetoric that emphasizes tangible relational ties.

With regard to the Wal-Mart debate, a group like Wal-Mart Watch begins to make richer moral connections in its call for Wal-Mart to pay "family-sustaining wages." Such a claim ties Wal-Mart's wages to the institution of the family, which also offers a host of other value-laden issues that might be connected to these concerns for economic well-being—and would rate high on Hart's "temperature" scale. The importance of workers' investments in children and aging parents, for example, played a key role in creating support for the eventual passage of the Family and Medical Leave Act.[19] Thus progressives could argue that transcendent, humanist principles of care and nurture emphasize the importance of parents' ability to spend time with their children, and thus our society should be one in which parents shouldn't have to work more than one job to pay the bills. Likewise, a group like WMW could also emphasize themes woven into the very concept of the American Dream—the simple notion that hard work should beget tangible rewards of economic empowerment and intergenerational mobility. Similarly, even though Wal-Mart Watch is largely consistent in arguing that the retailer limits freedom, it mirrors Obama's remarks on the auto industry by focusing its arguments on questions of freedom that reside almost entirely within the realm of market activities, such as the legal rights of small businesses, workers, and state governments. Conversely, economic conservatives tend to create a discursive universe that addresses a wider range of freedoms (and issues) that exist both inside *and* outside the market simply by referencing countless examples of individual experiences within families and communities that potentially create richer issue links and thus promote a more expansive, compelling public discourse. To be sure, WMW makes a few such arguments, and does so in some of its most public pronouncements (most notably, mentioning the idea of a family-sustaining wage in a full-page ad in the *New York Times*). At the same time, the discourse produced by Wal-Mart Watch only begins to fully engage these connections. When these progressive activists do work to link their policy positions to other domains, they tend to focus on civil-societal links to things like legal precedents in instances of alleged workplace discrimination. It's very possible that these resources are less compelling to their audience than the more individual-centered, experiential narratives of Wal-Mart's advocates.

Robert Wuthnow has argued that an ideal moral discourse is one that proves "capable of challenging economic norms and providing alternative ways of thinking," adding that "these arguments should be based on something other than economic calculations or assumptions about economic laws alone."[20] Yet in further investigations into the moral thought and discourse of a diverse sample of Americans, Wuthnow finds that most people are not able to give morally rich accounts of their economic behavior. In turn, this leaves a vapid space in which the scripts offered by institutions like the workplace and the market come to dominate moral thought about economic issues. Further, he proposes that more Americans view work and family as somewhat oppositional, with family representing a haven from the pressures and anxieties of the paid labor market. It should come as little surprise, then, that progressive economic critics find it difficult to connect issues of wage inequality to the institution of the family, and instead tend to occupy their discussion of fairness with concerns about potential monopoly power and preservation of the free market. Put a slightly different way, groups like Wal-Mart Watch tend to focus more of their attention on the end goals of a campaign—like raising Wal-Mart's workers' wages, or urging more environmentally friendly development—than evaluating the moral merit of the different means that might be used to achieve these goals. Wal-Mart and its supporters, in contrast, fare slightly better in creating a coherent and expansive moral discourse. Tight linkages between individual expressions of freedom and the market create connections between individuals and a key institution of American society. Wal-Mart supporters' remarks about freedom of choice and expression resonate well with the themes of expressive individualism that play key roles in American thought and political culture.[21] These linkages, then, may prove both more expansive and more resonant than those attempted by their opponents.

Further, conservative economic advocates are more likely to create tight linkages between these freedoms and their expression in consumerist society, which further undermines the ability of progressives to challenge these claims. As Glickman has demonstrated, historical struggles for "a living wage" have been inextricably bound up in Americans' rising standards of consumption—a story in which Wal-Mart plays a starring role as a perennial hero. In Glickman's analysis, socialist concerns with the natural value of labor were eventually eclipsed by the pursuit of higher standards of living that began developing in the antebellum era.[22] Accordingly, the present investigation reveals that conservative activists continue to emphasize the connections between freedom and consumption—in other words, the freedom to buy more and varied consumer goods—while progressives often struggle to articulate a morally rich argument about fairness in workers' wages and compensation. Given this historical legacy (along with Americans' difficulty in articulating moral warrants to evaluate economic behavior), progressives face steep challenges in creating a rich, expansive discourse about economic issues. The next chapter turns from the characteristics of the discourse among these "backstage" actors to the "frontstage" venue of American media, exploring how national newspapers take up these ideas and moral concepts in their coverage of issues related to Wal-Mart and its challengers, and the public debate surrounding these economic dilemmas created by global capitalism.

# PART 3

Market Morality in Media and Politics

# 6

## How Wal-Mart Wins the War of Words

The left is returning to its historic mission of being the avatar of genuine democracy in the teeth of a class-dominated, business-oriented society. It is the dedicated opponent of inequality, democracy's invariable cancer. . . . But this struggle to reduce inequality and to strengthen democracy will be incomplete for any prospective U.S. left without a vision of a more democratic media system, a program for media reform, and a strategic plan to organize around the issue.

—Robert McChesney, *Rich Media, Poor Democracy*

Wal-Mart's critics, like most social movement activists, have a common goal: to be noticed in the press. For groups like Wal-Mart Watch, earning recognition in larger spheres of discourse is a prerequisite for success because these groups have no real constituency, such as a local chapter that meets regularly to discuss goals, tactics, and future endeavors. At best, their core "constituency" is individuals who have given the organization an email address at which they receive periodic updates and urgings to contact an elected representative, sign a petition, or send an email to Wal-Mart's CEO. At the same time, they have a much larger target constituency in the broader public, through whom changes may be accomplished by convincing them that an everyday activity (shopping) carries with it a larger moral significance. This can happen only when their arguments and activities become of interest to the national media.

The national media is the master sphere in which the "primary claims" of activist groups are transformed into "secondary claims" by the national press.[1] The media are considered "secondary claims" makers because "the press does not merely transmit claims; it translates and transforms them."[2] In other words, the way claims take shape in the public sphere is not accidental or arbitrary. In like manner, Myra Marx Ferree and colleagues have argued that the media represent a kind of "master forum" in which various forums of speech—such as the public arena, the gallery of observers, and the backstage forum where actors strategically craft their messages—are contested.[3] Accordingly, they argue:

> The mass media forum is *the* major site of political contest because all of the players in the policy process *assume* its pervasive influence (whether justified or not). The mass media present—often in a highly selective and simplified way—discourse from other forums. The participants in these other forums look to the mass media forum to assess their effectiveness. . . . To have one's preferred framing of an issue increase significantly in the mass media forum is both an important outcome in itself and carries a strong promise of a ripple effect.[4]

In the Wal-Mart debate, as I have argued in the preceding chapters, activists on both sides of the divide have framed the issue in notably different ways. Progressive groups like Wal-Mart Watch, for example, frame the debate largely in terms of citizens and benevolence, arguing that it is not fair for a large corporation like Wal-Mart to skirt its responsibilities to its employees and force them to depend on state-funded entitlements at taxpayer expense. In contrast, Wal-Mart's supporters frame their arguments more often in terms of the needs of average working families who can maximize their individual freedoms in a market system whose fairness remains largely unquestioned. Yet the ultimate fate of these arguments depends on just how they are transformed by and appropriated within the public sphere of the national media. This raises important questions about both the future of these activist groups as well as how key media outlets present debates such as this one to the public. Informed by the preceding chapters, which examine how activist groups themselves talk about the moral issues raised by capitalism, this chapter asks how the media contributes to such debates through its coverage of the discourse of corporations and the activists who may challenge them. Accordingly, in this chapter I analyze coverage of Wal-Mart in 1,242 articles sampled from the *New York Times*, the *Wall Street Journal*, and *USA Today* during 2000–2006.[5]

Of course, most Americans don't get their news from these three newspapers, and most Americans' information about Wal-Mart almost surely comes from other avenues, whether television news sources, the Internet, or their own shopping experiences. Yet SMOs like Wal-Mart Watch do count it as success when their activities earn journalistic coverage in these print sources with the highest rates of national circulation—particularly in elite newspapers like the *New York Times* (arguably the paper of record for the United

States) and the *Wall Street Journal* (the paper of record for financial reporting). Examining Wal-Mart discourse in leading print sources thus promises to tell us more about how discourse about the economy is performed and enacted at these highest levels of the public sphere. My concern in this chapter is therefore not so much to identify what discourse is most likely received among the American public, but instead to describe the kind of discourse that is produced and reproduced in key domains within the public sphere, and theorize what this means for Americans' deliberations surrounding contentious economic issues.

We have good reason to believe that the media plays a key role as a gatekeeper in shaping both the content and the quality of public discourse about market dilemmas, such as those raised by Wal-Mart and its business practices. The preeminent media sociologist Herbert Gans has written extensively about the connection between journalism and democracy, arguing that despite journalists' implicit desire to encourage democracy by informing the citizenry, news media is, in practice, too focused on politics as a means of this empowerment, and as a result pays too "little attention to the other parts of society that affect the country's democracy."[6] Chief among these exclusions, Gans argues, is a sustained investigation of the economy and the influence of economic institutions and processes on American citizens and democracy itself. This is not to say that journalists are in the pocket of corporations, or that journalists avoid the economy as a subject of news. Rather, Gans argues that a set of institutional conventions generally encourage certain *forms* of economic reporting at the expense of others that might expose more fully the hidden connections between economic and political power that serve to undermine democratic freedom. To be sure, recent developments in the economy and prominent social movements like Occupy Wall Street may challenge some of Gans's conclusions, but his general argument about economic reporting is that journalists tend to package economic stories into at least one of four frames: the funding sources of election campaigns and political lobbying; corporations' legal troubles; quantitative economic indicators such as unemployment rates, inflation, consumer confidence, and so on; and general business coverage of corporate performance and stock market earnings. Gans reasons that journalists may "believe the news audience to be uninterested in most economic news," and suggests that "economic journalists could make economic news more appealing by borrowing some leads from the folk economics with which people make sense of their personal experiences in the economy."[7]

The media historian and communications scholar Robert McChesney is even more pessimistic about the potential role of the news media in furthering economic democracy.[8] As such, he has argued that the commercial ownership of national media outlets in the United States has ultimately created a less fruitful public discourse, particularly for issues of inequality wrought by capitalism. In this for-profit news environment, McChesney argues, "the corporate sector is increasingly exempt from any sustained critical examination from a public interest perspective," although he quickly adds that providing corporate information "to the investment community, of course, is one of the main functions of the business press."[9] In other words, in an environment in which newspapers seek to both report the news and sell newspapers, media outlets are less prone to be critical of the same market system that determines their ultimate fate; therefore, "as commercial journalism almost always stays within the parameter of mainstream opinion, the tenor of journalism has become less conciliatory toward ideas critical of capitalism and the 'free market' and less receptive of ideas laudatory of social spending, poor people's social movements, and regulation of business."[10] In this view, journalists are predisposed to write about the economy in ways that ultimately favor the existing economic order.

The Wal-Mart controversy of the mid-2000s offers a useful test case for exploring just how the national media covers economic critiques launched by SMOs like Wal-Mart Watch in their attempt to reform the world's largest corporation. As the preceding chapters have argued, the backstage discourse of these SMOs does attempt to create the discourse "from the perspective of employees and consumers" that Gans hopes to see reflected in media coverage. At the same time, Wal-Mart is a powerful corporation that clearly enters this media debate with a wealth of resources, financial and otherwise, at its disposal in telling its story to the press. Can groups like Wal-Mart Watch succeed in having their positions proclaimed and reiterated in elite national newspapers? And how does media coverage potentially change and redact the arguments that social actors make in "backstage," social movement venues when journalists write about the controversy in the public sphere? The answers to these questions promise not only to tell us more about the outcome of the Wal-Mart debate, but also to reveal larger conclusions about the national media and how it discusses these different dimensions of inequality in a capitalistic society.

## Claims-Making in the Public Sphere

The first question to answer in our analysis of leading national newspapers concerns whether the media even takes notice of economically progressive movements such as those created by Wal-Mart Watch. Can progressive

*Table 6.1. Descriptive statistics of variables in media article analysis (N=1,242)*

|  | 2000–2004 | 2005–2006 |
|---|---|---|
| Total number of articles | 606 | 636 |
| Speakers' claims | 667 | 951 |
| Wal-Mart reps | 248 (37%) | 4II (43%) |
| Civic group leaders | 32 (5%) | 123 (13%) |
| Industry analysts | 134 (20%) | 175 (18%) |
| Others | 253 (38%) | 242 (25%) |

Note: Due to rounding, percentages do not add up to I00.

groups like this earn attention in national newspapers, particularly in light of the capitalistic bias often attributed to national media? Answering this question requires that we explore both *who* gets covered in national news—in other words, whose claims journalists include or repeat in their stories—as well as *what* these stories cover. To evaluate both of these aspects of newspapers' content, I coded the frequency of different kinds of speakers' claims in stories about Wal-Mart for all years of the sample, from 2000 to 2006. Table 6.1 summarizes the descriptive statistics for claims of speakers reported in this sample.

A quick look at the percentages of different kinds of speakers' claims suggests that Wal-Mart's critics garnered increasing attention in the media between 2000–2004 and 2005–2006. First, the *New York Times*, the *Wall Street Journal*, and *USA Today* clearly devoted more coverage to Wal-Mart in 2005–2006, with the volume of coverage per year in 2005–2006 increasing more than twofold relative to each year in the period 2000–2004. These years also saw increases in the proportion of claims made in this coverage by both representatives of Wal-Mart and civic group leaders. Although not all civic group leaders are representing WMW (or even progressive activists necessarily), this change suggests that a growing discourse about Wal-Mart was indeed occurring during this time period, especially when compared to the years prior to the founding of WMW in 2005: of the claims made by speakers quoted in articles sampled in the years 2005–2006, 13% were made by representatives from civic organizations, as compared to 5% made by civic groups in the years 2000–2004. A slightly smaller portion of the claims reported in news stories came from industry analysts (those experts who evaluate things like Wal-Mart's stock performance and growth strategies). Wal-Mart's own representatives also found more frequent representation in media stories, with the percentage of claims increasing slightly from 37% to 43% by

2005–2006. Most important, these findings demonstrate that representatives from civic groups like Wal-Mart Watch did indeed succeed in getting more airtime in the press; the time period witnessed more coverage for activists both large and small who seek to have a voice in national debates about Wal-Mart and its role in civic life. If we think of discourse in terms of the range of voices involved in a discussion, these findings show that the years 2005–2006 incorporated more contributions to this civil discourse.

Yet we should also ask a related question about the content of these different claims in a national conversation about Wal-Mart. Specifically, when national newspapers reported the claims made by Wal-Mart representatives as well as civic group leaders, what was the content of their coverage? Table 6.2 examines the changing content of claims made by Wal-Mart representatives and by civic group leaders during this seven-year period, with particular attention to four key areas: mentions of public pressure or image problems for Wal-Mart, concerns about the environment, references to workers' issues, and allusions to larger market processes.

As table 6.2 illustrates, the content of discourse about Wal-Mart among these two groups of speakers has changed in some ways and remained constant in others. In particular, these claims appear to have been particularly

*Table 6.2. Changing content of speaker' claims in media article analysis (N=1,242)*

|  | 2000–2004 | 2005–2006 |
|---|---|---|
| Portion of claims made by WM reps that . . . | | |
| Referenced workers | 8% | 15% |
| Referenced environment | 0% | 5% |
| Referenced public image | 3% | 5% |
| Referenced market | 36% | 34% |
| Total number of claims | 248 | 411 |
| Portion of claims made by civic group leaders that . . . | | |
| Referenced workers | 31% | 27% |
| Referenced environment | 0% | 6% |
| Referenced public image | 6% | 9% |
| Referenced market | 34% | 33% |
| Total number of claims | 32 | 123 |

Note: Percentages do not add up to 100 due to the omission of some categories.

effective at injecting more discourse about workers into the media debate, particularly on the part of Wal-Mart's own representatives. This is no small accomplishment in a media environment that many allege has become increasingly inhospitable to the concerns of the left, particularly organized labor.[11] Moreover, although civic groups' claims concerned workers in roughly equal proportions between 2000–2004 and 2005–2006, the proportion of Wal-Mart representatives' claims that referenced workers' issues nearly doubled during this same period. This period clearly inculcated not just more voices from civil society, but also more talk about certain key issues, like labor.

Accordingly, the environment also earned increasing mention in claims as covered by the media; however, both groups appear to have referenced the environment in roughly equal proportions—not at all in 2000–2004, and in about 5% of their claims in 2005–2006. We could interpret this as another success for progressives: although the portion of claims that concern these topics is still quite small, they succeeded not only in infusing national newspapers with the voices of civic activists on both environmental and workers' issues, they also elicited a similar movement among conservative spokespersons, who reference the environment in increasing proportions and devoted more of their claims, proportionally, to issues faced by Wal-Mart's workforce. Finally, examining the changing content of claims over time shows that speakers quoted in newspapers devoted a slightly increased portion of their claims to concerns about Wal-Mart's public image, although civic groups did this more often than did Wal-Mart's own spokespersons. Civic group leaders' claims in 2005–2006, for example, referenced the retailer's public image almost 10% of the time, compared to 5% of the time for those speaking to the media as formal representatives of Wal-Mart.

What remains largely unchanged, however, is the proportion of claims that reference market processes, such as market competition, Wal-Mart's market influence, or the introduction of new goods and services into the marketplace. Across both groups of speakers and both periods of media coverage, about one-third of all claims reported in the media have to do with economistic matters. Thus it might be said that during the mid-2000s, SMOs critical of Wal-Mart witnessed some notable changes in the content of discourse about Wal-Mart, in that coverage during the heightened controversy made significantly greater mention of workers and devoted slightly more attention to the environment and Wal-Mart's public image. At the same time, this did not result in less discourse about Wal-Mart's market activities—this portion of the discourse as presented in the media remains virtually unchanged.

Narrating Wal-Mart Watch

Of course, these changes cannot be directly attributed to Wal-Mart Watch; other notoriously public forms of censure plagued Wal-Mart during this period and likely contributed to increased journalistic reporting on issues such as workers' rights. How then does Wal-Mart Watch succeed in disseminating its particular narrative about Wal-Mart's role in the global marketplace? Within the narrative structures of economic reporting, how does a progressive group like WMW succeed in telling its story to the press? As Ferree and colleague have noted, SMOs consistently aim to have "their" version of the story reproduced in the national media, and count it as success when their claims are picked up and disseminated to a broader audience. As such, the preceding discussion of the content of journalistic coverage of Wal-Mart does not necessarily tell us everything we need to know about the success of Wal-Mart Watch in earning recognition in larger spheres of discourse. After all, only a minority of these newspaper articles explicitly mentions Wal-Mart Watch or its United Food and Commercial Workers–funded counterpart, Wake-Up Wal-Mart. Although these organizations almost certainly played some role in changing the content of journalistic coverage of Wal-Mart, discerning their exact impact is much more difficult, given that other events—a growing environmental movement that placed Wal-Mart in its sights, several high-profile class action lawsuits pending against the company, and so on— were also taking place simultaneously. Therefore, we can get a better idea of how key media outlets covered the Wal-Mart debate by paying close analytical attention to the small subset of forty-six articles that explicitly mention Wal-Mart Watch in 2005–2006. Although these are not the only ways that Wal-Mart Watch attempted to reach the general public, studying the ways the *New York Times*, the *Wall Street Journal*, and *USA Today* frame the activities of Wal-Mart Watch can tell us more about *how* these national newspapers convey the story of Wal-Mart's critics in these elite spheres of speech. In other words, how do these newspapers cover WMW itself? And in doing so, what terms, metaphors, and narratives did journalists adopt to describe this controversy?

These questions are important because the *form* of journalistic coverage can be every bit as important as the *content* of the stories; how knowledge is communicated in newspaper stories shapes how those stories create a given portrait of empirical events. In his analysis of economic reporting, for instance, Gerald Suttles finds that journalistic reporting on market activities tends to coalesce around distinct metaphors that frame the economy itself in a particular way. For instance, during the 1980s the most prominent metaphor for the economy was that of a "machine," in which "the economy does things largely on its own, relying upon its internal guidance and self-regulation."[12] A second metaphor, that of medical emergency, also appears in journalistic reporting on economic matters, particularly when the economy is in need of some kind of intervention to "revive" sluggish growth in times of weakness or strain.[13] Such metaphors do more than simply represent reality, however—they also affect our ability to apprehend that reality. Language represents a fundamental aspect of cognition, and a long literature in the sociology of knowledge emphasizes the correspondence between socially constructed packages of meaning and mental structures of psychological cognition. Accordingly, Suttles argues that earlier warnings of financial collapse that began in 2008 were indeed present in the news, but ultimately went unnoticed in part because the new metaphors were not the ones key policy makers were accustomed to looking for. Against the earlier metaphors of "machine" and "medical emergency," the more recent financial crisis suggests a shift to the fundamental metaphor of an "information system" beset with "illness" in the form of "toxic assets" that spread "virally."[14] As a result, key industry analysts' warnings may have been ineffective because they did not coincide cognitively with the default assumption of looking at the system through a different metaphor. As Mark Jacobs explains, "Although the press covered the contrarian warnings of Buffett, Volcker, and Soros, among others, the warnings could not gain public traction because not just their substance but also their mnemonic frames were too dissonant from the emergent practice. We could not see the impending malfunctions in part because we were looking for problems of a natural or mechanical sort."[15]

In studying the coverage of Wal-Mart Watch in national media outlets, my research suggests that these sources overwhelming adopt the metaphor of *politics* as the narrative through which to relate this controversy. Here I use the term "narrative" to mean a representation of experience that places events in sequence through the telling of a story, typically offering a resolution to complicating action.[16] In other words, a narrative is a retelling of events in a temporal sequence—a plot with a beginning, middle, and end—in which the story is propelled forward through the actions of specific actors, often in the established literary forms of protagonists, villains, and heroes. In writing about Wal-Mart and the growing controversy surrounding the retailer in the mid-2000s, national newspapers might have chosen other metaphors through which to convey these events—for instance, a historical framework that drew comparisons between earlier populist movements and the growing criticism surrounding Wal-Mart. Another metaphor might have been the "machine" metaphor identified by Suttles, in which critics like Wal-Mart Watch are attempting to tinker with key workings of a global market system, as WMW frequently declared its intentions to urge Wal-Mart to "set a better example" throughout its global supply chain, which would presumably lead other companies in the global marketplace to follow suit.

Yet the predominant metaphor for this controversy that I find in all three newspapers is one of political struggle; this metaphor is also set within a narrative structure that includes common characters, complicating action, and, eventually, a resolution. In this case, I find that the "debate" over Wal-Mart itself thus becomes a form of complicating action, and actors like WMW clearly play a starring role in this recounting of events. And at first glance, this would seem to be a victory for WMW, because the organization's own framing of its mission tends to emphasize politically charged dimensions of its activities—such as state-based legislative reforms around employer-sponsored health care, and the generalized notion of grassroots action practiced by citizen activists. As I have argued in the preceding chapters, Wal-Mart Watch tends to address its arguments to an audience constructed as primarily citizens, taxpayers, and activists. Moreover, WMW emphasizes the needs and perspectives of larger groups of social actors who have allegedly been harmed by Wal-Mart's retail practices, such as women, African Americans, and small business owners. The political metaphor, therefore, would initially appear to be one favored by these activists themselves, so seeing this form of framing reproduced in national media outlets should represent a kind of victory for Wal-Mart's critics.

However, I contend that this particular telling of the story turns out to work against progressive activists, even though their politicized, grassroots-movement style of critique is very close to the politicized metaphor that the media eventually selects in its rendering of events. This is due to several factors, among them the fact that in telling this story, journalists tend to simplify this back-and-forth struggle as one that generally pits the group-based category of Wal-Mart's workers against the larger constituency of consumers themselves; this particular narrative does little to link the needs of workers as such with their purchasing power as consumers, a chasm that allows Wal-Mart ample room to exploit this politicized narrative for their own political gain. In effect, Wal-Mart and its representatives can rejoinder, "They're for politics and special interests [read: labor unions], while we're on the side of the great mass of consumers." Further, the introduction of the complicating action of a debate also allows—even encourages—the interpretation of Wal-Mart's reactions to its critics as heroic transformations that render Wal-Mart the embattled hero in a story with a happy ending.

*Political Metaphor*

One way that the journalistic reporting about Wal-Mart Watch adopts the metaphor of political struggle comes through the repeated use of the construct of "debate" itself to describe Wal-Mart Watch and its desire to challenge the giant retailer. In the very first article mentioning Wal-Mart Watch in the *New York Times*, for instance, the stage is set with the following opening paragraph (emphases added):

> With most of Wal-Mart's workers earning less than $19,000 a year, a number of community groups and lawmakers have recently teamed up with labor unions in *mounting an intensive campaign* aimed at prodding Wal-Mart into paying its 1.3 million employees higher wages.[17]

After describing Wal-Mart Watch's full-page advertisement of April 20, 2005, and referencing two other high-profile moments of criticism, the story continues:

> Among workers at Wal-Mart's 3700 stores across the United States, *the debate is also heating up.*

The *New York Times* account goes on to narrate the back-and-forth format of a debate by offering quotes from two different Wal-Mart employees, one who is grateful for her Wal-Mart job that pays $9.43 an hour, and another who believes he is underpaid. This back-and-forth framework—in which Wal-Mart's critics have their say, and Wal-Mart issues a rejoinder—continues throughout the article, until the story's author declares, "The debate is far from over." Accordingly, the article concludes with the standard "give both sides" model by quoting two Wal-Mart workers, one who says simply, "They don't pay a living wage," followed by another who praises the company and concludes the article with the words, "As soon as I heard about this store opening, I jumped. It's perfect for me right now."

The "giving both sides" model of journalistic writing certainly encourages this kind of framing. Coupled with words that signal political processes—the idea of an "intensive campaign," a debate that "is heating up" and is "far from over"—the political narrative is easily accessible. Moreover, the actual people involved in the controversy (both among WMW and at Wal-Mart itself), and the tactics they employ as a result, are imported directly from political operations. Thus this politicized form of journalistic coverage emphasizes this dimension of the controversy, which serves to further develop this politicized model of economic reporting. For instance, a front-page *New York Times* article adopted the political metaphor in a particularly pronounced way with the headline "A New Weapon for Wal-Mart: A War Room."[18] The article begins by describing the scene inside a "stuffy, window-less room" where "veterans of the 2004 Bush and Kerry presidential campaigns sit, stand and pace around six plastic folding tables," surrounded by half-eaten snacks, laptops and cell phones, and a TV in the corner. The story's author then interjects:

> A scene from a campaign war room? Well, sort of. It is a war room inside the headquarters of Wal-Mart, the giant discount retailer that hopes to sell a new, improved image to reluctant consumers. Wal-Mart is taking a page from the modern political playbook. Under fire from well-organized opponents who have hammered the retailer with criticisms of its wages, health insurance and treatment of workers, Wal-Mart has quietly recruited former presidential advisers, including Michael K. Deaver, who was Ronald Reagan's image-meister, and Leslie Dach, one of Bill Clinton's media consultants, to set up a rapid-response public relations team in Arkansas.

If journalists who cover Wal-Mart Watch for the country's leading newspapers adopt a politicized frame of reference to describe the controversy, they clearly do so in part because the starring characters in this story are individuals who once played leading roles in national political contests.

Sociologists invoke the "neoinstitutional" school of organizational analysis to explain why we observe this kind of similarity across organizations and their respective fields of activity. For instance, scholars have asked why different kinds of organizations have so many rules and structures in common—both public and private schools, for example, generally seat students at desks, assign work to be completed at home, and award letter grades of *A–F* as a method of evaluation. One answer to this question emphasizes the norms of professionalization that are conveyed to people in positions of leadership, who, in turn, act in similar ways even when working in different organizations.[19] For instance, to continue with the example of educational systems, prospective teachers must take courses in education departments taught by education specialists who share a common discourse and training. When teachers enter classrooms, they take these common skills and approaches with them into bureaucracies that have developed similar assumptions about the "best" and "most appropriate" ways of doing things. Innovation is stifled, and the result is a set of organizations that look and act in increasingly similar ways.

The narrative of Wal-Mart Watch that I find in the journalistic record suggests that this kind of professional diffusion has indeed helped to politicize the Wal-Mart debate. For instance, a 2006 *Wall Street Journal* story notes that both Wal-Mart Watch and Wake-Up Wal-Mart "are top-heavy with former Democratic operatives from the 2004 presidential campaigns of John Kerry and Howard Dean."[20] Later in the year, another story explained

> If Mr. Scott, the chief executive of Wal-Mart Stores, Inc. seems like he's running for office, it's no accident. For the last 15 months, the Edelman public-relations firm, led by seasoned political operatives, has been directing a campaign it calls "Candidate Wal-Mart." The goal: Rescue the battered image of the world's largest retailer.[21]

The tactics described hail directly from the political campaigns in which individuals like Deaver and Dach had previously worked:

> In their "Candidate Wal-Mart" Pitch, Messrs. Dach and Deaver of Edelman described a campaign with all the trappings of a U.S. presidential bid. A war room of publicists would respond quickly to attacks or adverse news. Operatives would be assigned to drum up popular support for Wal-Mart via Internet blogs and grass-roots initiatives. Skeptical outside groups, such as environmentalists, would be recruited to team up with Wal-Mart. Edelman won and quickly put its plan into practice, with three dozen staffers working on the account in Washington, D.C., and Bentonville.[22]

In light of these approaches and the professionals directing them, it's not surprising that Wal-Mart even briefly adopted a plan to expand voter registration among its employees in the fall of 2006, an action that prompted Wal-Mart Watch to respond by explicitly pitting "politics" against the allegedly more lasting forms of change that the organization sought to bring about through its campaign against the retailer. Quoting Nu Wexler, a WMW spokesman, a *Wall Street Journal* article concluded with Wexler's words on behalf of his organization: "Wal-Mart's problems with health care, wages and gender discrimination go beyond politics, and they have the potential to last well beyond the 2006 and 2008 election cycle."[23]

Yet even as WMW attempted to tag Wal-Mart itself with the negative associations of "playing politics," much of the political metaphor in this smaller body of articles stems from references to WMW's union-based funding. Thus the political metaphor of national newspapers' coverage of WMW further develops this presentation of the Wal-Mart debate by emphasizing

Wal-Mart Watch's ties to organized labor. Sometimes this comes from adopting the words of Wal-Mart's own spokespeople, as when the *New York Times*
repeats Lee Scott's claim that "a coalition of labor unions and others are
spending $25 million to do whatever they have to do to damage this com-
pany."[24] Of course, unions need not necessarily be framed as political entities,
but the political dimensions of union funding are underscored throughout
these articles, as when Wal-Mart's Sarah Clark is quoted when responding to
criticisms about the company's health care programs, saying, "This is just the
latest negative attack from Washington union leaders."[25] Further, the mon-
iker extends beyond Wal-Mart's own sound bites. The following examples
are typical of the ways national newspapers present Wal-Mart Watch in their
reporting (emphases added):

> Wal-Mart's community activist and *organized labor critics* said the envi-
> ronmental goals failed to address what they said were the company's most
> pressing problems.[26]

> Wal-Mart opponents gave the company's effort a mixed grade. "They are to
> be commended for presenting negative research," says Tracy Sefl, spokes-
> woman for Wal-Mart Watch, an activist group that is among the retailer's
> most vocal critics and is *funded by groups including the Service Employees
> International Union*.[27]

> "The so-called Bank of Wal-Mart has been dealt another heavy blow," says
> *union-backed* Wal-Mart Watch.[28]

> Wal-Mart Watch, *a group backed by unions* and foundations that is press-
> ing Wal-Mart to enhance its wages and benefits.[29]

This "union-funded" tagline is reminiscent of Working Families for Wal-
Mart's refrain (discussed in the preceding chapters) about Wal-Mart's critics
being mere servants of a special interest group seeking more dues for its narrowly defined cause. While such constructs are communicating something
about empirical reality—after all, Wal-Mart Watch did receive significant
union-based sources of funding—I argue that this narrative ultimately weakens progressive claims by connecting them to the larger domain of special
interest politics, in this case the goals and aims of "union-funded" groups that
presumably would seek to organize Wal-Mart's workers for their own gains.

Moreover, emphasizing the role of organized labor in the Wal-Mart opposition also fits into an ideological categorization that emerges in this media

discourse, where the debate becomes one that pits Wal-Mart workers against consumers. Some of Wal-Mart's critics had initially worked hard to present a message that linked workers and consumers, as when the *New York Times* quoted William McDonough of the UFCW as saying, "Henry Ford made sure he paid his workers enough so that they could afford to buy his cars. . . . Wal-Mart is doing the polar opposite of Henry Ford. Wal-Mart brags about how its low prices help poor Americans, but its low wages are helping increase the number of Americans in poverty."[30] But the later discourse produced in the media is one that rarely links the categories of worker and consumer in this way—a failure that mirrors the separate core categories produced by the respective SMOs in backstage spheres of discourse.

Just as Wal-Mart Watch emphasizes the core identity categories of citizens and taxpayers, and Wal-Mart Inc. focuses on "average working families," these categories are rarely connected in the national newspaper coverage of Wal-Mart Watch itself. Instead, the "giving both sides" journalistic model actually helps to reify these opposing camps, particularly in highlighting Wal-Mart's benefits for consumers in contrast to the problems faced by its workers, as in the following example:

> Wal-Mart's rapid expansion made it a lightning rod in some corners of labor and the political left for a long list of grievances against big business. Wal-Mart and its supporters argue that the big retailer offers an enormous boon to Americans—particularly lower-income consumers—by driving down the price of household goods, appliances and thousands of other products.[31]

In this instance, for example, the *Wall Street Journal* emphasizes the contours of the debate as being about the needs of workers (who see Wal-Mart's success as a "lightning rod" for other issues affecting labor) versus the consumption needs of a larger group of "Americans" and especially "lower-income consumers." Likewise, Lee Scott, as quoted in the *New York Times*, emphasizes the company's commitment to and support among lower-income American consumers, saying, "Wal-Mart's focus has been on lower income and lower-middle income consumers. . . . In the last four years or so, with the price of fuel being what it is, that customer has had the most difficult time. The upper-end customer got a tremendous number of tax breaks about four years ago. They have been doing very well in this economy."[32] Thus Wal-Mart's decision to pursue more energy-efficient trucks along with other environmentally friendly goals can be easily framed in terms of this divide, such that Lee Scott can declare that "embracing energy-conscious and environmentally conscious goals will help both the company's bottom line and its customer's needs."[33] Likewise, this framework can even allow Lee Scott to support congressional efforts to raise the minimum wage not on the grounds that it would help Wal-Mart's *workers*, but instead by saying "We can see first hand at Wal-Mart how many of our customers are struggling to get by."[34] Further, because Wal-Mart seeks to develop support among the consumers who keep it in business, and cultivates its audience as "average working families" who need the store for their consumption, Wal-Mart can more successfully combine these categories of worker and consumer on its own terms—terms that refer only vaguely to the struggles of "working families" whose workers are not Wal-Mart workers, and whose struggles are sequestered away from the impersonal forces of the global economy and interpreted primarily in terms of their consequences for the family.

This particular mode of framing—which generally pits workers against consumers, and when combining the two categories tends to favor a conservative stance on these issues—stems from the political metaphor, and is ultimately an ironic victory for a more conservative, pro-business story. With these two "camps" presented as "the two sides," the larger narrative of "the debate" itself becomes a form of complicating action. Within this particular narrative construction, Wal-Mart can actually emerge as an embattled hero, a company that does the right thing in response to its critics. In this larger narrative of politicized struggle, the attacks of critics like Wal-Mart Watch actually became an early point of plot development in the larger arc of a developing narrative, as when a 2005 *New York Times* article declared, "For years, unions hurled little more than insults at the chain. But over the last year, two small groups—Wal-Mart Watch and Wake Up Wal-Mart—set up shop in Washington with the goal of waging the public relations equivalent of guerilla warfare against the company."[35] These descriptions of the actions of Wal-Mart's critics play a key role in the developing story of the controversy surrounding the retailer, and further solidify the representation of this story *as a story*, where "events become meaningful because of their placement in a narrative."[36] As a result, this depiction of the controversy over Wal-Mart invites readers to consider the debate as a dramatized version of struggle between Wal-Mart's critics on one hand, and the retailer itself. Stories such as these emphasize the novelty of Wal-Mart's more recent critics, whose actions have moved beyond the "little more than insults" that unions had formerly "hurled" at the retailer. Here the plot thickens: although Wal-Mart had long been a target of labor unions' designs for organizing the service sector, these newer critics have successfully "stung" the retailer and mounted "an intensive campaign" in response.[37]

Such a narrative ironically functions to paint Wal-Mart itself as a kind of victim—a questionable rendering of events, to be sure, but one that none-theless allows the story to take a new turn. Francesca Polletta has written extensively about the role of victim narratives in protest movements and political activism.[38] Focusing on narratives of victimization in domestic violence cases, for instance, Polletta paradoxically observes that while vic-tim narratives are not always successful in garnering broader support for a social movement, they simultaneously need not always be disempower-ing. In her words, "Familiar criticisms [of victimhood] underestimate both the advantages and the dangers of telling stories of victimization. To claim oneself a victim is not necessarily to trade agency for passivity. The vic-tims of social injustice have sometimes cast themselves as political irritants rather than supplicants and as tutors of moral uplift rather than objects of pity."[39] Although Polletta is writing largely about women's narratives in legal trials and court proceedings, this same principle may be applied to the ways an organization—in this case, Wal-Mart—is cast as a kind of vic-tim in newspaper reporting about its dialogue with critics—in this case, Wal-Mart Watch.

Within this narrative, when reporters for leading national newspapers describe the complicating action of Wal-Mart's critics' growing successes, the story begins to frame Wal-Mart as a somewhat victimized protagonist beset with a new challenge. Therefore, groups like Wal-Mart Watch have placed Wal-Mart "under assault as never before," the beleaguered retail giant has "come under withering criticism," and it must therefore respond and "com-bat critics."[40] In the format of a story placed within the larger metaphor of politicized struggle, Wal-Mart plays the role of an errant but still-good-deep-down hero who must institute some kind of change in response. As a result, this narrative of potential victimization ultimately invites Wal-Mart to play the role of an embattled consumers' hero—the large and sometimes wayward global retailer that has successfully responded to its critics on behalf of its consumers' needs.

In an October 2005 *New York Times* article, for instance, the story predict-ably begins with the complicating action and moves very quickly to its reso-lution: "Wal-Mart, which has long been criticized for the benefits it offers to its workers, is introducing a cheaper health insurance plan, with monthly premiums as low as $11, that the company hopes will greatly increase the number of its employees who can afford coverage."[41] Similarly, in April 2006 (a year after Wal-Mart Watch's founding), a series of articles covering WMW began to document Wal-Mart's attempts to respond to some of its alleged worst offenses:

Mr. Scott called Wal-Mart a company "in transformation" and offered what a year ago would have seemed an unthinkably long list of changes under way at the company, the nation's largest retailer. In just the last six months, the company has expanded health insurance to the children of part-time workers, committed to sweeping reductions in energy use and is planning to support local businesses, including competitors, near its proposed urban stores.[42]

Trying to become a leader on two issues that have bedeviled it for decades, Wal-Mart Stores is developing an extensive program to teach its 1.3 million employees in the United States how to take better care of themselves and the environment, people briefed on the plans said yesterday.[43]

"Leslie [Dach] has been a part of our transformation over the last year," Mr. Scott said. "He brings new perspective, diverse talents and tremendous expertise to his role as a member of our strategic and executive teams. I look forward to his continued involvement as we transform our business for the future." In a brief interview, Mr. Dach said he was joining Wal-Mart because he has been impressed by what he says is the company's transformation, especially on issues such as sustainability. "On the big issues, Wal-Mart has said government can't do it alone," Mr. Dach said. "Wal-Mart wants and will be part of the solution, and I find that intriguing."[44]

If the story renders Wal-Mart's critics as the agents of complicating action, then the narrative structure encourages some form of resolution; in this case, the resolution comes in the form of Wal-Mart's "transformation" that has launched what previously "would have seemed an unthinkably long list" of reforms. If Wal-Mart Watch and its campaign represents the complicating action in the larger process of plot development, then Wal-Mart, which is the bigger and in many ways more "newsworthy" object of reporting, must become the eventual protagonist. And at the end of the story, the protagonist saves the day.

Leslie Dach's claim that "on the big issues, Wal-Mart has said government can't do it alone," noted above, also suggests a related finding: in this larger narrative arc, Wal-Mart can successfully frame the controversy surrounding its workers, business model, and general role in a globalized market economy as being about a kind of special interest politics versus rank-and-file consumers. An April 2006 article about Wal-Mart's change illustrates this point very well. After describing some of the key changes Wal-Mart had recently introduced, *New York Times* reporter Michael Barbaro poses the question: "Why so much change so quickly?" Barbaro continues:

> Wal-Mart is loathe to credit its critics with influencing the company, but Mr. Scott's message of change—he used the word "transformation" five times in his speech—coincides with the one-year anniversary of the formation of two union-backed groups, Wal-Mart Watch and Wake Up Wal-Mart, which have helped turn the company into a social, political and economic issue.[45]

The article also considered the Fair Share Health Care law passed in Maryland (it was later overturned in U.S. district court), and Barbaro quoted Lee Scott saying the following about that outcome:

> "It is going to be tough to legislate Wal-Mart out of a community," Mr. Scott said at the close of a two-day media conference here, just a few miles from the company's headquarters in Bentonville, in northwest Arkansas. . . . Power over Wal-Mart's future, Mr. Scott said, "is not with the legislature," but with more than 100 million Americans who shop at the company's 3,500 stores every week.[46]

Examining the Wal-Mart debate through the lens of articles that mention Wal-Mart Watch thus reveals a narrative that ultimately empowers consumers, pitting the store's hardworking, penny-pinched shoppers against the politicized entities of labor unions, state legislatures, and special interest politics.

In sum, national newspapers adopt the politicized narrative of Wal-Mart's critics, but they do so in such a way that the struggle is framed as not just between Wal-Mart and its opponents, but also between the rights and needs of workers as represented by organized labor, and the desires and expectations of American customers. Wal-Mart Watch may have succeeded in seeing its particular method of framing become more prevalent in the news—a politicized, guerilla-warfare-style struggle with a key emblem of global capitalism—but these terms may be interpreted as paradoxically favoring Wal-Mart because the selection of workers as a category demands a corresponding locus of conflict, which turns out to be the consumer. As a result, we see few linkages between the categories of worker and consumer, and thus little in the way of a discourse that might successfully create a new portrayal of the interdependent identities of workers and consumers, shoppers and citizens. The narrative of political conflict is ready-made, but far removed from the interdependent needs and expectations of families and citizens, workers and consumers.

## Conclusion

What does this analysis tell us about how the national media creates a larger discourse about economic issues? First, examining the content of claims made by key activists as presented in this media sample suggests that the most notable change between 2000 and 2006 concerns the increasing discussion of workers' issues among Wal-Mart's own spokespeople. The environment also received more coverage during this period by activists and Wal-Mart representatives alike, but the increased concern for workers is a particularly notable change since, as demonstrated in earlier chapters, the rationalized category of the worker lies close to the heart of Wal-Mart Watch's discursive strategies. Although we cannot isolate the impact of Wal-Mart Watch itself on this shift, the general environment of 2005–2006 was indeed one in which workers' issues received comparatively greater mention in leading national newspapers.

Studying how these national news outlets cover Wal-Mart Watch itself in a smaller body of articles reveals a number of interesting findings—about both the coverage of Wal-Mart Watch as well as the larger narrative of politicized economic debate into which this particular controversy falls. As I have argued above, the elites involved in this debate on both sides hail from national political undertakings, and the resultant emphasis on political features (e.g., "war rooms" and "campaigns") are borne out in their discourse. But this political metaphor also has other, more subtle dimensions. In particular, I have argued that the political metaphor that guides news reporting on Wal-Mart Watch ultimately weakens the group's presentation in the press, because it allows Wal-Mart Watch to be linked to the tainted domain of "special interest politics," as a mere extension of labor unions that seek to line their own coffers with increased dues paid by potential new members. Wal-Mart itself can thus become the hero that stands up for "everyday American consumers" in the face of this elite-driven agenda.

Within this narrative, Wal-Mart has a surprising ability to present itself as something of a victim. Within the confines of *the story* itself, Wal-Mart Watch's criticisms of the retailer become a form of complicating action that sets the stage for Wal-Mart's eventual transformation; the sheer size and scope of Wal-Mart lends itself to being framed as the protagonist, with a starring role as the wayward retailer turned reformed hero, which frames the company's reforms as a way of furthering its long-standing mission to empower consumers and enhance their lives through consumption. Workers ultimately become the adversary here, positioned against the low costs that the store hopes to be able to maintain on behalf of its shoppers.

This case study also suggests some of the hidden pitfalls and enduring challenges endemic to progressive critiques of market entities and processes. Critiquing a giant multinational corporation like Wal-Mart will always be an uphill battle, if only because such entities posses such an asymmetry of power and influence. Wal-Mart is narrated not just by these national newspapers, but also via advertising on television, in print, and as an actual embodied experience of consumption for the masses of shoppers who pass through its doors on any given day. Groups like Wal-Mart Watch face so much organizational asymmetry that their attempts to pin lasting criticisms to the retailer might initially look like little more than a fool's errand. In this light, the fact that the group received so much notice in leading national newspapers (which frequently cited the group's campaign as a motivation for Wal-Mart to institute some key changes to its health care policies and environmental initiatives) is nothing short of remarkable.

At the same time, I wish to suggest that progressive market criticisms, especially those that target a particular entity or organization, face additional asymmetries that are more cognitive than organizational or institutional. Just as I argued in chapter 3 that both sides of this debate frame Wal-Mart in personified ways—as an entity that alternatively "reaches out" to consumers or "bullies its way" through small town America—this journalistic coverage also adopts some of these person-based terms in describing Wal-Mart as "stung" or "beleaguered" by criticism, being "under assault" and eventually experiencing a "transformation" to "become a leader" on things like environmental sustainability and worker health and wellness. This represents yet another iteration of corporate personhood, in which the corporation can enjoy all the benefits of its power and market influence while still embodying traits that can be exploited to claim a kind of submissive status as withering victim. In this case, even small changes at Wal-Mart—in part because they seem so unthinkable in light of the company's long-standing problems with environmental activists and employee benefits—can be framed as laudable metamorphoses.

My concern here is not to denigrate or downplay these reforms on Wal-Mart's part; things like expanding health insurance access for employees and promoting fuel-efficient trucks are laudable initiatives, to be sure. Rather, I want to emphasize the subtle cognitive dimensions of this form of storytelling; these less-apparent aspects of the journalistic narrative—which ultimately favor Wal-Mart as a protagonist beset by challenge and seeking pardon through its eventual "transformation"—represent yet another way in which the corporation can capitalize on the notion of personhood to exercise rhetorical power, in this case as an unlikely "victim" at the hands of "special interest politics." Groups like labor unions, or SMOs like Wal-Mart Watch, cannot claim this image in quite the same way, which paradoxically advantages the corporation in a David versus Goliath kind of contest.

The media narrative of Wal-Mart Watch also reifies the camps prioritized in each body of discourse as I have described them in the preceding chapters. Most important, the triumphant category championed by Wal-Mart throughout the narrative is that of the consumer, such that Wal-Mart Inc. can actually issue statements in support of a higher minimum wage on the grounds that it would help Wal-Mart shoppers! As I discuss in the next and final chapter, creating more cognitive linkages between workers and consumers—two categories that ultimately emerge as generally hostile and contradictory in this analysis of the media—will be crucial to any kind of lasting progressive movement that seeks to fully address the inequalities wrought by the tumultuous forces of global capitalism, with Wal-Mart at the center of the storm.

7

## Moral Populism in the Twenty-First Century

As long as "the people" remain united more by what they wish to consume than by their grievances as producers, resentment of the new world order will probably not alter the centrist course of American politics. For most citizens, global capitalism is not a visceral danger but, at worst, the symbolic marker of a reality they cannot hope to control.

—Michael Kazin, *The Populist Persuasion*

The joke goes something like this: A union member, a member of the Tea Party, and a corporate CEO are sitting around a table looking at a plate that holds a dozen cookies. The CEO reaches across and takes eleven cookies, looks at the Tea Partier, and says, "Look out for that union guy, he wants a piece of your cookie." Circulated on political blogs and social networking sites in early 2011, this wry story betrays a core assumption of much progressive politics: at best, that poor and middle-class conservatives simply misunderstand reality, or at worst, that they are duped by the subversive powers of manipulation wielded by big business. The political left's seeming inability to convince middle Americans on such economic issues—particularly matters having to do with unionization and tax policy—was what led pundits like Thomas Frank to ask, in exasperation, just "what's the matter with Kansas?"[1] Middle American conservatives, Frank argued, lean Republican because they prioritize social issues—abortion and same-sex marriage, for instance—over and above their economic self-interests, which would presumably be better served by Democratic economic policies.

I believe that such views of the American political landscape fundamentally misunderstand both the empirical and the moral foundations of conservative populism. To begin with, much of Frank's argument has been tested with empirical data and found wanting. In their book *The Truth about Conservative Christians*, Andrew Greeley and Michael Hout demonstrate that the dichotomy Frank posits between "values voters" (those who prioritize conservative social issues, like restricting abortion and same-sex marriage) and "interest voters" (those who prioritize policies promising economic benefits) is much more complicated than Frank concludes. Using data from the General Social Survey, Greeley and Hout find that while conservative Christians have become somewhat more likely to vote Republican over the past three decades, class cleavages also influence Christian conservatives' voting patterns. In fact, poor and lower-middle class Christian conservatives are not more likely to vote Republican; rather, they are the *least* likely conservative Christians to say they voted for a Republican presidential candidate.[2] Instead, the likelihood of voting Republican increases for conservative Christians according to income, and higher-status people of all religious traditions are more likely to support the GOP. In other words, economic interests are not cast aside at the voting booth; both income and values affect voting patterns at the presidential level.

At the same time, however, the consensus among many observers of American political life is that Democrats are somehow unable to connect in a sustained and meaningful way with the "real Americans" who fill the aisles of Wal-Mart on Saturdays and conservative evangelical churches on Sundays. Although Frank may be mistaken about the "values voters," another part of his argument presciently describes the inadequacies of progressive language. As Frank concludes, "Democrats no longer speak to the people on the losing end of a free-market system that is becoming more brutal and more arrogant by the day."[3] Accordingly, survey evidence suggests that while the current political climate is marked by no small amount of idiosyncratic volatility, Democrats continue to lose support among lower- and middle-class whites. As of 2008, white Americans with households earning between $30,000 and $75,000 annually preferred Republicans by only about 1%; by 2011 this gap had widened to 16%.[4]

In this concluding chapter, I argue that the left's failure to connect with middle Americans on economic issues is a twin shortcoming of both organization and imagination; moreover, it is a failure nearly a century in the making that is dramatized mostly clearly in the language of progressive economic activism. In his history of American populism, Michael Kazin argues that progressives throughout the twentieth century increasingly failed to connect with middle-class Americans, whose very real economic worries were too often obscured by Democrats' prioritization of liberal social issues, only adding to the perception that Democrats were wealthy elites who couldn't fully empathize with "real Americans."[5] In the moments when Democratic candidates did attempt to address middle-class economic angst, Kazin argues that their efforts were too far removed from the kind of grassroots activism that might have infused this rhetoric with a vocabulary truly capable of resonating with the white middle class. Instead, Democrats' language "remained a strategy hatched by candidates and their consultants," which as a result "was not connected in any organic way to the 'working men and women' whose sentiments candidates ritually invoked."[6] Instead, progressives at the end of the twentieth century set their sights on a new villain in the form of American corporations that both exploited the global marketplace and abandoned American workers; for a new coalition of progressive activists, led by organized labor, "'the people' was a rich, multicultural abstraction and could only be represented as such."[7] However, this conception of "the people"—and thus, of progressives' audience—ultimately missed the mark. Kazin argues that in celebrating the worker (and concurrently denigrating the new economic order), progressive activists simply misunderstood the present reality, in which unions' power had diminished, and with it the economic fortunes of middle Americans.

This book's study of recent Wal-Mart debates helps to continue this analysis of populist politics by exploring how and why such political rhetoric succeeds or fails; in the process, I have offered an interpretive portrait of conservative economic discourse that attempts to move beyond superficial progressive interpretations that portray conservative Americans as either hoodwinked by big business or woefully unaware of their economic self-interests. Most important, a central argument of this book is that "the family" is not just a flashpoint in the culture wars—a topic to be debated with regard to same-sex marriage, the boundaries of abortion, or regulations on sexual activity and behavior. Rather, *the family is also a discursive context that shapes how conservative and progressive organizations talk about economic issues.* Understood in this way, the family is not just a moral project, but also an economic one that has deeply moral significance. To that end, Wal-Mart's own discourse emphasizes not just "the family" but "the average working family," discussing economic issues in a moral framework that brings the family and the economy together. Thus the family is a powerful rhetorical construction in economic debates precisely because so many of our everyday economic actions—most notably the ritual of consumption—take place within the bounds of this social institution.[8] A key contribution of my analysis of recent Wal-Mart debates has been to emphasize how this concept—along with the related discourses of individualism, thrift, and freedom—creates a broader moral framework for evaluating the economic dilemmas that face the American public. Resurgent populism of the sort embodied by conservatives—be they Wal-Mart's supporters or Tea Party activists—forges new connections between the institutional legacies of conservatism and free market fetishism to imbue a much older economic understanding of the family with a new moral and ideological significance. In doing so, it sanctifies the family as the core unit of economic activity, and succeeds in ways that progressive rhetoric cannot, particularly because it constructs an audience of "average working families" against the allegedly out-of-touch elites who simply cannot understand the economic realities of middle-class Americans facing an increasingly uncertain future. Accordingly, Greeley and Hout note that in both 1992 and 1996 Bill Clinton earned more votes from religious conservatives with low incomes than did either of his Republican opponents, and conclude by predicting that "to repeat Clinton's success in future elections, Democrats need to appeal to the economic needs of those Conservative Protestants who share the values announced by their leaders but who vote their families' interests on election day."[9] Understood in this way, populist rhetoric that can successfully connect with the needs and interests of voters in conjunction with their familial roles, experiences, and identities will be better able to appeal to their economic concerns.

This kind of discursive construction is fundamentally a cognitive project. Assigning different kinds of worth to persons and priorities requires social actors to distinguish between different categories (such as families and citizens) in evaluating specific practices and policies. Codes of ethics in the workplace, for example, dictate what kinds of behaviors are deemed morally acceptable between different categories of persons, such as romantic relationships between a manager and a subordinate.[10] Language dramatizes both power and priorities as they are shared between people and various social structures; as Josée Johnston has succinctly explained, "Critically-oriented discourse analysis is not simply interested in how social reality is discursively constructed, but has a particular focus on how discursive activities create, sustain, and legitimate relationships of power and privilege."[11] Thus examining worldview construction through discourse also invites questions about the power of ideas and institutions to create the enduring structures of both political and economic life.

As I have argued in the preceding chapters, the debate over Wal-Mart represents only one particular economic debate, although it offers a valuable window into understanding how moral ideas animate the political project of constructing moral visions of the market in public life. Although both sides of the Wal-Mart debate share a common moral lexicon, they prioritize its application in very different ways that have important implications for how Americans structure their public talk about contentious economic policies. Both sides conduct this debate in terms of the dialectics of individualism and community, thrift and benevolence, and freedom and fairness. Yet they apply these values in such different ways that they ultimately create two separate discursive moral frameworks. Wal-Mart's supporters prioritize the *average working family* as the main unit of reference in their discourse, and build around it a moral worldview in which the market is fair, and thus "hardworking" or "average Americans" need only equal access to its institutions to be able to benefit from its bounteous provisions. For this group of activists, the moral terms of this debate are shouldered primarily by individuals and their families, who are rhetorically cloistered from the punishing disruptions of the larger market and other institutional forms of disadvantage, such as racism, discrimination, or global outsourcing. Full participation in capitalist America—and its commonplace trope of the American Dream—is accomplished by the yin and yang of thrift and consumption, a paradox that is reconciled by Wal-Mart and its mantra of everyday low prices.

To the contrary, progressive groups like Wal-Mart Watch build a moral framework around the category of the *benevolent citizen*. To that end, they repeatedly censure Wal-Mart for its alleged selfishness and monopolistic perversion of market freedom in ways that harm larger groups in society. Wal-Mart's size and scale, for these activists, threaten various forms of freedom such that they render the marketplace inherently unfair to entire classes of people, particularly women, African Americans, and small business owners who are driven out of business by Wal-Mart's relentless bottom line. The mirror image of Wal-Mart's focus on the Gemeinschaft of family, Wal-Mart's most public detractors tend to focus on larger Gesellschaft categories such as the worker, the taxpayer, and the citizen—all of which are rationalized, collective groups deprived of revenue and freedom due to Wal-Mart's allegedly poor care and provision for its employees.

The two groups are not without similarities, of course. Both take for granted the centrality of a theoretically free market in their discussions, and even Wal-Mart Watch does not seek to dismantle capitalism as we know it. As such, Wal-Mart Watch's critique of the retailer as the world's preeminent example of capitalism does not so much seek to run Wal-Mart into the ground but to harness its massive power to use the market itself to spawn a diffusion of initiatives that the group views as desirable for the capitalist system at large: improved health benefits for employees, better working conditions for global suppliers, and protections for the environment. And both groups use person-based metaphors and talk of community in ways that prove highly contentious upon closer analysis.

Yet despite their commonalities, these discourses remain largely conflictual because of the different categories at the root of their discursive worldviews. In this way, the kinds of populist debates epitomized by Wal-Mart have much in common with the abortion debate as analyzed by Kristin Luker in her influential book *Abortion and the Politics of Motherhood*. Here, Luker argues that two different worldviews lie at the heart of the debate about the morally ambiguous status of a human fetus: the two groups don't just disagree on whether the fetus is a person endowed with human rights, but engage in a conflict that stems from the different ways each group prioritizes motherhood, sexuality, and the institution of marriage. For pro-lifers, their position revolves around a moral center that prioritizes God and divine providence, in which motherhood is a central source of meaning in women's lives, and thus sexuality and reproduction exist to serve a biological goal within the protective institution of marriage. In contrast, Luker argues that pro-choice women hold a moral worldview built on a primary belief in human ability and the primacy of reason. For these women, their status as reproductive agents is subordinated to their belief in the importance of human potential and flourishing outside the family unit, all of which are facilitated by their access to resources—particularly education and incomes—which they gain by working alongside men.[12]

Such debates illustrate both the power and conflict created by a discourse that sees the family as the core building block of economic society. Although the evidence in this book draws mostly from recent debates over Wal-Mart, I have argued that these frameworks inform other recent economic controversies as well, such as the Tea Party's call for lower taxes, the debate over health care reform, and the public outcry over the bailouts for American auto companies facing economic collapse. For economic conservatives, the importance of the family lies at the heart of a moral outlook that looks to individual effort as the means of achieving the American Dream. Not surprisingly, thrift and freedom are the primary moral values trumpeted throughout their discourse, particularly because thrift is practiced at the level of the family, and as witnessed by the enduring stories of Poor Richard, one that has a long and noble history in rags-to-riches tales played out against a backdrop of American freedom—such as the one that surrounds Wal-Mart's own patriarch, Sam Walton. For economic progressives, the family is often secondary. Although Wal-Mart Watch does make some efforts to ground its claims on behalf of workers in terms of the needs of their families, the bulk of their moral claims-making places broader societal categories at its center—particularly the needs and concerns of citizens, tax-payers, and workers, and the priorities of the larger economic system. For this group of activists, key moral values are benevolence and distributive conceptions of fairness.

## Institutionalism and Cognition in Moral Discourse

Understanding the genesis of these different rhetorical frameworks requires a careful consideration of the institutional underpinnings of the language of both progressive and conservative activists. For instance, Wal-Mart Watch was funded primarily by unions, and thus is heir to labor-infused organi-zational repertoires and approaches to solving social problems. Although organized labor groups have moved beyond the single-minded "organize Wal-Mart" plan of action, the institutional legacy of unionization still looms large in their discourse. Even when they are not explicitly noted, institutional logics exert a powerful influence on the frames and tactics that actors use in social movements.[13] Discursively, this influence appears in Wal-Mart Watch's references to the ways the retailer negatively affects collective identities, for not only workers but also citizens and taxpayers. This discourse also reflects organized labor's uneven attention to the nexus of work–family concerns,[14] particularly in light of labor's historical tendency to downplay concerns about women and families in favor of more "patriarchal" preoccupations with power and confrontational modes of action.

To be sure, unions are responding to their increasingly precarious position in the globalized economy with new attention to women and other forms of challenge, including greater attention to policies that concern families, such as health benefits, sick leave, and vacation time.[15] At the same time, the discourse produced by union-funded groups like Wal-Mart Watch suggests that the institutional legacy of the labor movement perseveres in its focus on empowering collectivities through an agenda that seeks gains primarily in terms of wages and benefits rather than family-friendly policies such as family leave and child care. Simultaneously, the legacy of unionization favors more collective forms of discourse because unions and progressive consum-ers' movements have always sought to unite individuals in collective action against powerful corporations, which, in contrast, seek to isolate workers and consumers to dilute their power and reduce their influence.

For pro-Wal-Mart activists, discourse that emphasizes the family also stems from Wal-Mart's southern roots, along with its historical legacy of agrarian patriarchy, evangelicalism, and celebration of free enterprise. For instance, the historian Bethany Moreton has chronicled how Wal-Mart's founder, Sam Walton, brought a distinctly patriarchal form of management to his early chain of discount stores, which employed male managers to supervise their female employees in ways that reinvigorated the masculinity undermined through the decline of family farming in the early twentieth century.[16] This patriarchal model of the family—men benevolently in charge, women gladly following their lead—also drew on the region's evangelical heartbeat and the emerging concept of "servant leadership," in which austere patriarchy is recast as benevolent submission to others.[17] In the context of the region's growing service economy, Moreton shows how this ideology wove religious significance into the "how may I help you?" ethos of service work—and subtly justifies employees' lack of authority and ownership in its larger economic project. The lasting legacy of this shop-floor culture came to a particularly ugly head in the *Dukes* lawsuit, in which Wal-Mart's allegedly gendered view of women as primarily domestic consumers, not economic producers, permeated all aspects of the company's approach to the management and promotion of its female employees.[18]

Understood in this way, economic dilemmas such as this one echo longstanding regional and ideological divisions between the evangelical, service-oriented Sunbelt and the manufacturing-rich legacy of the Rustbelt. Therefore, this clash represents divisions in American political life that run far deeper than just attitudes about Wal-Mart, and draw instead on very different institutional legacies within each region. Most important, the progressive rhetoric of union-led coalitions bespeaks the Northeast and Midwest's long history with organized labor, collective forms of representation, and a Democratic Party that has historically championed the rights of other marginalized groups, such as women and African Americans. In contrast, the conservative rhetoric of Wal-Mart's supporters draws on the very different legacies of suburban conservatism, evangelicalism, and the long-standing absence of unionization in service industries and "right to work" states.

In a pronounced way, this case study also points to the larger institutional legacies of the related discourses of conservatism, individualism, and free market ideology that have become increasingly intertwined in American society over the past half century. Most important, the conservative movement claims deep roots in an interrelated set of ideas about family, religion, autonomy, and individualism. The regional context of the Sunbelt—in which suburbanization and evangelicalism were often intertwined—allowed these different institutional discourses to coalesce and forge new connections among related domains.[19] In the case of Wal-Mart, the store's long-standing relationship with evangelical shoppers (not to mention the evangelical identity typically attributed to the store's founder) provides fertile ground for ideas about the family, individualism, patriotism, and entrepreneurship to cohere and become mutually reinforcing.[20] Scholars of religion, for instance, emphasize the individualistic ethos inherent in evangelicalism, which sees salvation as a personal decision that resides between the individual and Jesus Christ.[21] Accordingly, this individualistic ethos can color other views and attitudes, diverting attention away from the structural causes of economic inequality.[22]

For this reason, economic conservatives' embrace of the family may carry more "sticking power" in that it calls forth a host of other moral ideals that have implications not only for consumption (such as thrift) but also deeply held accompanying moral discourses about strength, self-reliance, and freedom. Moreover, economic discourse that places the family at its center can simultaneously construct normative models of "the family" through language about consumption. The narratives produced by Wal-Mart's supporters, for instance, tend to reify a certain conception of family—a married, heterosexual household with a male breadwinner. These discourses need not be explicitly acknowledged to be strong motivators of moral reasoning; such "deep frames" (or mere common sense) may undergird activists' moral messages without their explicit recognition.[23] Similarly, these deeply held moral concepts may affect the resonance of activists' discursive strategies without explicit knowledge on the part of their target audience—one may simply hear Wal-Mart's messages about helping a family "save money and live better" without fully understanding why it's morally appealing. The centrality of the family in recent social movements, not to mention our everyday experiences, make the Wal-Mart discourse even more compelling because it is rooted in this central category of social life.

Moreover, constructing an economic paradigm that begins with the family makes it moral to prioritize thrift, which also serves to render the globalizing processes that bring low prices to Wal-Mart as part of a larger, moral process of familial survival and self-determination. A moral framework built around the citizen, conversely, emphasizes larger social processes—the activities of larger market systems and democratic politics, the equal treatment of social groups, and the legal protections afforded to key social groups, like workers. This core difference helps explain why the conservative discourse seems to worry so little about the influence of larger economic disturbances—the outsourcing of jobs, for example, or declining opportunities for skilled labor in the United States—and instead frames economic upheaval in terms of familial disruption. When these tropes are frequently wedded to a conservative religious discourse of evangelicalism and its celebration of individualism, the deeper cognitive foundations of these ways of viewing the world carry even greater structuring power. In like manner, progressives' comparatively greater emphasis on workers and taxpayers fits in with a moral worldview that prioritizes the citizen: if workers receive adequate compensation from companies like Wal-Mart that are allegedly exploiting citizens and their tax revenues, the well-being of families will simply follow suit.

The media's narration of Wal-Mart Watch (and the debate it represents) as indicative of a larger struggle between workers and consumers speaks to the power of institutions to shape the key categories of public discourse. The previous chapter also described some of the challenges that groups like WMW face if they attempt to connect discourse about workers with the rich and morally saturated discourse connected to families, who enter the market first and foremost as consumers. Other contentious public issues—abortion, same-sex marriage, or recent military interventions—have more obvious connections to familial life; even critics of the war in Iraq took pains to mention the intense burden borne by military families that assumed multiple deployments as the country's armed forces experienced increasing strain. Connecting the needs of families and consumers to the rights of workers may present a greater challenge, as I argued earlier, in part because of the institutional legacy of unions' contractual rhetoric. The changing nature of the American Dream—one that more often than not requires two incomes—has meant that family life and work life face increasing compartmentaliza-tion.[24] Particularly in a cultural context that divides the realms of family and work,[25] progressives face new challenges in creating a discourse that success-fully forges such connections between economic aspects of paid work and the larger context of family well-being. As a result, many Americans seek to insulate their home and family lives from the tumultuous pressures of the workplace, which means that groups that seek to use family-based moral lan-guage to actually critique the market (rather than to celebrate consumption) face additional cognitive challenges. Debates about Wal-Mart are not unique in this regard but are rather an example of the kind of discourse that has long pervaded American life when the topic concerns consumers and consump-tion. At the same time, such discourse faces both institutional and cognitive limitations; I turn my attention to these paradoxes, along with some possi-bilities for the future, in the remainder of this chapter.

## The Potential and Limits of Civic Consumerism

Progressive populism faces an uphill battle in a political and economic cli-mate that historically tends to prioritize reducing inflation (preserving "low prices"), and in which many Americans regularly live beyond their means via readily accessible lines of credit. A large and growing group of scholars has begun wrestling with the question of how Americans might change this system through a combination of social, political, and rhetorical activism. In particular, how could both social activism and moral discourse help Americans to recognize and build on the connections that exist between our familial buying power as consumers and our social identities as workers and citizens? Historians like Meg Jacobs, for instance, would remind us that things has not always been so: the fortunes of middle-class families were once inextricably connected to a political agenda that argued not only for low prices, but also for high wages and strong "purchasing power" to accompany them.[26] This early part of the twentieth century was actually marked by strong cooperation and mutual activism among grassroots consumers, labor unions, and political parties. These coalitions sought the common goal of helping the electorate afford the consumer goods deemed necessary for a good life, creating both discourse and politics that viewed strong wage growth as essential to a successful economy.[27] However, Jacobs argues that this "purchasing power" agenda that once allied middle-class American families with organized labor has steadily declined in an increasingly globalized economy, in which Wal-Mart emerges as an example par excellence of corporations' eroding commitments to their workforce. Here, the economic fortunes of a new generation of families lie not so much in seeking higher wages for workers, but rather in ensuring low prices for consumers.

Accordingly, Jacobs observes that present-day consumer movements tend to vacillate between short-lived "buy American" campaigns, conscientious consumption movements (such as "no-sweat" clothing or fair trade products), and NIMBY movements that focus on big-box stores at the local, grassroots level. Though perhaps admirable, Jacobs notes that these "Wal-Mart politics" characterizing the present era "draw few connections between what people earn, the prices they pay for retail products, and the state of the larger economy."[28] Even though my findings from the media analysis in the previous chapter suggest that groups like WMW may have been somewhat successful in reinvigorating a discursive focus on Wal-Mart workers and their provisions, this language focuses less on how to help workers live the "good life" via high wages, and more on how their low wages ultimately stick taxpayers with a bill that should, it is argued, be the responsibility of their employer.

Instead, as Lizabeth Cohen argues in her meticulously documented history of mass consumption in the postwar era, the identities of consumer and citizen have become so fused in contemporary American life that "consumption has become entwined with the rights and obligations of citizenship."[29] The consumer remains a powerful voice in the political marketplace: refrains of "it's the economy, stupid" only remind us how forcefully the American electorate may express their disappointment with a president's economic leadership. Moreover, many consumer decisions do indeed help to serve the larger goals of good citizenship. Buying hybrid vehicles, fair trade coffee, and no-sweat clothing may represent small but important avenues for directing public policy in moral directions. For instance, although Michael Schudson argues that "political choices and consumer choices are not just the same," he also views consumption as one potential avenue "to enlarge the points of entry to political life."[30]

However, the normative value of this citizen–consumer marriage for the health of a democracy remains controversial—if citizens care primarily about their own pocketbooks, for example, won't the public good inevitably suffer? For his part, Benjamin Barber advocates a slightly different, more pessimistic view of the citizen–consumer model in the ominously titled Con$umed. Although he voices some approval for the progressive goals achieved through consumer advocacy, he expresses mostly skepticism about the potential of consumer movements and boycotts to create lasting change—and more importantly, to correct the deep and abiding inequalities wrought by a capitalist system that seeks perpetual expansion by manufacturing new wants and needs for well-heeled consumers in developed nations. What Barber calls "civic consumerism" emerges as ultimately inadequate because it relies on the market alone to regulate the distribution of private goods: consumers demand fair trade coffee, for example, and so companies like Starbucks hurry to supply it. Discourse about collective public goods—clean water in developing countries, safe working conditions in Asian sweatshops—fall outside the market's purview, and require more sustained collective (often governmental) efforts to be fully achieved.[31] Other scholars see similar shortcomings in the "citizen–consumer hybrid" model because, unlike the real responsibilities of citizens as taxpayers and law-abiders, the citizenship responsibilities of consumer choices are largely voluntary and thus individual, ignoring the possibilities of organized, collective action.[32] Furthermore, discourse about socially responsible consumerism is frequently infused with elitist overtones that ignore the very real influence of social class; astute observers note that an identical basket of monthly food goods would cost $564 at Whole Foods Market versus $232 at Wal-Mart.[33] The point here is this: whether termed civic consumerism or something else, activism that relies on changed consumer behavior in the market alone tends to be erratic and individual, and does not offer all people access to this form of critique. Although Barber mentions discourse only in passing, rhetoric that could successfully elevate human concerns above market goals, in challenging some of the central principles of market logic, would be essential to any such project.

In the case of Wal-Mart, have progressive activists found a language that can potentially elevate human concerns over and above a hostile economic order? Yes and no. On the one hand, Wal-Mart's chief critics do challenge some key tenets of market logic by asserting that Wal-Mart should be more benevolent to its workers, providing them with better pay and benefits simply because the company could afford to do so. This claim strikes at the heart of Wal-Mart's low-cost, razor-thin-profit-margin business model. Shifting the focus of the debate to workers represents a key victory as well—Wal-Mart Watch's claim that Wal-Mart should "use some of its profits to help some of its people" offers a similar challenge. At the same time, when Wal-Mart justifies its decision to change certain aspects of its business practices, they tend to do so with reference to thrift, claiming that Wal-Mart has made its health insurance benefits more "affordable" for its workers. Far from augmenting the purchasing power that an earlier generation of workers once enjoyed, these labor victories are achieved not by raising wages but by lowering prices.

A more expansive discourse would be one that unites these various discourses by breaking down the rhetorical divisions between workers and consumers, and in the process connecting concerns about the family with claims about the market. Although it is difficult to say exactly what such claims would look like in the public sphere, arguments that are rooted in the family but draw meaningful connections with economic processes would have greater moral power in populist rhetoric. Progressives do make such claims in some instances, and I believe that these are effective and should be a key strategy for progressive economic activists in the future. Rhetoric about children being denied life-saving medical treatments by insurance companies or working in sweatshops abroad offers one powerful example of this kind of claim—allegations of this type receive quick notice in the media (as in the Kathie Lee Gifford scandal) because images of little children who are suffering from treatable illnesses, or toiling over Wal-Mart garments prompt public disgust based on generally widespread collective ideas about what is moral regarding the well-being of children. The "living wage" parlance offers a similar opportunity for critics to connect economistic concerns about wages with the tangible needs of families—if critics of capitalism like Barber argue for a discourse that reminds us that not everyone needs to be a shopper (at least not all the time), labor advocates would be wise to remind onlookers that not everyone is always a worker, and that the category of "working families" itself represents, in actual practice, a web of tangible social ties with both economic and emotional significance.

For progressive activists, however, this means more than simply including the word "family" in press releases and organizational statements. Progressives must do more to successfully convince the American public that their would-be leaders truly identify with their lived experiences as families confronting economic scarcity but still striving for the American Dream. Poorly paid workers are also mothers and fathers, caregivers of elderly relatives, or young people contributing to a family's economic survival. Much in the same way that Marx argued for the human being's multifaceted potential, labor activists have much to gain by augmenting a discourse that is focused primarily on economistic victories to include the multidimensional needs of workers as members of families. The labor movement has long worried that corporate concessions that take the form of family and medical leave would ultimately cost unions the meatier benefits of higher wages and expanded benefits; although these fears may have some merit, it is also possible that expanding the discourse around labor issues in the United States to prioritize such issues would also expand the cognitive frameworks in which these discursive struggles are currently fought.

Regardless of the outcome of this particular debate over Wal-Mart, the persistently slow growth of wages in the United States, coupled with the weak economy that lingers as of this writing, indicates that these dilemmas will persevere. Growing economic inequality and slow market growth offer both advantages and disadvantages to all sides of any economic debate—activists will argue all the more for needed changes from Wal-Mart even as consumers take continued advantage of the low prices that Wal-Mart promises, particularly in hard economic times. The categories of family and worker, citizen and consumer, offer the building blocks for a rich moral vocabulary accessible to populist activists of all persuasions; perhaps we need only to discover that all Americans can still speak this common language.

# Methodology

In studying public discourse over economic issues, defining the universe for analysis presents an immediate methodological challenge. In the case of debate over Wal-Mart, numerous actors and institutional spheres are engaged in public dialogue surrounding these issues. For example, not only do the contributions of the national media and national advocacy groups like Wal-Mart Watch or Wake-Up Wal-Mart immediately come to mind, but so do countless other actors ranging from local activists and union chapters to bloggers and local journalists, to name but a few.

Because I am interested primarily in the ways actors make public, moral claims in such debates, I chose to focus the analysis first and foremost on the deliberate and public presentations of the actors who were most involved in directing the outcome of this controversy. Although one approach would have been to conduct fieldwork among activists opposing Wal-Mart in a particular town or suburb, or to examine newspaper coverage of anti-Wal-Mart activism in various locales around the country, I chose instead to focus my attention on the claims and arguments made in the public sphere by actors whose legitimacy and institutional connections grant them access to policy makers and other national elites, namely, journalists in leading newspapers with national circulation. In this way, my analysis avoids the methodological pitfall of confounding NIMBY-type activism on smaller, local levels with the larger ideological movement that challenges Wal-Mart and related issues of economic inequality in a nationally prominent way.

## Selection of Advocacy Groups

For this reason I initially chose to limit my analysis of the "major players" in this debate to groups such as Wal-Mart Watch, Working Families for Wal-Mart, and Wal-Mart Inc. itself. Although Wake-Up Wal-Mart had also been a vocal participant in this debate, its strategies were more connected to local union chapters, protests, and membership drives conducted "on the ground." For this reason, I chose to focus exclusively on Wal-Mart Watch as an example of the discourse produced by national anti-Wal-Mart activists, as it yielded a richer range of discourse, and was less beholden to the concerns of local union chapter members, as with Wake-Up Wal-Mart and its UFCW constituency.

Limiting the analysis to WMW, WFWM, and to a limited extent Wal-Mart Inc. (as I discuss below) has several main benefits. First, it isolates potentially conflicting variables such as size, national prominence, and social location. By holding these factors largely constant, the analysis can focus more closely on the ways these actors use similar tools to construct larger moral claims in their discursive strategies. Both Wal-Mart Watch and Working Families for Wal-Mart, for example, are mainly "paper" advocacy groups with large lists of email supporters, funding from larger, influential organizations (like the SEIU and Wal-Mart Inc.), and office addresses squarely within the "K Street" region of Washington, DC–based lobbying organizations.

Second, because these groups are single-purpose issue groups, they offer a body of text materials that are largely compatible, allowing comparisons that would be more difficult between the AFL-CIO, for example (i.e., an organization with particular concerns about Wal-Mart but a host of other, potentially competing agendas as well), and a single-issue group like WFWM. Because both groups waged their campaigns largely through the media and advertisements designed to sway public opinion on this issue, they offer data well-matched to the kind of investigations I undertake here. Although Wal-Mart Inc. is clearly a large corporation pursuing multiple goals and interests, excluding the corporation's own response to its attackers would miss an important aspect of this public debate. For that reason, I also include Wal-Mart Inc.'s press releases—those documents prepared explicitly for public dissemination in the media and beyond—in the analysis.

Finally, limiting the analysis to the discourse of similar but competing advocacy groups facilitates the analysis of the deeper cognitive and moral underpinnings of each group's particular discursive strategies. Because I am interested primarily in moral claims, discursive strategies, and the ways the components of each hold together (and diverge) for both groups, I chose to focus the analysis on text itself—even though this excludes other worthy and rich investigations of the role of discursive mediums, social locations, and discursive fields in shaping moral discourse.

To be sure, a challenge common to all projects of social scientific investigation includes constraining the data in a way that produces significant breadth for investigation but also limits the project to a manageable size.

Because the Wal-Mart debate gained traction and arguably reached a fever pitch in the period 2005–2006, I limit the analysis to this two-year time frame, and to the discourse produced by Wal-Mart Watch, Working Families for Wal-Mart, and, as noted above, the press releases disseminated by Wal-Mart Inc. during this same period. After limiting the universe in this way, the data I collected from WMW, WFWM, and Wal-Mart Inc. included almost one thousand organizational documents for analysis (941 total)—a corpus significantly large to conduct rich investigations, but significantly small enough to facilitate complete and exhaustive analysis. These documents included press releases, emails, and website content created by these organizations during the two-year period of 2005–2006.

## Method of Analysis

I approached this body of organizational texts with the analytical techniques of grounded theory and initially moved through them with an "open coding" strategy that did not bring to the analysis a specific goal or theoretical question, but allowed questions for analysis and salient themes to emerge from the data themselves.[1] Accordingly, throughout the analysis I supplemented my coding with the discipline of memo-writing about emerging themes, questions, and, above all, theory. Through these deliberations, the three sets of themes that I focus on in chapters 3–5 emerged as the central, orienting concepts for the analysis. Influenced by Gamson's work on political language, I began to think of the central moral concepts of thrift, freedom, and the rights of the individual not as isolated frames, but as key themes in both this discourse and larger American political culture that are accompanied by "counterthemes" of benevolence, fairness, and community.[2]

Having identified these three thematic dialectics as emergent in the data, I used these findings to guide my analysis of the remaining data and to revisit earlier documents with these three dialectics in mind. Along the way, the analysis was sharpened, refined, and documented through regular commenting on specific textual excerpts and memo-writing about larger patterns. In chapters 3–5, which emerged from this analysis, I report my findings with a particular concern for how each group of actors invoked these themes, what other concepts they link to these larger moral values, and how the strategies used differ between the two groups. Above all, my predominant concern is for the use of language as a cultural medium that communicates a larger conception of the symbolic and moral order; accordingly, in these chapters I focus less on the *frequency* of certain strategies and more on the *range* of discursive strategies used and dimensions of the language each group invokes in doing so.

## Moral Claims in the Media

After examining the ways in which moral claims are constructed in chapters 3–5, I turn my attention in chapter 6 to the ways such claims are represented in the national media. The claims and discursive strategies of actors like WMW and WFWM are certainly interesting in their own right, but the larger relevance of their actions is best evaluated through a close examination of the ways such "backstage" claims fare once they reach the "master sphere" of the national media.[3] For this reason, in chapter 6 I introduce a broader analysis of the ways these larger dialectics take shape in the national media.

Based on statistics of national circulation, I focus on the three most popular national newspapers (*USA Today*, the *Wall Street Journal*, and the *New York Times*). I investigated the possibility of including articles in other periodicals, either general weeklies like *Newsweek* or political periodicals of differing ideological persuasions such as *The Nation* or *National Review*. However, coverage of Wal-Mart in these periodicals was surprisingly thin. *Newsweek*, for example, published articles concerned primarily with Wal-Mart only nineteen times between 2000 and 2006; any mention of Wal-Mart at all appeared in *The Nation* only twelve times during the same period. I ultimately concluded that this sample size would be too small to produce enough variation worthy of analysis. Focusing the analysis on daily newspapers provides comparable "newshole" coverage—they are published daily, unlike periodicals, which may circulate weekly, bimonthly, or monthly.

I obtained these articles by searching for stories in which Wal-Mart was referenced in key topical fields for each search engine. Although different databases have different means of cataloging articles (e.g., "key terms" fields, reference in the citation and article abstract, mention in lead paragraph), I selected the search tools most comparable between search engines, and those that provided the largest universe of media coverage explicitly focused on Wal-Mart. For the *New York Times* and the *Wall Street Journal* I used the "Citation and Abstract" field in ProQuest; for *USA Today* I used the "Headline and Lead Paragraph" field in Factiva. To focus on articles that were more potentially content rich in their description of Wal-Mart and its role in the economy, I excluded those that were dedicated solely to changes in stock prices or other "boilerplate" financial reporting that did not include additional journalistic coverage. Similarly, those articles that included some measure of commentary on particular companies' performance or larger economic trends were likewise included. I also excluded corrections, op-eds,

Table A.1. Newspapers included in media analysis

| | 2000–2004 | | | 2005–2006 | | |
|---|---|---|---|---|---|---|
| | Mentioned Wal-Mart | Met criteria | Sampled | Mentioned Wal-Mart | Met criteria | Sampled |
| USA Today | 146 | 110 | 110 | 95 | 75 | 75 |
| Wall Street Journal | 1,064 | 535 | 268 | 756 | 596 | 296 |
| New York Times | 1,019 | 455 | 228 | 722 | 550 | 265 |
| Total | – | – | 606 | – | – | 636 |

letters to the editor, and articles in which Wal-Mart was mentioned only once and not in relation to the article's main content (articles that mentioned Wal-Mart only once but did so in connection to a larger issue in retailing, such as online DVD sales or holiday shopping deals, were included). I also included all articles in which a short business briefing mentioned a development in Wal-Mart's business operations. When business briefings included Wal-Mart along with a list of other corporations, I analyze only the text that refers to Wal-Mart.

The table below summarizes the publications available for inclusion in this portion of the analysis, and details the number of articles sampled per the criteria above. For the *Wall Street Journal* and the *New York Times*, my sample included every other article for both 2000–2004 and 2005–2006.

Coding of Data

The purpose of this media analysis was twofold. My first objective was to examine how claims about Wal-Mart change during the period in which Wal-Mart Watch was founded and began its most pointed attacks on the company. The first part of this inquiry concerns how the claims made about Wal-Mart during the period 2000–2004 compare to those made in 2005–2006. To examine this question, I coded *speakers' claims* about Wal-Mart for every year of the sample. A speaker's claim includes any reference in an article to an utterance by an outside source—for example, the remarks of an industry analyst, a statement by a representative of Wal-Mart, or a press release from an organization. Because I am most interested in the ways that claims about Wal-Mart move from the backstage sphere of primary claims-makers and into the secondary sphere of the national media, this analysis not only illustrates the changing content of speakers' claims during this six-year period, but also the relationship between spheres of discourse: for example, how speakers' claims as quoted in the national media may resemble those made by primary activists in the backstage sphere in which claims are tested and constructed. Accordingly, I subsequently coded the content of speakers' claims concerning whether the claim concerned workers, the environment, the company's public image, or generalized market processes (including market competition, economic development, profitability, and Wal-Mart's market influence). The second purpose of this analysis was to examine how these same newspaper sources covered Wal-Mart Watch itself. This smaller subsection of articles (forty-six total) were selected for more open-ended analysis, using the methods of grounded theory discussed above, which ultimately generated the arguments about political metaphor and narrative structure that I develop in chapter 6.

# NOTES

## NOTES TO THE PREFACE

1. For a fuller description of this analysis of the Panel Study of Income Dynamics, see Boddie et al., "Did the Religious Group Socioeconomic Ranking Change?"
2. Making Change at Walmart, "'Walmart 1 Percent' among Leading Supporters of Right-Wing ALEC."

## NOTES TO CHAPTER 1

1. Strasser, "Woolworth to Wal-Mart."
2. Dicker, *United States of Wal-Mart*, 164–167.
3. Cohen, *Consumer's Republic*.
4. Fourcade and Healy, "Moral Views of Market Society," 300.
5. See ibid.
6. Zelizer, "Beyond the Polemics"; *Purchase of Intimacy*, 13.
7. Zelizer, *Purchase of Intimacy*, 27.
8. See, for example, Swidler, "Culture in Action"; and *Talk of Love*.
9. See, for example, Gamson, *Talking Politics*.
10. Gusfield, *Culture of Public Problems*, 187.
11. Wuthnow, *Poor Richard's Principle*, 52.
12. Abend, "Two Main Problems," 118.
13. For a useful discussion of this perspective, see Vaisey, "Motivation and Justification."
14. Lakoff, *Moral Politics.*
15. DiMaggio, Evans, and Bryson, "Have Americans' Social Attitudes Become More Polarized?"
16. Ibid. See also Fiorina, Abrams, and Pope, *Culture War?*; Wolfe, *One Nation, After All.*
17. Fiorina, Abrams, and Pope, *Culture War?*
18. Smith, *Moral, Believing Animals*, 26–27.
19. Polletta, *It Was Like a Fever*, 13.
20. Wagner-Pacifici, *Discourse and Destruction*, 5.
21. Goldman and Girion, "Wal-Mart's Memo Blurs Its Message."
22. Bloomberg News, "Bankers Urge Congress"; Paletta, "FDIC Halts Acceptance."
23. Barbaro and Greenhouse, "Andrew Young Resigns"; Goldman, "Young to Quit"; McGhee, "Young Resigns."
24. Goldman, "Wal-Mart Hires Clinton Aide"; Hudson, "Campaign Tactics."

25. Goldman, "Wal-Mart to Raise and Limit Wages."
26. Maher, "Wal-Mart Joins Health-Care Call"; Barbaro and Pear, "Wal-Mart and a Union Unite."
27. Dash, "Wal-Mart Abandons Bank Plans."
28. Ball, "Wal-Mart Asks Suppliers to Rate Energy Use"; Friedman, "Lead, Follow, or Move Aside."
29. Barbaro, "Health Plan Overhauled."

## NOTES TO CHAPTER 2

1. Slater, *Wal-Mart Decade*.
2. Ibid., 183.
3. Soderquist, *Wal-Mart Way*, 211.
4. Fishman, *Wal-Mart Effect*.
5. Petrovic and Hamilton, "Making Global Markets," 122n25; Slater, *Wal-Mart Decade*, 185; Halebsky, *Small Towns and Big Business*.
6. Slater, *Wal-Mart Decade*, 185.
7. Fishman, *Wal-Mart Effect*.
8. *The Economist*, "Wal-Mart."
9. *Raw Story*, "Kerry Slams 'Swiftboating.'"
10. Cavanagh and Anderson, "Ten Reasons Why Wal-Mart Pundits Are Wrong."
11. Tierney, "Shopping for a Nobel."
12. *Wall Street Journal*, "Oh, No, Low Prices."
13. Kazin, *Populist Persuasion*, 1.
14. Nagourney and Barbaro, "Eye on Election, Democrats Run as Wal-Mart Foe."
15. Ibid.
16. U.S. Department of Health and Human Services, "2007 HHS Poverty Guidelines."
17. Barbaro and Abelson, "Wal-Mart Says Health Plan Is Covering More Workers."
18. Featherstone, *Selling Women Short*, 239–240.
19. Cited in Karjanen, "Wal-Mart Effect."
20. Ibid.
21. Featherstone, *Selling Women Short*, 245.
22. *Los Angeles Times*, "Wal-Mart Ordered to Pay Workers"; Covert, "Wal-Mart Loses Pennsylvania Suit"; Greenhouse, "Wal-Mart Told to Pay"; Associated Press, "Wal-Mart Loses."
23. *Chicago Tribune*, "Judge Denies Illinois Wal-Mart Workers' Class Action."
24. Greenhouse, "Wal-Mart Faces Fine in Minnesota."
25. Paletta, "FDIC Delay of Wal-Mart Bank Bid."
26. Paletta, "FDIC Halts Acceptance"; Sidel and Zimmerman, "Can Wal-Mart Cash In?"
27. *Wall Street Journal*, "FDIC Seeks Input on Limited Wal-Mart Plan"; Goldman, "Sides to Square Off on Bank."
28. Paletta, "FDIC Delay of Wal-Mart Bank Bid."
29. Janofsky, "U.S. Discloses Wal-Mart Fine."
30. Gunther, "Green Machine"; *New York Times*, "Build Green, Make Green."
31. Simon, "Business, Labor Aligning on Health Care."
32. Goldberg, "Selling Wal-Mart."
33. At its zenith, for example, A&P had nearly five times as many stores as Wal-Mart did in 2004. See Strasser, "Woolworth to Wal-Mart," 44. For a thorough discussion

of the history of consumerism and mass merchandizing in the United States, see Cohen, *Consumer's Republic*; Strasser, "Woolworth to Wal-Mart"; Petrovic and Hamilton, "Making Global Markets."

34. Petrovic and Hamilton, "Making Global Markets," 108.
35. See, for example, Lichtenstein, "Wal-Mart."
36. Centeno, "Observing Trade."
37. Dollar, "Globalization, Poverty, and Inequality since 1980"; Findlay and O'Rourke, "Commodity Market Integration."
38. Dollar, "Globalization, Poverty, and Inequality since 1980."
39. Bhagwati, *In Defense of Globalization*.
40. Firebaugh and Goesling, "Accounting for the Recent Decline in Global Income Inequality."
41. Dollar, "Globalization, Poverty, and Inequality since 1980."
42. Ibid. See also Rodrik, "Has Globalization Gone Too Far?"
43. Dollar, "Globalization, Poverty, and Inequality since 1980"; Findlay and O'Rourke, "Commodity Market Integration"; Millstone and Lang, *Penguin Atlas of Food*; Pomeranz and Topik, *World That Trade Created*.
44. Bonacich, "Wal-Mart and Logistics Revolution," 165–168; Centeno, "Observing Trade."
45. Goetz and Swaminathan, "Wal-Mart and Country-Wide Poverty"; Hudson and Bellman, "Wal-Mart to Enter India"; Linebaugh, "Wal-Mart to Buy Grocer-Retail Chain in China"; Rai and Giridharadas, "Wal-Mart's Superstores Gain Entry into India."
46. Barboza, "Wal-Mart Will Unionize in All of China"; Dickerson, "In Mexico, Wal-Mart Is Counting on Banking"; Malkin, "Wal-Mart Will Offer Retail Banking in Mexico."
47. Soderquist, *Wal-Mart Way*.
48. Dicker, *United States of Wal-Mart*.
49. Soderquist, *Wal-Mart Way*; Petrovic and Hamilton, "Making Global Markets."
50. Hoopes, "Growth through Knowledge."
51. Carroll and Hannan, *Demography of Corporations and Industries*.
52. Of course, this move has not gone without controversy, as critics warn that this practice disrupts family life, makes it difficult to arrange child care or transportation, and potentially moves workers from predictable full-time hours to precarious part-time schedules. See *Los Angeles Times*, "Wal-Mart Rolls Out Scheduling Software"; Maher, "Wal-Mart Joins Health-Care Call."
53. Fishman, *Wal-Mart Effect*; Goldberg, "Selling Wal-Mart."
54. Bonacich, "Wal-Mart and Logistics Revolution."
55. Ibid.
56. Ibid.
57. Williams, *Inside Toyland*.
58. Fishman, *Wal-Mart Effect*, 4.
59. Barbaro, "No Playtime."
60. Bonacich, "Wal-Mart and Logistics Revolution."
61. Fishman, *Wal-Mart Effect*, 80–81.
62. Ibid., 249.
63. Ibid., 175–179.
64. Ibid., 179.

65. Moreton, *To Serve God and Wal-Mart.*

66. Soderquist, *Wal-Mart Way.*

67. Dicker, *United States of Wal-Mart.*

68. Bai, "New Boss."

69. National Public Radio, "Analysis."

70. For instance, see Bellah et al., *Habits of the Heart*; Lichterman, *Search for Political Community.* See, by way of comparison, Gamson, *Talking Politics*, on self-reliance versus mutuality.

71. For instance, see Bellah et al., *Habits of the Heart*; Putnam, *Bowling Alone.*

72. For instance, see Lakoff, *Moral Politics*, 65–107.

73. Gusfield, *Culture of Public Problems.*

74. Armstrong, *Conceiving Risk, Bearing Responsibility.*

75. Global Insight, "Economic Impact of Wal-Mart."

76. Hausman and Leibtag, "CPI Bias from Supercenters"; Fishman, *Wal-Mart Effect*, 147–153.

77. Barber, *Consumed.*

78. Fishman, *Wal-Mart Effect*, 222.

79. Ibid., 224.

80. Soderquist, *Wal-Mart Way*, 83.

81. Dicker, *United States of Wal-Mart.*

82. Goldberg, "Selling Wal-Mart."

83. Soderquist, *Wal-Mart Way.*

84. Barbaro and Story, "Two Hired to Overhaul"; Elliott, Barbaro, and Story, "Wal-Mart Fires Marketing Star"; McWilliams, Vranica, and Boudette, "Bad Fit."

85. Barbaro, "Bare-Knuckle Enforcement."

86. Gunther, "Green Machine."

87. Ibid.

88. Johnston, "The Ultra-Rich Give Differently."

89. Soderquist, *Wal-Mart Way*, 4.

90. Slater, *Wal-Mart Decade*, 32.

91. Lynn, "Breaking the Chain."

92. From public hearings regarding the deposit insurance application of Wal-Mart Bank, held by the FDIC in Arlington, Virginia (April 10, 2006).

## NOTES TO CHAPTER 3

1. Benford and Snow, "Framing Processes and Social Movements."

2. Frank and Meyer, "Profusion of Individual Roles."

3. Meyer and Jepperson, "The 'Actors' of Modern Society."

4. Ibid.

5. Wuthnow, *America and the Challenges of Religious Diversity*, 96.

6. Polletta and Jasper, "Collective Identity and Social Movements," 298.

7. Ibid.; Lichterman, *Search for Political Community.*

8. All quotations attributed to the Working Families for Wal-Mart website were accessed by the author through the website (forwalmart.com) during the research-gathering phase of this book, although at the time of printing the website was no longer accessible. Quotations attributed to WFWM press releases, Wal-Mart press releases, and WFWM emails were also accessed via the Internet or email and

correspond to the appropriate date listed. In order to be faithful to these texts in their original form, I have chosen not to correct errors in spelling and grammar that appear in the personal stories collected by WFWM. Additionally, these stories refer to Wal-Mart, Walmart, Wal-mart, Wal Mart, and Wal*Mart, and I have elected not to standardize those references.

9. All quotations attributed to the Wal-Mart Watch website were accessed by the author through the website during the research-gathering phase of this book, although some may no longer be available. Wal-Mart Watch resources are now housed at makingchangeatwalmart.org. Quotations attributed to WMW press releases, their faith-based letters, and emails were also accessed via the Internet or email and correspond to the appropriate date listed.

10. See, for example, Habermas, *Structural Transformation*; Walzer, *Thick and Thin*; Lichterman, *Search for Political Community*, 17.

11. Wuthnow, *Poor Richard's Principle*.

12. Greene et al., "An fMRI Investigation."

13. Goodwin, Jasper, and Polletta, "Introduction."

14. Suttles, *Front Page Economics*.

15. Coleman, *Asymmetric Society*.

16. Ibid., 154.

17. Waddock, "Corporate Citizenship."

18. Alexander, *Performance of Politics*, 89.

19. Ibid.

20. In a few instances, WMW did attempt to explain how the actions of one individual were indicative of a larger, group-based corporate culture. For instance, in commenting on the departure of a Wal-Mart PR exec who had allegedly created an offensive television ad invoking Nazi imagery, WMW explained, "Scrambling to fix yet another stunning public relations gaffe, Wal-Mart has certainly done the right thing by accepting the resignation of Peter Kanelos. He of course bore responsibility by approving the company's now-infamous Nazi ad and we commend his resignation. However, let me emphasize two things about the corporate culture of this company: first, the level to which Wal-Mart would stoop in its insatiable pursuit of corporate growth. And second, that Wal-Mart has a long history of conducting stealth, cash-rich campaigns against local citizens. This is why Wal-Mart Watch remains committed to aiding community groups in their battles to reform Wal-Mart's business practices. The company's days of unchecked steamrolling over local communities are officially over" (WMW press release, June 9, 2005). However, such larger commentary was observed less frequently than the more person-based strategies discussed in the text.

21. Brooks, "Broken Society"; Rich, "Grand Old Plot."

22. Associated Press, "Palin Rips Taxes."

23. Berger and Neuhaus, *To Empower People*.

24. Zernike, "In Nevada, Tea Party Ramps Up Efforts."

25. Alexander, *Performance of Politics*, 199–200.

26. As quoted in ibid., 201.

27. Excerpts from Sarah Palin's convention speech throughout this chapter are from *Huffington Post*, "Sarah Palin RNC Convention Speech."

28. Zernike, "In Nevada, Tea Party Ramps Up Efforts."

29. McGirr, *Suburban Warriors*, 272.
30. Lepore, *Whites of Their Eyes*.
31. Wuthnow, "Taking Talk Seriously."
32. Cerulo, *Never Saw It Coming*.

NOTES TO CHAPTER 4

1. These and other quotations in this chapter are from cited from Franklin, *Poor Richard's Almanack*.
2. Wuthnow, *Poor Richard's Principle*, 3–4.
3. Miller, *Theory of Shopping*.
4. Maitland, "Great Non-Debate"; Miller, *Dialectics of Shopping*.
5. Frank, *Purchasing Power*.
6. Fishman, *Wal-Mart Effect*, 218. See also Featherstone, *Selling Women Short*, 230.
7. Miller, *Dialectics of Shopping*, 134.
8. Tönnies, *Community and Society*.
9. Soderquist, *Wal-Mart Way*, 83.
10. Moreton, "It Came from Bentonville"; and *To Serve God and Wal-Mart*.
11. Friedland, "Religious Nationalism."
12. Ibid., 134.
13. Ibid., 137.
14. See, for example, Zelizer, *Purchase of Intimacy*.
15. See, for example, Wuthnow, *Poor Richard's Principle*, 241–264, on the realms of work and family.
16. Wuthnow, *Poor Richard's Principle*.
17. See, for example, Luker, *Abortion and Politics of Motherhood*; Hunter, *Culture Wars*; Friedland, "Religious Nationalism."
18. Berke and Seeyle, "Gore Calls Bradley."
19. Williams, *Inside Toyland*.
20. See chapter 3, note 8.
21. Kohut, Allen, and Keeter, *Holiday Greeting Flap*.
22. See, for example, Frank, *Purchasing Power*; Cohen, "From Town Center to Shopping Center."
23. For example, one speaker explained Wal-Mart's benefits within the context of job losses in the wake of NAFTA: "Wal-Mart has been a God-send for my small community. After losing our textile and hosiery plants due to the NAFTA agreement during the Clinton administration, many of our citizens were left without jobs . . . or hope. Wal-Mart provided many jobs for these displaced employees at a time when very few other jobs were available." Another referenced economic difficulties brought on by inflation and high gas prices. However, even these accounts frame Wal-Mart as the savior, maintaining a strict separation between the store as it is experienced by the speaker of the narrative and the Wal-Mart corporation, which has been an active participant in the economic processes referenced in these narratives. Wal-Mart, for example, has almost certainly benefited from the opportunities for cheaper production and transit created by NAFTA—the very economic transformation that made members of the speaker's hometown need jobs at the new Wal-Mart.
24. Mills, *Sociological Imagination*. See also Armstrong, *Conceiving Risk, Bearing Responsibility*.

25. For example, see Wuthnow, *Poor Richard's Principle*, 130–131.
26. See chapter 3, note 9.
27. Excerpts from President Obama's health care address throughout this chapter are from *New York Times*, "Obama's Health Care Address to Congress."
28. Palin, "Statement on Current Health Care Debate."
29. Gramm, "Resistance Is Not Futile."

NOTES TO CHAPTER 5

1. Rasmussen Reports, "Just 53% Say Capitalism Better Than Socialism."
2. CNN, "Bush: Our Economy Is in Danger."
3. As quoted in Sanger, Zeleny, and Vlasic, "GM to Seek Bankruptcy."
4. *Wall Street Journal*, "Obama Autoworks."
5. Lepore, *Whites of Their Eyes*, 157.
6. Wuthnow, *God and Mammon in America*, 206.
7. Hayek, *Road to Serfdom*, xv–xvi.
8. Gamson, *Talking Politics*.
9. Clay-Warner, Hegtvedt, and Roman, "Procedural Justice, Distributive Justice," 90.
10. Ibid.
11. Ibid.; Barry and Tyler, "Other Side of Injustice."
12. In a few instances, WMW adopts strategies similar to its opponents in showcasing individual stories as evidence of larger patterns of discrimination—as in response to the rhetorical question "Why a Vigil?" on WMW's website's "Faith Community" section. It reads, "We are in a vigil for all the women like Betty Dukes who suffered and are suffering from sexual discrimination while working at Wal-Mart. We are in a vigil for disabled people like Steve Bradley, Jr. who was discriminated by Wal-Mart because of his cerebral palsy. We are in a vigil for people like Cindy Bowling who worked faithfully for Wal-Mart until she was injured on the job and then fired because of the injury." However, such vignettes are few and far between; instead, the discourse associated with WMW tends to provide an abundance of facts about discrimination and about Wal-Mart.
13. Of course, individualizing arguments have long been accused of diluting workers' power relative to larger institutions, while unions emphasize "collective" bargaining as a source of greater power and influence. I address this point more fully in chapter 7.
14. *National Post*, "Still the Same Old Auto Game."
15. Sanger, Zeleny, and Vlasic, "GM to Seek Bankruptcy."
16. Brooks, "Money for Idiots."
17. White House, "Remarks by the President."
18. Hart, *Cultural Dilemmas of Progressive Politics*.
19. Wexler, "Work/Family Policy Stratification."
20. Wuthnow, *Poor Richard's Principle*, 55.
21. Bellah et al., *Habits of the Heart*.
22. Glickman, *Living Wage*.

NOTES TO CHAPTER 6

1. Best, *Threatened Children*.
2. Ibid., 88.
3. Ferree et al., *Shaping Abortion Discourse*.

4. Ibid., 10.
5. For a full discussion of the sampling and analytical procedures used for this data, please see the appendix.
6. Gans, *Democracy and the News*, 61.
7. Ibid., 67.
8. McChesney, *Rich Media, Poor Democracy*.
9. Ibid., 58.
10. Ibid., 62.
11. Ibid.
12. Suttles, *Front Page Economics*, 53.
13. Ibid., 54.
14. Ibid.
15. Ibid., xvi.
16. Riessman, *Narrative Analysis*.
17. Greenhouse, "Parrying Its Critics."
18. Barbaro, "New Weapon for Wal-Mart."
19. DiMaggio and Powell, "Iron Cage Revisited."
20. Zimmerman, "In Wal-Mart's Case, Its Enemies Aren't Terribly Good Friends."
21. Hudson, "Campaign Tactics."
22. Ibid.
23. Hudson, "Wal-Mart to Launch Campaign."
24. *New York Times*, "Holders Hear Wal-Mart Defy Critics."
25. Barbaro, "Wal-Mart in Their Sights" (emphasis added).
26. Barbaro and Barringer, "Wal-Mart to Seek Savings in Energy."
27. Zimmerman, "Wal-Mart Sets Seminar to Assess Economic Impact."
28. Grant, "Wal-Mart Maintains Bank Hopes."
29. Barbaro, "Wal-Mart Begins Quest for Generals in PR War."
30. Greenhouse, "Parrying Its Critics."
31. Zimmerman, "In Wal-Mart's Case, Its Enemies Aren't Terribly Good Friends."
32. Greenhouse and Barbaro, "On Private Web Site, Wal-Mart Chief Talks Tough."
33. Barbaro and Barringer, "Wal-Mart to Seek Savings in Energy."
34. Ibid.
35. Barbaro, "New Weapon for Wal-Mart."
36. Riessman, *Narrative Analysis*, 18.
37. Zimmerman, "Wal-Mart Sets Seminar to Assess Economic Impact"; Greenhouse, "Parrying Its Critics."
38. Polletta, *It Was Like a Fever*.
39. Ibid., 111.
40. Barbaro, "Wal-Mart Enlists Bloggers in Its Public Relations Campaign"; Barbaro, "Wal-Mart Begins Quest for Generals in PR War"; Zimmerman, "Wal-Mart Taps Image Maven for a New In-House Position."
41. Barbaro, "Wal-Mart to Expand Health Plan."
42. Barbaro, "Chief's Tone Reflects Change at Wal-Mart."
43. Barbaro, "Wal-Mart Effort on Health and Environment Is Seen."
44. Zimmerman, "Wal-Mart Taps Image Maven for a New In-House Position."
45. Barbaro, "Chief's Tone Reflects Change at Wal-Mart."
46. Ibid.

## NOTES TO CHAPTER 7
1. Frank, *What's the Matter with Kansas?*
2. Greeley and Hout, *The Truth about Conservative Christians.*
3. Frank, *What's the Matter with Kansas?* 245.
4. Pew Research Center for the People and the Press, "GOP Makes Big Gains among White Voters."
5. Kazin, *Populist Persuasion.*
6. Ibid., 279.
7. Ibid., 281
8. As Bethany Moreton observes, "Outside of the desert island that neoliberal economics assumes, we all conduct our survival strategies within a web of human relations." See *To Serve God and Wal-Mart,* 80–81.
9. Greeley and Hout, *The Truth about Conservative Christians,* 68 (emphasis added).
10. Zelizer, *Purchase of Intimacy.*
11. Johnston, "Citizen–Consumer Hybrid," 233.
12. Luker, *Abortion and the Politics of Motherhood.*
13. Binder, *Contentious Curricula.*
14. Gerstel and Clawson, "Unions' Responses to Family Concerns."
15. Clawson and Clawson, "What Has Happened to the U.S. Labor Movement?"; Milkman and Voss, *Rebuilding Labor*; Milkman, *LA Story.*
16. Moreton, *To Serve God and Wal-Mart.*
17. Ibid.
18. Meyer, "Wal-Mart's Conundrum."
19. McGirr, *Suburban Warriors.*
20. Massengill, "Why Evangelicals Like Wal-Mart."
21. Smith, *American Evangelicalism*; Emerson and Smith, *Divided by Faith.*
22. Starks and Robinson, "Two Approaches to Religion and Politics."
23. Lakoff, *Thinking Points,* 29.
24. Wuthnow, *Poor Richard's Principle.*
25. On the competing domains of work and family, see ibid.; Hochschild, *Time Bind*; Blair-Loy, *Competing Devotions* .
26. Jacobs, *Pocketbook Politics.*
27. Ibid.
28. Ibid., 265.
29. Cohen, *Consumer's Republic,* 408.
30. Schudson, "Troubling Equivalence of Citizen and Consumer," 202–203.
31. Barber, *Con$umed.*
32. Johnston, "Citizen–Consumer Hybrid."
33. Ibid., 256–257.

## NOTES TO THE APPENDIX
1. Glaser and Strauss, *Discovery of Grounded Theory.*
2. Gamson, *Talking Politics.*
3. Ferree et al., *Shaping Abortion Discourse.*

# BIBLIOGRAPHY

Abend, Gabriel. "Two Main Problems in the Sociology of Morality." *Theory and Society* 37 (April 2008): 87–125.

Alexander, Jeffrey C. *The Performance of Politics: Obama's Victory and the Democratic Struggle for Power.* New York: Oxford University Press, 2010.

Armstrong, Elizabeth M. *Conceiving Risk, Bearing Responsibility: Fetal Alcohol Syndrome and the Diagnosis of Moral Disorder.* Baltimore: Johns Hopkins University Press, 2003.

Associated Press. "Palin Rips Taxes with Boston Tea Partiers." MSNBC. April 14, 2010.

———. "Wal-Mart Loses Big Labor Verdict: Employees Worked through Breaks, off the Clock, Jury Finds." *Chicago Tribune,* October 14, 2006.

Bai, Matt. "The New Boss." *New York Times,* January 30, 2005.

Ball, Jeffrey. "Wal-Mart Asks Suppliers to Rate Energy Use." *Wall Street Journal,* September 24, 2007.

Barbaro, Michael. "Bare-Knuckle Enforcement for Wal-Mart's Rules." *New York Times,* March 29, 2007.

———. "Chief's Tone Reflects Change at Wal-Mart in the Last Year." *New York Times,* April 20, 2006.

———. "Health Plan Overhauled at Wal-Mart." *New York Times,* September 19, 2007.

———. "A New Weapon for Wal-Mart: A War Room." *New York Times,* November 1, 2005.

———. "No Playtime on Recovery Road." *New York Times,* November 19, 2006.

———. "Wal-Mart Begins Quest for Generals in PR War." *New York Times,* March 30, 2006.

———. "Wal-Mart Effort on Health and Environment Is Seen." *New York Times,* June 22, 2006.

———. "Wal-Mart Enlists Bloggers in Its Public Relations Campaign." *New York Times,* March 7, 2006.

———. "Wal-Mart in Their Sights, States Press for Health Benefits." *New York Times,* January 5, 2006.

———. "Wal-Mart to Expand Health Plan for Workers." *New York Times,* October 24, 2005.

Barbaro, Michael, and Reed Abelson. "Wal-Mart Says Health Plan Is Covering More Workers." *New York Times,* January 11, 2007.

Barbaro, Michael, and Felicity Barringer. "Wal-Mart to Seek Savings in Energy." *New York Times,* October 25, 2005.

Barbaro, Michael, and Steven Greenhouse. "Andrew Young Resigns Job as Wal-Mart Image-Builder." *New York Times,* August 18, 2006.

Barbaro, Michael, and Robert Pear. "Wal-Mart and a Union Unite, at Least on Health Policy." *New York Times*, February 7, 2007.

Barbaro, Michael, and Louise Story. "Two Hired to Overhaul Marketing Leave Their Posts at Wal-Mart." *New York Times*, December 6, 2006.

Barber, Benjamin. *Con$umed: How Markets Corrupt Children, Infantilize Adults, and Swallow Citizens Whole*. New York: Norton, 2007.

Barboza, David. "Wal-Mart Will Unionize in All of China." *New York Times*, August 10, 2006.

Barry, Heather, and Tom R. Tyler. "The Other Side of Injustice: When Unfair Procedures Increase Group-Serving Behavior." *Psychological Science* 20 (August 2009): 1026–1032.

Bellah, Robert Neelly, Richard Madsen, William M. Sullivan, Ann Swidler, and Steven M. Tipton. *Habits of the Heart: Individualism and Commitment in American Life*. Berkeley: University of California Press, 1985.

Benford, Robert D., and David A. Snow. "Framing Processes and Social Movements: An Overview and Assessment." *Annual Review of Sociology* 26 (August 2000): 611–639.

Berger, Peter L., and Richard John Neuhaus. *To Empower People: The Role of Mediating Structures in Civil Society*. Washington, DC: American Enterprise Institute for Public Policy, 1977.

Berke, Richard L., and Katharine Q. Seeyle. "Gore Calls Bradley to More Debates." *New York Times*, October 10, 1999.

Best, Joel. *Threatened Children: Rhetoric and Concern about Child–Victims*. Chicago: University of Chicago Press, 1990.

Bhagwati, Jagdish N. *In Defense of Globalization*. New York: Oxford University Press, 2004.

Binder, Amy. *Contentious Curricula: Afrocentrism and Creationism in American Public Schools*. Princeton: Princeton University Press, 2004.

Blair-Loy, Mary. *Competing Devotions: Career and Family among Women Executives*. Cambridge: Harvard University Press, 2003.

Bloomberg News. "Bankers Urge Congress to Stop Wal-Mart Bank." *Chicago Tribune*, July 25, 2006.

Boddie, Stephanie Clintonia, Rebekah Peeples Massengill, and Anne Shi. "Did the Religious Group Socioeconomic Ranking Change Going into the Great Recession?" *Research in the Sociology of Work* 23 (2012): 27–47.

Bonacich, Edna. "Wal-Mart and the Logistics Revolution." In *Wal-Mart: The Face of Twenty-First-Century Capitalism*, edited by Nelson Lichtenstein, 163–187. New York: New Press, 2006.

Brooks, David. "The Broken Society." *New York Times*, March 16, 2010.

———. "Money for Idiots." *New York Times*, February 19, 2009.

Carroll, Glenn R., and Michael T. Hannan. *The Demography of Corporations and Industries*. Princeton: Princeton University Press, 2000.

Cavanagh, John, and Sarah Anderson. "Ten Reasons Why the Wal-Mart Pundits Are Wrong." *The Nation*, September 29, 2006.

Centeno, Miguel A. "Observing Trade: Overview of Changes, 1980–2001." *Observing Trade: Revealing International Trade Networks and Their Impacts*. Princeton Institute for International and Regional Studies, March 9, 2006.

Cerulo, Karen A. *Never Saw It Coming: Cultural Challenges to Envisioning the Worst*. Chicago: University of Chicago Press, 2006.

*Chicago Tribune*. "Judge Denies Illinois Wal-Mart Workers' Class Action." March 10, 2007.

Clawson, Dan, and Mary A. Clawson. "What Has Happened to the U.S. Labor Movement? Union Decline and Renewal." *Annual Review of Sociology* 25 (1999): 99–119.

Clay-Warner, Jody, Karen A. Hegtvedt, and Paul Roman. "Procedural Justice, Distributive Justice: How Experiences with Downsizing Condition Their Impact on Organizational Commitment." *Social Psychology Quarterly* 68 (March 2005): 89–102.

CNN. "Bush: Our Economy Is in Danger." Transcript. Posted September 24, 2008, on http://articles.cnn.com/.

Cohen, Lizabeth. *A Consumer's Republic: The Politics of Mass Consumption in Postwar America.* New York: Knopf, 2003.

———. "From Town Center to Shopping Center: The Reconfiguration of Community Marketplaces in Postwar America." *American Historical Review* 101 (October 1996): 1050–1081.

Coleman, James Samuel. *The Asymmetric Society.* Syracuse: Syracuse University Press, 1982.

Covert, James. "Wal-Mart Loses Pennsylvania Suit on Rest Breaks." *Wall Street Journal,* October 13, 2006.

Dash, Eric. "Wal-Mart Abandons Bank Plans." *New York Times,* March 17, 2007.

Dicker, John. *The United States of Wal-Mart.* New York: Jeremy P. Tarcher, 2005.

Dickerson, Marla. "In Mexico, Wal-Mart Is Counting on Banking." *Los Angeles Times,* August 27, 2006.

DiMaggio, Paul, John Evans, and Bethany Bryson. "Have Americans' Social Attitudes Become More Polarized?" *American Journal of Sociology* 102 (November 1996): 690–755.

DiMaggio, Paul, and Walter Powell. "The Iron Cage Revisited: Institutional Isomorphism and Collective Rationality in Organizational Fields." *American Sociological Review* 48 (April 1983): 147–160.

Dollar, David. "Globalization, Poverty, and Inequality since 1980." *World Bank Research Observer* 20 (September 2005): 145–175.

*The Economist.* "Wal-Mart: From Both Sides Now." November 25, 2006.

Elliott, Stuart, Michael Barbaro, and Louise Story. "Wal-Mart Fires Marketing Star and Ad Agency She Chose." *New York Times,* December 8, 2006.

Emerson, Michael, and Christian Smith. *Divided by Faith: Evangelical Religion and the Problem of Race in America.* New York: Oxford University Press, 2000.

Featherstone, Liza. *Selling Women Short: The Landmark Battle for Workers' Rights at Wal-Mart.* New York: Basic Books, 2004.

Ferree, Myra Marx, William Anthony Gamson, Jurgen Gerhards, and Dieter Rucht. *Shaping Abortion Discourse: Democracy and the Public Sphere in Germany and the United States.* New York: Cambridge University Press, 2002.

Findlay, Ronald, and Kevin H. O'Rourke. "Commodity Market Integration, 1500–2000." In *Globalization in Historical Perspective,* edited by Michael D. Bordo, Alan M. Taylor, and Jeffrey G. Williamson, 13–62. Chicago: University of Chicago Press, 2003.

Fiorina, Morris P., Samuel J. Abrams, and Jeremy Pope. *Culture War? The Myth of a Polarized America.* Upper Saddle River, NJ: Pearson Education, 2006.

Firebaugh, Glenn, and Brian Goesling. "Accounting for the Recent Decline in Global Income Inequality." *American Journal of Sociology* 110 (September 2004): 283–312.

Fishman, Charles. *The Wal-Mart Effect: How the World's Most Powerful Company Really Works—and How It's Transforming the American Economy.* New York: Penguin, 2006.

Fourcade, Marion, and Kieran Healy. "Moral Views of Market Society." *Annual Review of Sociology* 33 (August 2007): 285–311.

Frank, Dana. *Purchasing Power: Consumer Organizing, Gender, and the Seattle Labor Movement, 1919–1929*. New York: Cambridge University Press, 1994.

Frank, David John, and John W. Meyer. "The Profusion of Individual Roles and Identities in the Postwar Period." *Sociological Theory* 20 (March 2002): 86–105.

Frank, Thomas. *What's the Matter with Kansas? How Conservatives Won the Heart of America*. New York: Henry Holt, 2004.

Franklin, Benjamin. *Poor Richard's Almanack*. Mount Vernon, VA: Peter Pauper, 1987.

Friedland, Roger. "Religious Nationalism and the Problem of Collective Representation." *Annual Review of Sociology* 27 (August 2001): 125–152.

Friedman, Thomas L. "Lead, Follow or Move Aside." *New York Times*, September 26, 2007.

Gamson, William A. *Talking Politics*. New York: Cambridge University Press, 1992.

Gans, Herbert. *Democracy and the News*. New York: Oxford University Press, 2003.

Gerstel, Naomi, and Dan Clawson. "Unions' Responses to Family Concerns." *Social Problems* 48 (May 2001): 277–297.

Glaser, Barney G., and Anselm L. Strauss. *The Discovery of Grounded Theory: Strategies for Qualitative Research*. Chicago: Aldine, 1967.

Glickman, Lawrence B. *A Living Wage*. Ithaca: Cornell University Press, 1997.

Global Insight. "The Economic Impact of Wal-Mart." Global Insight Advisory Services Division, November 2, 2005.

Goetz, Stephan J., and Hema Swaminathan. "Wal-Mart and County-Wide Poverty." *Social Science Quarterly* 87 (June 2006): 211–226.

Goldberg, Jeffrey. "Selling Wal-Mart." *New Yorker*, April 12, 2007.

Goldman, Abigail. "Sides to Square Off on Bank." *Los Angeles Times*, April 10, 2006.

———. "Wal-Mart Hires Clinton Aide to Handle Criticism." *Los Angeles Times*, August 30, 2006.

———. "Wal-Mart to Raise and Limit Wages." *Los Angeles Times*, August 8, 2006.

———. "Young to Quit Wal-Mart Group after Racial Remarks." *Los Angeles Times*, August 18, 2006.

Goldman, Abigail, and Lisa Girion. "Wal-Mart's Memo Blurs Its Message on Benefits." *Los Angeles Times*, October 27, 2005.

Goodwin, Jeff, James M. Jasper, and Francesca Polletta. "Introduction: Why Emotions Matter." In *Passionate Politics*, edited by Jeff Goodwin, James M. Jasper, and Francesca Polletta, 1–24. Chicago: University of Chicago Press, 2001.

Gramm, Phil. "Resistance Is Not Futile." *Wall Street Journal*, March 25, 2010.

Grant, Lorie. "Wal-Mart Maintains Bank Hopes despite Greenspan Urging Change in Law." *USA Today*, January 27, 2006.

Greeley, Andrew, and Michael Hout. *The Truth about Conservative Christians: What They Think and What They Believe*. Chicago: University of Chicago Press, 2006.

Greene, Joshua D., R. Brian Sommerville, Leigh E. Nystrom, John M. Darley, and Jonathan D. Cohen. "An fMRI Investigation of Emotional Engagement in Moral Judgment." *Science* 293 (September 14, 2001): 2105–2108.

Greenhouse, Steven. "Parrying Its Critics, Wal-Mart Says Its Wages Must Stay Competitive." *New York Times*, May 4, 2005.

———. "Wal-Mart Faces Fine in Minnesota Suit Involving Work Breaks." *New York Times*, July 2, 2008.

———. "Wal-Mart Told to Pay $78 Million." *New York Times*, October 14, 2006.

Greenhouse, Stephen, and Michael Barbaro. "On Private Web Site, Wal-Mart Chief Talks Tough." *New York Times*, February 17, 2006.

Gunther, Marc. "The Green Machine." *Fortune*, August 7, 2006.

Gusfield, Joseph R. *The Culture of Public Problems: Drinking-Driving and the Symbolic Order*. Chicago: University of Chicago Press, 1981.

Habermas, Jürgen. *The Structural Transformation of the Public Sphere: An Inquiry into a Category of Bourgeois Society*. Cambridge: MIT Press, 1989.

Halebsky, Stephen. *Small Towns and Big Business: Challenging Wal-Mart Superstores*. Lanham, MD: Rowman and Littlefield, 2009.

Hart, Stephen. *Cultural Dilemmas of Progressive Politics: Styles of Engagement among Grassroots Activists*. Chicago: University of Chicago Press, 2001.

Hausman, Jerry, and Ephraim Leibtag. "CPI Bias from Supercenters: Does the BLS Know That Wal-Mart Exists?" MIT and Economic Research Service, U.S. Department of Agriculture, 2005.

Hayek, Friedrich A. von. *The Road to Serfdom*. Chicago: University of Chicago Press, 1994.

Hochschild, Arlie Russell. *The Time Bind: When Work Becomes Home and Home Becomes Work*. New York: Metropolitan Books, 1997.

Hoopes, James. "Growth through Knowledge: Wal-Mart, High Technology, and the Ever Less Visible Hand of the Manager." In *Wal-Mart: The Face of Twenty-First-Century Capitalism*, edited by Nelson Lichtenstein, 83–105. New York: New Press, 2006.

Hudson, Kris. "Campaign Tactics: Behind the Scenes, PR Firm Remakes Wal-Mart's Image." *Wall Street Journal*, December 7, 2006.

———. "Wal-Mart to Launch Campaign Urging Its U.S. Workers to Vote." *Wall Street Journal*, September 20, 2006.

Hudson, Kris, and Eric Bellman. "Wal-Mart to Enter India in Venture." *Wall Street Journal*, November 28, 2006.

*Huffington Post*. "Sarah Palin RNC Convention Speech." September 3, 2008.

Hunter, James Davison. *Culture Wars: The Struggle to Define America*. New York: Basic Books, 1991.

Jacobs, Meg. *Pocketbook Politics: Economic Citizenship in Twentieth-Century America*. Princeton: Princeton University Press, 2005.

Janofsky, Michael. "U.S. Discloses Wal-Mart Fine of $3.1 Million." *New York Times*, May 13, 2004.

Johnston, David Cay. "The Ultra-Rich Give Differently from You and Me." *New York Times*, July 2, 2006.

Johnston, Josée. "The Citizen–Consumer Hybrid: Ideological Tensions and the Case of Whole Foods Market." *Theory and Society* 37(June 2008): 229–270.

Karjanen, David. "The Wal-Mart Effect and the New Face of Capitalism: Labor Market and Community Impacts of the Megaretailer." In *Wal-Mart: The Face of Twenty-First Century Capitalism*, edited by Nelson Lichtenstein, 143–162. New York: New Press, 2006.

Kazin, Michael. *The Populist Persuasion: An American History*. Rev. ed. New York: Basic Books, 1995.

Kohut, Andrew, Jodie Allen, and Scott Keeter. *Holiday Greeting Flap: Ho Ho Hum*. Washington, DC: Pew Research Center for the People and the Press, 2005.

Lakoff, George. *Moral Politics: What Conservatives Know That Liberals Don't*. Chicago: University of Chicago Press, 1996.

———. *Thinking Points: Communicating Our American Values and Vision*. New York: Farrar, Straus and Giroux, 2006.

Lepore, Jill. *The Whites of Their Eyes: The Tea Party's Revolution and the Battle over American History*. Princeton: Princeton University Press, 2010.

Lichtenstein, Nelson. "Wal-Mart: A Template for Twenty-First-Century Capitalism." In *Wal-Mart: The Face of Twenty-First-Century Capitalism*, edited by Nelson Lichtenstein, 3–30. New York: New Press, 2006.

Lichterman, Paul. *The Search for Political Community: American Activists Reinventing Commitment*. New York: Cambridge University Press, 1996.

Linebaugh, Kate. "Wal-Mart to Buy Grocer-Retail Chain in China." *Wall Street Journal*, October 17, 2006.

*Los Angeles Times*. "Wal-Mart Ordered to Pay Workers." October 14, 2006.

———. "Wal-Mart Rolls Out Scheduling Software." January 4, 2007.

Luker, Kristin. *Abortion and the Politics of Motherhood*. Berkeley: University of California Press, 1984.

Lynn, Barry C. "Breaking the Chain: The Antitrust Case against Wal-Mart." *Harper's*, July 2006.

Maher, Kris. "Wal-Mart Joins Health-Care Call: Unlikely Coalition of Labor, Business Pushes for Overhaul." *Wall Street Journal*, February 8, 2007.

Maitland, Ian. "The Great Non-Debate over International Sweatshops." *British Academy of Management Annual Conference Proceedings* (1997): 240–265.

Making Change at Walmart. "The 'Walmart 1 Percent' among Leading Supporters of Right-Wing ALEC." Posted February 29, 2012, on http://makingchangeatwalmart.org/.

Malkin, Elisabeth. "Wal-Mart Will Offer Retail Banking in Mexico, an Underserved Market." *New York Times*, November 24, 2006.

Massengill, Rebekah Peeples. "Why Evangelicals Like Wal-Mart: Education, Region, and Religious Group Identity." *Sociology of Religion* 72 (Spring 2010): 50–77.

McChesney, Robert. *Rich Media, Poor Democracy: Communication Politics in Dubious Times*. Urbana: University of Illinois Press, 1999.

McGhee, Bernard. "Young Resigns from Wal-Mart Committee amid Criticism of Remarks." *Chicago Tribune*, August 19, 2006.

McGirr, Lisa. *Suburban Warriors: The Origins of the New American Right*. Princeton: Princeton University Press, 2001.

McWilliams, Gary, Suzanne Vranica, and Neal E. Boudette. "Bad Fit: How a Highflier in Marketing Fell at Wal-Mart." *Wall Street Journal*, December 11, 2006.

Meyer, John W., and Ronald L. Jepperson. "The 'Actors' of Modern Society: The Cultural Construction of Social Agency." *Sociological Theory* 18 (March 2000): 100–120.

Meyer, Margaret. "Wal-Mart's Conundrum: Women—Friend or Foe?" Unpublished paper, Princeton University, 2010.

Milkman, Ruth. *LA Story: Immigrant Workers and the Future of the U.S. Labor Movement*. New York: Russell Sage Foundation, 2006.

Milkman, Ruth, and Kim Voss, eds. *Rebuilding Labor: Organizing and Organizers in the New Union Movement*. Ithaca: Cornell University Press, 2004.

Miller, Daniel. *The Dialectics of Shopping*. Chicago: University of Chicago Press, 2001.

———. *A Theory of Shopping*. Cambridge, MA: Polity Press, 1998.

Mills, C. Wright. *The Sociological Imagination*. New York: Oxford University Press, 1959.

Millstone, Erik, and Tim Lang. *Penguin Atlas of Food*. New York: Penguin, 2003.

Moreton, Bethany. "It Came From Bentonville: The Agrarian Origins of Wal-Mart Culture." In *Wal-Mart: The Face of Twenty-First-Century Capitalism*, edited by Nelson Lichtenstein, 57–82. New York: New Press, 2006.

———. *To Serve God and Wal-Mart*. Cambridge: Harvard University Press, 2009.

Nagourney, Adam, and Michael Barbaro. "Eye on Election, Democrats Run as Wal-Mart Foe." *New York Times*, August 17, 2006.

*National Post.* "Still the Same Old Auto Game." June 4, 2009.

National Public Radio. "Analysis: Organized Labor in a Debate Over Its Survival." *All Things Considered*, March 5, 2005.

*New York Times.* "Build Green, Make Green." August 11, 2006.

———. "Holders Hear Wal-Mart Defy Critics." June 4, 2005.

———. "Obama's Health Care Address to Congress." Transcript. Posted September 10, 2009, on http://www.nytimes.com/.

Paletta, Damian. "FDIC Delay of Wal-Mart Bank Bid Stymies Others: Home Depot, GM Are among Companies to Take a Hit by Moratorium on Approvals." *Wall Street Journal*, August 7, 2006.

———. "FDIC Halts Acceptance, Action on Industrial-Bank Applications." *Wall Street Journal*, July 29, 2006.

Palin, Sarah. "Statement on Current Health Care Debate." Posted August 7, 2009, on http://www.facebook.com/.

Petrovic, Misha, and Gary Hamilton. "Making Global Markets: Wal-Mart and Its Suppliers." In *Wal-Mart: The Face of Twenty-First Century Capitalism*, edited by Nelson Lichtenstein, 107–141. New York: New Press, 2006.

Pew Research Center for the People and the Press. "GOP Makes Big Gains among White Voters." July 22, 2011.

Polletta, Francesca. *It Was Like a Fever: Storytelling in Protest and Politics*. Chicago: University of Chicago Press, 2006.

Polletta, Francesca, and James M. Jasper. "Collective Identity and Social Movements." *Annual Review of Sociology* 27 (August 2001): 283–305.

Pomeranz, Kenneth, and Steven Topik. *The World That Trade Created: Society, Culture, and the World Economy, 1400–the Present*. Armonk, NY: M. E. Sharpe, 1999.

Putnam, Robert D. *Bowling Alone: The Collapse and Revival of American Community*. New York: Simon and Schuster, 2000.

Rai, Saritha, and Anand Giridharadas. "Wal-Mart's Superstores Gain Entry into India." *New York Times*, November 28, 2006.

Rasmussen Reports. "Just 53% Say Capitalism Better Than Socialism." April 9, 2009.

*Raw Story.* "Kerry Slams 'Swiftboating' of Democrats by Wal-Mart Front Group Member." October 23, 2006.

Rich, Frank. "The Grand Old Plot against the Tea Party." *New York Times*, October 30, 2010.

Riessman, Catherine. *Narrative Analysis*. Newbury Park, CA: Sage Publications, 1993.

Rodrik, Dani. *Has Globalization Gone Too Far?* Washington, DC: Institute of International Economics, 1997.

Sanger, David E., Jeff Zeleny, and Bill Vlasic. "GM to Seek Bankruptcy and a New Start." *New York Times*, May 31, 2009.

Schudson, Michael. "The Troubling Equivalence of Citizen and Consumer." *Annals of the American Academy of Political and Social Science* 608 (November 2006): 193–204.

Sidel, Robin, and Ann Zimmerman. "Can Wal-Mart Cash In on Financial Services?" *Wall Street Journal*, July 6, 2006.

Simon, Scott. "Business, Labor Aligning on Health Care." *Weekend Edition*, National Public Radio, February 10, 2007.

Slater, Robert. *The Wal-Mart Decade: How a New Generation of Leaders Turned Sam Walton's Legacy into the World's #1 Company*. New York: Penguin, 2003.

Strasser, Susan. "Woolworth to Wal-Mart: Mass Merchandising and the Changing Culture of Consumption." In *Wal-Mart: The Face of Twenty-First Century Capitalism*, edited by Nelson Lichtenstein, 31–55. New York: New Press, 2006.

Smith, Christian. *American Evangelicalism: Embattled and Thriving*. Chicago: University of Chicago Press, 1998.

———. *Moral, Believing Animals: Human Personhood and Culture*. New York: Oxford University Press, 2003.

Soderquist, Don. *The Wal-Mart Way: The Inside Story of the Success of the World's Largest Company*. Nashville: Thomas Nelson, 2005.

Starks, Brian, and Robert V. Robinson. "Two Approaches to Religion and Politics: Moral Cosmology and Subcultural Identity." *Journal for the Scientific Study of Religion* 48 (December 2009): 650–669.

Suttles, Gerald D. *Front Page Economics*. Chicago: University of Chicago Press, 2010.

Swidler, Ann. "Culture in Action: Symbols and Strategies." *American Sociological Review* 51 (April 1986): 273–286.

———. *Talk of Love: How Culture Matters*. Chicago: University of Chicago Press, 2001.

Tierney, John. "Shopping for a Nobel." *New York Times*, October 17, 2006.

Tönnies, Ferdinand. *Community and Society (Gemeinschaft und Gesellschaft)*. New York: Harper and Row, 1963.

U.S. Department of Health and Human Services. "The 2007 HHS Poverty Guidelines: One Version of the (U.S.) Federal Poverty Measure." Washington, DC. http://aspe.hhs.gov/poverty/07poverty.shtml.

Vaisey, Stephen. "Motivation and Justification: A Dual-Process Model of Culture in Action." *American Journal of Sociology* 114 (May 2009): 1675–1715.

Waddock, Sandra. "Corporate Citizenship: The Dark-Side Paradoxes of Success." In *The Debate over Corporate Social Responsibility*, edited by Steve May, George Cheney, and Juliet Roper, 74–86. New York: Oxford University Press, 2007.

Wagner-Pacifici, Robin. *Discourse and Destruction: The City of Philadelphia versus MOVE*. Chicago: University of Chicago Press, 1994.

*Wall Street Journal*. "FDIC Seeks Input on Limited Wal-Mart Plan." April 12, 2006.

———. "The Obama Autoworks." March 31, 2009.

———. "Oh, No, Low Prices." September 28, 2006.

Walzer, Michael. *Thick and Thin: Moral Argument at Home and Abroad*. Notre Dame: University of Notre Dame Press, 1994.

Wexler, Sherry. "Work/Family Policy Stratification: The Examples of Family Support and Family Leave." *Qualitative Sociology* 20 (June 1997): 311–322.

White House (Office of the Press Secretary). "Remarks by the President on the American Automotive Industry." Posted March 30, 2009, on http://www.whitehouse.gov/.

Williams, Christine L. 2006. *Inside Toyland: Working, Shopping, and Social Inequality*. Berkeley: University of California Press.

Wolfe, Alan. *One Nation, After All: What Middle-Class Americans Really Think about God, Country, Family, Racism, Welfare, Immigration, Homosexuality, Work, the Right, the Left, and Each Other.* New York: Viking, 1998.

Wuthnow, Robert. *America and the Challenges of Religious Diversity.* Princeton: Princeton University Press, 2005.

———. *God and Mammon in America.* New York: Free Press, 1994.

———. *Poor Richard's Principle: Recovering the American Dream through the Moral Dimension of Work, Business, and Money.* Princeton: Princeton University Press, 1996.

———. "Taking Talk Seriously: Religious Discourse as Social Practice." *Journal for the Scientific Study of Religion* 50 (March 2011): 1–21.

Zelizer, Viviana A. "Beyond the Polemics on the Market: Establishing a Theoretical and Empirical Agenda." *Sociological Forum* 3 (Autumn 1988): 614–634.

———. *The Purchase of Intimacy.* Princeton: Princeton University Press, 2005.

Zernike, Kate. "In Nevada, Tea Party Ramps Up Efforts to Beat Reid." *New York Times*, April 5, 2010.

Zimmerman, Ann. "In Wal-Mart's Case, Its Enemies Aren't Terribly Good Friends." *Wall Street Journal*, January 11, 2006.

———. "Wal-Mart Sets Seminar to Assess Economic Impact." *Wall Street Journal*, November 4, 2005.

———. "Wal-Mart Taps Image Maven for a New In-House Position." *Wall Street Journal*, July 25, 2006.

# INDEX

abortion, 180
abstraction, 62, 148, 177
advertising, 13, 26, 98, 163, 173, 190, 199n20
advocacy groups: "paper" advocacy groups,
   27, 190; selected for study, 189–91. *See
   also* Wal-Mart Watch (WMW); Working
   Families for Wal-Mart (WFWM)
affirmative action, 34–35, 119
Alexander, Jeffrey, 65
American Dream, 35, 39, 49, 53–54, 149, 179,
   180, 184, 188
Americans with Disabilities Act, 141
anecdotes. *See* personal narratives
"asymmetric society," 63, 69
audience: citizens as, 111, 162; community
   identity and, 70; consumers or "working
   families" as, 52–53, 59, 83, 87, 111, 168, 178,
   183; core categories and, 14, 16, 47–48,
   70, 83, 111; divided, 59, 61; for economic
   news, 155; as imagined communities,
   47–49; media and access to, 160; person-
   centered rhetoric and appeal to, 49, 70,
   149; rhetorical framing and construction
   of, 45–47; thrift/benevolence and, 37;
   us-against-them rhetoric and appeal to,
   72–73
auto industry, federal intervention in, 115–17,
   120, 146–49, 180
"average working family": as audience for
   discourse, 52–53, 70, 83, 168, 178; as category, 14–16, 36, 74, 167; and discussion of
   economic issues in a moral framework,
   177, 179; as identity in personal narrative,

88–89, 123; as imagined community,
   49–50, 52–55; in Tea Party ideology, 72

bailouts, xvi, 7, 79, 115–17, 146–48, 180
Barbaro, Michael, 170–71
Barber, Benjamin, 36, 186–87
Bayh, Evan, 23
Beck, Glenn, 77–78
benevolence, 37–38, 76, 180–81; in progressive
   rhetoric, 111–13, 154; *vs.* thrift in discourse
   (*see* thrift/benevolence moral dialectic);
   as voluntary, 38, 97–98, 109; in Wal-Mart's
   discourse, 79–80, 127–28; Wal-Mart's
   philanthropic efforts as, 38, 127
benevolent citizen concept, 14, 83, 154, 179
Ben Franklin variety stores, 27, 39–40
Biden, Joe, 23, 46
Brooks, David, 146–48
business model, Wal-Mart's, 39; impact of
   low profit margin on suppliers, 32; profit
   margin in, 187; religion and, 82–83
"Buy American" programs, 13, 26, 185

capitalism: American preference for, 115,
   118–19; family as defense against, 82–83;
   inequality as inherent in, 22–23, 137–38,
   156, 174, 186; media bias and, 150, 156–57;
   as moral issue, 4–5, 9, 22–23, 34–35,
   117, 154–56; Protestant ethic and, 37, 78;
   trends in 21st century, 28; Wal-Mart as
   anti-capitalist, 96–98; Wal-Mart as exem-
   plar of global, 3, 15, 34, 41–42, 107–8, 171,
   179. *See also* market freedom

Chambers, Susan, 68–69, 101
China: as emerging market for Wal-Mart, 29–30; globalization and economic development in, 29; labor violations charges, 106; manufacture of goods in, 26; product safety issues, 105–6
choice: benevolence as moral, 38, 97–98, 109; consumer choice, 121–22, 129, 139, 186; as freedom in Wal-Mart discourse, 121–22, 150; as individual freedom, 128–29; mandatory union membership as violation, 65, 123–24; market freedom as, 128–30, 139, 145; school choice as issue, 73; Wal-Mart and limits on consumer, 139
citizenship: "benevolent citizen" concept, 14, 83, 154, 179; citizens as audience, 111, 162; "civic consumerism" and, 186–87; collectivity and, 70, 111–12; "corporate citizenship," 63; family/citizen moral dialectic, 74; as identity, 70, 167; WMW and citizen/taxpayer in discourse, 167
*Citizens United v. Federal Election Commission*, 63
"civic consumerism," 186–87
class, economic: "class warfare," xvi; elite/average opposition in Wal-Mart's discourse, 178; and ideological voting patterns, 176, 178; lower or middle class referents in Wal-Mart discourse, 51–55, 59, 74, 85; political appeal to, 72; and political orientation, 176; as theme in personal narratives, 87–88; Wal-Mart consumers as lower or lower-middle class, 167
Clean Water Act, 25
Clinton, Bill, 23, 178, 200n23
Clinton, Hillary Rodham, 23
Cohen, Lizabeth, 185–86
Coleman, James, 63–64, 69
collectivity: American cultural tradition and, 7, 34, 147; citizenship and, 70, 111–12; collective bargaining (*see* unions); collective categories and framing of WMW arguments, 17, 120, 136–37, 140–41, 181; collectives as imagined communities, 48; conservative opposition to, 73–74; empowerment and, 57, 181; *Gesellschaft* and, 179; government intervention

and, 147; identity movements and, 47; individual/collective moral dialectic, 15, 34–37, 45–46, 62, 70–71, 76, 128, 145–46; in Obama's discourse, 147; public good and collective effort, 186; social movements and, 48–49; workers as, 141
communities, 34; audience as community, 47–49, 70; "average working family" as community, 49–50, 52–55; collectives as, 48; customers as community, 48; divisiveness and construction of community identities, 47–49; as imagined, 47–49; individual/collective moral dialectic, 34, 48–49; and small-town values in conservative rhetoric, 45, 73; WFWM and community identity, 47–48
competition: as beneficial to market participants, 128; fairness and, 41, 142; market forces and, 22, 40; Wal-Mart and, 40, 149, 159; and Wal-Mart as monopolistic power, 14
conservatism: conservative populism, 175–76, 178; and construction of economic morality, 22; and deployment of moral values in rhetoric, 15; environmental issues and, 159; evangelical religion and, 183; fairness as framed by, 119–20; and family as category, 14–15, 17; and family as discursive context for economic issues, 177, 183; and framing of economic issues, xiii, 119–20; free market principles and, 119–20, 145–47, 150, 182; individual freedoms and responsibilities as focus of, 14–15, 146–47, 150, 175–76, 182, 183; institutionalism and moral discourse, 181–84; moral warrants deployed by, 150; and objection to government intervention, 7, 74, 114–17, 146–46; and personal responsibility as value, 146–47; and person-based rhetoric, 71–74; social issues and, 9, 175–76; and "Strict Father" as moral metaphor, 8; thrift as conservative value, 77–80, 110. *See also* Tea Party
Constitutionalism, 75
consumerism: "civic consumerism," 186–87; consumption as freedom issue, 150; consumption as normative behavior,

183; critiques of consumption search, 36; freedom linked to consumption, 150; individualism and, 36; shopping as moral activity, 80–81, 87, 153

consumers: as audience, 52–53, 59, 83, 87, 111, 168, 178, 183; as category in Wal-Mart discourse, 174; as community, 48; as identity category, 174; as wage-earners, 29–30, 150, 167–68, 174, 185; Wal-Mart and empowerment of, 122–23; women as, 87, 182; worker/consumer moral dialectic, 83, 106, 166–68

Corcoran, Terry, 146

Costco, 107

"culture wars," 8, 72, 74, 177

customers. *See* consumers

Dach, Leslie, 13, 164–65, 170

"death panels," 112–13

Deaver, Michael K., 164–65

disabled workers, 82, 125, 141, 201n12

discrimination, workplace, 24, 127–28, 133, 135, 141, 149, 165, 179, 201n12

divisive rhetoric, xvi

Dukes, Betty, 24, 201n12

*Dukes vs. Wal-Mart Stores Inc.*, 12–13, 24, 108, 141, 182, 201n12

economic disruption, 90–92, 109, 183–84; as context for Wal-Mart debate, xv–xvi; systemic financial crisis, 4–5, 10, 16, 20, 115–16, 118, 161

economic inequality, 188; capitalism and, 22–23, 137–38, 156, 174, 186; globalization, 29; market freedom and, 137; wage inequality as threat to free-market, 149–50

economic symbols, 3–6, 148

Edelman (Wal-Mart's PR firm), 27, 50, 87, 165

education: school choice, 73

Edwards, John, 23, 54–55

elites: identity politics and the other, xvi; populism and perception of, xvi, 22, 54–55, 176–78; role in public discourse, 8–9, 160, 172, 189; unions framed as elitist "other," 71–72

emotion: person-centered rhetoric and emotional appeal, 49, 62–63, 148

employee benefits: family and medical leave, 148, 188; unions and collective bargaining for, 139; Wal-Mart and health benefits, 57–58, 108

employees: as "associates" or "team members," 33. *See also* workers

empowerment: employment opportunity as, 123; individual freedom and personal, 121; as theme in personal narratives, 122–23; as theme in Wal-Mart discourse, 122–23, 127–28, 129–30, 133–35, 145, 171; Wal-Mart and empowerment of consumers, 122–23; WMW and focus on collective empowerment, 56–57, 181

enlightenment ideal and rationalized society, 82

environmental issues: Clean Water Act violations, 25; criticism of Wal-Mart linked to, 5, 20, 36, 41, 160, 166; in media coverage, 158–60, 172; thrift and, 95, 100; Wal-Mart and environmental violations, 25, 100; Wal-Mart's environmental initiatives, 38, 64–65, 167–68, 170, 173, 194

equality as value, 9, 34; and American economic policy, 118–19; capitalism and inequality, 22–23, 137–38, 156, 174, 186; "fairness" and, 131–37, 140–44; individualism and, 145, 183; inequality as lack of access to market, 134; political left and, 153; WMW and, 120. *See also* economic inequality

evangelical Christianity: individualistic ethos and, 182–83; thrift as value in, 82; Wal-Mart policies criticized by, 21

fairness, 34, 115–50; and business competition, 142; as collective rather than individual, 140–44; conservative framing of, 119–20; as equal access, 140–41; as equal access *vs.* just reward, 140–41; and equality as value, 131–37, 140–44; equal opportunity and, 131–36, 142; "fair wages," 104–5, 132, 139, 142; freedom/fairness moral dialectic, 34, 39–41; justice as, 132, 140–41, 145; market competition and, 41, 142; in progressive rhetoric, 154; as theme in personal narratives, 132

Fair Share Health Care Act, 58, 143–44
family: citizen as opposing category to, 74; as common term, 188; in conservative political rhetoric, 45–46, 72; economic discourse on, 5–6; as economic unit in WMW discourse, 104; as key theme in discourse, 84–89; normative models created through economic discourse, 183; parents as community, 48; in populist discourse, 45, 49, 51, 53–55, 73–74, 177–78; southern regional origins and emphasis on, 181–82; "Strict Father" *vs.* "Nurturant Parent" metaphors, 9; as theme in narratives, 83, 86–87; as theme in Wal-Mart's public relations messages, 92–93; unions framed as enemy of, 93–94; wages and family in discourse, 21, 82, 104–5, 142, 147–50, 187–88; in Wal-Mart's discourse, 53–55; and Wal-Mart's economic paradigm, 183–84; work and family as oppositional, 93, 149; worker's needs as members of, 188. *See also* "average working family"
family and medical leave, 148, 188
Family and Medical Leave Act, 148
Ferree, Myra Marx, 153–54, 160
financial crisis, 4–5, 10, 16, 20, 115–16, 118, 161
Fishman, Charles, 32, 36
Fourcade, Marion, 5
framing, 46–47
Frank, Thomas, 175–76
Franklin, Benjamin, 77–80, 94
freedom: as collective rather than individual, 140–45; for collectivities, 140–44; compulsory union membership as violation of, 124; consumption as freedom issue, 150; freedom/fairness moral dialectic, 34, 39–41; individualistic framing of by Wal-Mart, 126–27; justice and, 144–45; as moral value, 4, 39–41; in WMW discourse, 137–40, 144–45. *See also* market freedom
Friedland, Roger search, 82
Friedman, Milton, 118–19

Gamson, William, 119
Gans, Herbert, 155–56
*Gemeinschaft*, 103, 105, 179. *See also Gesellschaft/Gemeinschaft* opposition

gender: female role as consumer, 87, 182; gender-based discrimination and Wal-Mart, 24, 141, 165, 201n122; male role as breadwinner, 183; patriarchal management style and Wal-Mart culture, 181–82
*Gesellschaft*, 103, 105, 108, 179
*Gesellschaft/Gemeinschaft* opposition, 81–82, 94–98, 109; in conservative political rhetoric, 112–13; defined and described, 81–82; in personal narratives collected by WFWM, 89–94; in Wal-Mart debates, 179
Glass, David, 19
Glickman, Lawrence, 150
Global Insight, 36
globalization, 34, 81, 108; as business opportunity, 29–30; "Buy American," 26; and emerging markets, 29–30; NAFTA and job loss, 200n23; poverty and, 29; sweatshop scandals, 187; and wage suppression, 29; Wall Street bailout and, 115–16
Gramm, Phil, 113
greed, 51, 60, 67, 78–80, 96, 98–99, 102–3
Greely, Andrew, 176
Grossman, Andrew, 60, 99–100, 101, 142–43

Hart, Stephen, 148
Hayek, F. A., 118
health care: abortion and contraception, 180; debate over health care reform, 73–74, 77, 112–13; Fair Share for Health Care (FSHC), 107, 143; medical leave as employment benefit, 148, 188; pharmaceutical prices at Wal-Mart, 92–39, 130; unions and collective bargaining for benefits, 139; Wal-Mart and employee health benefits, 57–58, 108
Healy, Kieran, 5
heroes, Wal-Mart as heroic, 161–62, 168–69
Hout, Michael, 176

identity: "average working families" as identity category, 88–89, 123, 167; citizen/taxpayer as identity category, 70, 167; communities framed by Working Families for Wal-Mart, 47–48; conservative ideology and, 73–74; consumer as identity category, 174; divisiveness and group or community, 47; organizational identity of WMW, xiv–xv; Tea Party and, 74; unions and collective, 181; Wal-Mart and evangelical, 37, 82–83, 182–83; Wal-Mart customers as "average Americans," 52–55, 74, 123, 179

imagined communities of reference. *See* audience

India, 29; as emerging market for Wal-Mart, 29–30

individualism: in American political culture, 4, 35, 182; and benevolence as voluntary choice, 97–98; conservatism and, 14–15, 146–47, 150, 175–76, 182, 183; consumerism and, 36; and economic disruption as personal rather than systemic issue, 92, 109; empowerment and, 181; evangelical Christianity and, 182–83; and framing of Wal-Mart rhetoric, 128; freedom, individualistic framing of, 126–27; individual/collective moral dialectic, 15, 34–37, 45–46, 62, 128, 145–46; market freedom and individual freedom, 121, 128–31, 133, 150; and opposition to government intervention, 146–47; self-reliance and, 122–23, 127, 146–47; and use of person-based language in discourse, 67–68

Industrial Loan Corporations (ILCs), 24

institutionalism and moral discourse, 181–84

Jacobs, Mark, 161
Jacobs, Meg, 185
justice, 145. *See also* fairness

Kanelos, Peter, 199n20
Kazin, Michael, 22, 175, 176–77
Kerry, John, 21, 69

L. R. Nelson (sprinkler company), 32
labor, organized. *See* unions
Lakoff, George, 8
lawsuits, class-action suits against Wal-Mart, 24
legislation: Americans with Disabilities Act violations, 141; Clean Water Act, 25; Fair Share Health Care Act, 58, 143–44; Family and Medical Leave Act, 148; Patient Protection and Affordable Care Act, 77, 113

Lepore, Jill, 117
loyalty, customer, 121–22
Luker, Kristin, 180
Lynch, Courtney, 84–85, 124

Making Change at Wal-Mart, xv
market freedom: as American value, 7, 115–21, 144–45, 178, 179, 182; as choice, 128–30, 139, 145; commercial journalism and, 156; conservatism and, 178; contrast between discourse and policy, 118–19; difference in conservative and liberal discourse about, 145; and economic inequality, 137; fairness and, 136, 145–46; and government intervention, 115–17; ideology and, 119–20; individual freedoms and, 121, 128–31, 133, 150; justice and, 120, 144–45; and market as moral system, 4–6, 145, 147, 149–50; monopoly, Wal-Mart market power as, 137–39, 149–50; personal choice conflated with, 129–30; as political issue, 176; state power and limits to, 4, 7, 118; Tea Party (FreedomWorks) and, 117–18; wages and, 41; Wal-Mart as actor in, 21–22, 137–41 (*see also* monopoly *under this heading*); in WMW discourse, 137–40, 179–80

markets: moralization of (constructing moral markets), 4–6, 147; as social construction, 5. *See also* market freedom

Marxism, 32–33, 188
McChesney, Robert, 153, 155–56
McDonough, William, 167
McGirr, Lisa, 74
McLaughlin, Brian, 67–68
media: advertising, 13, 26, 98, 163, 173, 190, 199n20; commercial ownership of, 155–56; and construction of narrative, 161–62; economic news coverage by, 155–56; metaphors deployed by, 17, 160–61; moral discourse and coverage of Wal-Mart, 150; narrative construction in, 161–62, 168 (*see also* political struggle narrative); role in economic discourse, 19, 155, 184; Tea Party movement and, 46;

media (cont'd): "two sides" journalistic model, 168; Wal-Mart and advertising or public relations, 13, 26, 173, 190. *See also* newspapers

membership, 93–94

merchandising, push and pull systems of, 31–33

metaphors: of the body, 62–64; for the economy, 160–62; of illness, 161; of information system, 161; "little guy" and giant, 36, 66–67, 71; of machine, 160–62; and media coverage of Wal-Mart, 17, 47–49, 160; and moral discourse, 64–65; for nuclear family, 8; person-based, 62–64, 179–80; political, 8, 172 (*see also* political struggle narrative)

methodology: data coding for media analysis, 193–94; quotation sources, 198n8, 199n9; scope in time, 191; selection of advocacy groups, 189–91

Mexico: as emerging market for Wal-Mart, 29–30

military families, 27, 127–28, 184

Miller, Daniel, 81, 83, 92, 109

Mills, C. Wright, 92

minorities: charitable activities targeting, 127; employment of, 127–28; racial discrimination at Wal-Mart, 141; relationships with minority-owned businesses, 135

"moral dialectics," 15

moral discourse: in the media, 182–83; "thick" *vs.* "thin," 148; Wuthnow on ideal, 149

moral markets: American values and, 3–4; audience categories and visions of, 16; capitalism and, 4–5; debates over, 6–10; "free trade" and, 4; moral significance of economic symbols, 6; in public discourse, 2–5

Moreton, Bethany, 82, 181–82, 203n8

NAFTA, 200n23

narratives: American identity and shared, 75; complicating actions as element of, 161–62, 168–70, 172; and creation of meaning, 75, 161, 168; and cultural schemas, 9; family as theme in (*see under* family); and journalistic coverage and, 16–17, 161–62; media's role in framing and disseminating, 160; normative family in Wal-Mart, 183; and protagonist/antagonist dynamic, 161; resolution as element of, 161–62, 169–70; Sam Walton's narrative and public image, 19–20, 37, 39–40, 54, 55, 180; Tea Party and American, 75; victim narratives, 17, 65–68, 169, 172–73; Wal-Mart debate as politicized narrative (*see* political struggle narrative; politicization of Wal-Mart debates)

"neoinstitutional" organizational analysis, 164

newspapers: activist narratives as influence on, 150; advertising in, 13, 26; analysis of articles in, 16–17, 23; civic groups claims reported in, 158–59; commercial journalism and market freedom, 156; coverage of Wal-Mart and labor issues in, 16–17; form *vs.* content of reports in, 160–61; government intervention in economy as reported in, 26; included in media analysis, 193; journalistic model and reification of worker/consumer moral dialectic, 165–67; labor issues covered in national, 171–72; metaphors deployed by, 160–61; politicized frame for reportage, 162, 164; public debate reflected in, 20; as representative of public discourse, 154–55; as subject of discourse analysis, 154–55; Wal-Mart public relations efforts in, 26; WMW as depicted in, 166; WMW media strategy and, 13, 26

Obama, Barack, 73–74, 110–13, 115–17, 146–48

Occupy Wall Street (OWS), xiii–xvi, 63, 155

opportunity, 123; consumers and low prices as, 87, 89, 129–30; fairness and equal, 131–36, 142; freedom and, 119–21, 124–28; globalization as business, 29–20; thrift and opportunities for benevolence, 83, 94; Wal-Mart employment as, 54, 65, 90, 96–97, 124–26, 131, 132, 135–36

othering: populism and, xvi; us-against-them rhetoric and appeal to, 72–73

outsourcing, 183

Palin, Sarah, 45–49, 71–74, 112–13
parents, as community, 48
Patient Protection and Affordable Care Act, 77, 113
patriarchy and corporate culture of Wal-Mart, 180–82
Pelosi, Nancy, 46
personal narratives: economic disruption mentioned in, 90–92, 109; fairness as theme in, 132; freedom or choice as theme in, 129; gratitude toward Wal-Mart expressed in, 96–97; persuasive power of, 149; Sam Walton's life story and public image, 19–20, 37, 39–40, 54, 55, 180; self-sufficiency and empowerment themes in, 122–23; unions vilified in, 93; used by Wal-Mart for public relations, 27; used by WMW, 201n12; as WFWM website content, 50–55, 70, 122; women's role as described in, 87
person-based rhetoric: and collectivity held accountable for individual actors, 67–69; conservatism and, 62–70; individualism and, 67–68; metaphors, 62–64, 179–80
personhood of corporations, 49, 62–70, 63, 64
philanthropy/ charitable giving, 59; minorities as targets of, 127; scholarships, 127; Walton Family Foundation, 38
polarization: and media's framing of debate, 163–65; of public discourse and debate, 8–10, 72; Wal-Mart as polarizing, 12
Poletta, Francesca, 169
political debate: economic issues as polarizing, 8–10; Wal-Mart as issue in, 12, 23–24
political metaphors. See political struggle narrative
political struggle narrative: as disadvantage for progressive claims, 162, 166–67; identity categories deployed in, 167–68, 174; journalistic use of, 161–72; political discourse and involvement of political operatives, 172; and unions as "special interests," 166–67, 172; and victim narratives, 172; and Wal-Mart as hero, 162; and worker/consumer moral dialectic, 166–67
politicization of Wal-Mart debates: and

involvement of political campaign operatives, 165, 172
populism: citizen/taxpayer in populist discourse, 49, 56, 70, 74; competing discourses of, 49–55, 70–71, 74, 179–80, 190; conservatism and, xv–xvi, 175–78; divisiveness and, 70–72 (see also othering under this heading); economic concerns and, xvi, 41, 51, 175–77, 184; elites, perception of, xvi, 22, 54–55, 176–78; family in populist discourse, 45, 49, 51, 53–55, 73–74, 177–78; Occupy Wall Street, xiii–xvi; and othering, xvi, 45–46, 49, 59, 71–72; people vs. power dynamic in, 22–23, 52; person-centered rhetoric and, 49, 70, 179–80; progressivism and, 184–185; rhetoric and, 22–23, 187–88; Tea Party movement, xiii–xvi, 45–46, 71, 73–74; Wal-Mart and, 33–41, 49–55, 65, 74
poverty: globalization and, 29
product safety issues, 105–6
progressivism: benevolence as progressive value, 110–11; and "benevolent citizen" category, 14; and civic consumerism, 187–88; and collective categories, 17; collectivity and progressive ideology, 74; and construction of economic morality, 22, 147–49; and failure to understand appeal of conservative message, 175–77; and family as discursive context for economic issues, 177; framing of economic issues, xiii, 119–20; free market principles and, 119–20; institutionalism and moral discourse, 181–84; and "Nurturant Parent" as moral metaphor, 8
Protestant ethic, 5, 37–38, 78
public relations: benevolence and thrift linked in press releases, 95; personal narratives used in, 27, 87

Reid, Harry, 46
religion: faith in WMW discourse, 139; and ideological voting patterns, 176, 178; Wal-Mart and evangelical identity, 82–83, 182–83
research design. See methodology

scheduling, technology and employee, 31

Schudson, Michael, 186

Scott, Lee, 3, 14, 20, 25, 26, 50, 52, 69, 92–93, 108, 130, 133–34, 165–66, 168, 170–71

Service Employees International Union (SEIU), xii–xiv, 13, 14, 26, 34

shopping as moral activity, 80–81, 87, 153

Slater, Robert, 19, 20

small businesses, 5, 15; as category, 136; in conservative discourse, 45, 71; Wal-Mart as market for products, 85, 179; Wal-Mart unfair competition for, 120, 136, 139, 142–44; in WMW discourse, xv, 57–58, 120, 136, 139, 149, 162

Smith, Catherine, 50, 54

socialism, 115, 118

social issues, 9, 92, 180; liberal priorities, 176–77; values voters and, 9, 175–76

social movement organization (SMOs), xvi, 8, 15–16; framing of discourse by, 46–47. *See also specific organizations*

Soderquist, Don, 20, 33, 36–37, 39–40, 59, 82

Stern, Andrew "Andy," 14, 26, 34

Stewart, Jon, 19

Suttles, Gerald, 160–61

sweatshops, 19, 186, 187

symbolic language in economic discourse, xvi, 9, 42, 45, 109–10, 191–92; and thrift as moral value, 77–78, 98

taxes: in conservative political rhetoric, 46, 71; historical levies on chain stores, 4; as patriotic civic responsibility, 46; as political campaign issue, 45–46; in progressive political rhetoric, 46; "tax for living" *vs.* "work for a living" opposition in WFWM discourse, 51; taxpayer/citizen as identity category, 14–16, 49, 56–58, 70, 167; taxpayers as victim in narratives, 103; Tea Party fiscal conservatism and objection to, 3, 45–46, 71, 74, 117–18, 180; Wal-Mart and shifting of costs onto taxpayers, 13, 16, 20, 24, 26, 57–58, 98, 147–48, 185

Tea Party, xiii–xvi, 3, 15–16, 45–46, 49, 71–74, 75, 117–18, 175

technological innovation, Wal-Mart and, 30–31

"thick" *vs.* "thin" discourse, 148

thrift: *vs.* benevolence in discourse (*see* thrift/benevolence moral dialectic); Benjamin Franklin and American tradition of, 77–80, 94; in conservative rhetoric, 77, 113; as key theme in discourse, 84–89; and Protestant work ethic, 5, 26, 78; symbolic language in economic discourse and morality of, 77–78, 98; and Wal-Mart's business model, 37; women and, 80–81, 87

thrift/benevolence moral dialectic, 14, 16, 41, 84, 109, 179; audience and, 37; charity or philanthropy as voluntary, 95; citizenship and, 80 (*see also* benevolent citizen concept); as conflicting values resistant to reconciliation, 81–82; core categories and, 80–81, 80–84; and discourse analysis methodology, 191; in economic debates, 79–80; ethical shopping and, 81; family and, 78–84; and *Gesellschaft/Gemeinschaft*, 81–82, 94–98, 109; greed narratives in, 78–79; inhibition of benevolence by thrift, 34, 78, 84; personal-responsiblity narratives in, 77–79; Protestant ethic and, 37–38; reconciliation of, 79, 84–85, 94–98, 121, 128, 182; and Wal-Mart as benevolent actor, 38, 94–97, 127

Tönnies, Ferdinand, 81

Troubled Asset Relief Program (TARP), 115–16, 146

unions: collectivity and, 181–82; compulsory union membership as violation of freedom, 124; and family and medical leave as employee benefit, 188; framed as elitist "other," 71–72; framed as enemy of family, 93–94; framed as special interest group, 55, 166–67, 172; framed negatively in personal narratives collected by WFWM, 93, 124; individual/collective moral dialectic and, 145–46; role in shaping discourse, 181; union organization as freedom issue, 139; unions and work-family concerns, 181; Wal-Mart's opposition to, 28, 33–34; WMW as supported and influenced by, 165–67, 181

United Food and Commercial Workers (UFCW), xv, 167, 190
us-against-them rhetoric, 72–73
Useem, Michael, 116

victim narratives, 169; taxpayers as victim in, 103; Wal-Mart as victim in, 17, 65–68, 169, 172–73
Vlasic Pickles, 32

wages, 167; consumers as wage-earners, 29–30, 150, 167–68, 174, 185; culture and acceptance of lower, 82, 90; "fair wages," 41, 104–5, 132, 139, 142, 150; "family-sustaining wages" framed as moral issue, 21, 104–5, 142, 148–50; globalization and suppression of, 29; increases in Wal-Mart, 14; as issue in political debate, 23–24; and labor in Wal-Mart discourse, 121; legislative control of, 23, 168, 174; "living wage" and family in discourse, 82, 142, 147–48, 187–88; market freedom and, 41; profit margin and, 31, 98, 100–102; tax burden linked to lower, 98, 185; unions and collective bargaining, 139; wage inequality as threat to free-market, 149–50, 188; Wal-Mart as low-wage employer, 21, 23, 27–28, 31, 41, 82–83, 98, 100–102, 163; Wal-Mart hourly as above average, 23–24
Wake-Up Wal-Mart, 160, 165, 189–90
Wall Street bailout, 115–16
"Wal-Mart effect," 32
Wal-Mart Watch (WMW): advertising by, 13, 98, 163; and changes in Wal-Mart's policies, 4–5, 14; citizen/taxpayer identity and, 167; collective categories and framing of arguments, 15, 17, 120, 136–37, 140–41; effectiveness of narrative structure deployed by, 161–62; faith in discourse, 139; and family as economic unit, 104; freedom as framed by, 137–40, 144–45; and Making Change at

Wal-Mart, xv; market freedom as framed by, 137–40, 179–80; media as information channel for, 13, 16–17; mission of, xiii–xiv, 13–14; organizational identity of, xiv–xv; partner organizations of, 13; personal narratives used by, 201n12; as single-issue advocacy group, 190; as subject of discourse analysis, xiii–xiv; union influence and support of, 13, 16–17, 165–67, 181
Walton, Alice, 102–3
Walton, Sam: death of, 19; personal narrative and public image of, 19–20, 37, 39–40, 54, 55, 180; religious identity of, 37; WMW and citation of, 105
Walton Family Foundation, 38
Weber, Max, 5, 37–38, 78
Williams, Christine, 83
women: discourse on shopping, 80–81; gender discrimination and Wal-Mart, 24, 141, 165, 201n122; narrative emphasizing Wal-Mart as employment opportunity for, 90
workers: as "associates," 33–34; as collectivity, 141; as members of families, 188; worker/consumer moral dialectic, 83, 106, 165–68; "worker" vs. "family" in discourse, 105–6
Working Families for Wal-Mart (WFWM): community identities framed by, 47–48; dissolved as organization, xv, 27; and "family" as theme, 83–85; founded by Wal-Mart, xiv, 25–27; as "paper" advocacy group, 190; sample e-mail produced by, 84–85; as subject of discourse analysis, 189–91; and Wal-Mart as "little guy" in need of defense, 65–67; Young's resignation as head of, 13, 68
Wuthnow, Robert, 61, 118, 149

Young, Andrew, 13, 50, 68

Zelizer, Viviana, 5–6

ABOUT THE AUTHOR

Rebekah Peeples Massengill is Lecturer in the Princeton Writing Program at Princeton University.

WAL-MART WARS

DISCARDED